Rolling Back the Market

Rolling Back the Market

Economic Dogma and Political Choice

Peter Self

St. Martin's Press
New York

ROLLING BACK THE MARKET

Copyright © 2000 by the estate of Peter Self

All rights reserved. No part of this book may be used or reproduced in any manner whatsoever without written permission except in the case of brief quotations embodied in critical articles or reviews. For information, address:

St. Martin's Press, Scholarly and Reference Division, 175 Fifth Avenue, New York, N.Y. 10010

First published in the United States of America in 2000

This book is printed on paper suitable for recycling and made from fully managed and sustained forest sources.

Printed in Hong Kong

ISBN 0–312–22651–9 clothbound
ISBN 0–312–22652–7 paperback

Library of Congress Cataloging-in-Publication Data
Self, Peter.
Rolling back the market : economic dogma and political choice / Peter Self.
p.   cm.
Includes bibliographical references and index.
ISBN 0–312–22651–9 (cloth). — ISBN 0–312–22652–7 (pbk.)
1. Social choice.   2. Welfare economics.   3. Economic policy.
I. Title.
HB846.8.S463   1999
338.9—dc21   99–22160
                                                  CIP

To Diana Self, a kindly and helpful adviser

Contents

Preface

This book offers a comprehensive critique of the dominant place in our lives and societies now occupied by a largely uncontrolled capitalist market system operating on a global scale. It is not written from a Marxist perspective because I am not an economic determinist, but a social democrat who still believes or hopes in the capacity of reasoned discussion to influence policies and opinions. It does not question that there is value in the concept of 'competitive markets', but it does question strongly whether the present market system is the best or only way of realising this objective. In particular it argues that the present market system has expanded well beyond its desirable bounds and limits, to the detriment of other important values, and has become in Sir Geoffrey Vickers' phrase 'a dangerously self-exciting system', which needs to be reined back and kept within the bounds of a more balanced and sane society.

This prevailing market system is supported by a very influential set of economic dogmas which have come to occupy a dominant place in the lives of modern societies. These include the high importance attached to market-led economic growth; the value of complete free trade in money and capital as well as in goods and services; the need to subordinate social welfare to market requirements; the belief in cutting down or privatising government functions; the acceptability of profit as a test of economic welfare; and others as well.

The aim of this book is to challenge these beliefs, to show their adverse impacts on the life of society, and to suggest policies which can achieve a better balance between a narrow concept of economic efficiency and a broader concept of human welfare. The first four chapters pursue this aim on a broad front and through considering the impact of market dogmas in spheres which are usually kept distinct, namely those of economic thought, political thought, concepts of welfare and the operations of government. These subjects are usually handled separately by different disciplines, and I hope that by bringing them together I can offer a much broader critique of dominant economic beliefs and their impacts than is available elsewhere, and also help specialists to locate their subject within a broader context.

Chapter 1 deals with the relation of market beliefs and dogmas to economic theory, because that is the basis on which they are usually justified and it is necessary to confront them on their home ground. I have tried (as I have tried throughout) to make the exposition here as clear and simple as possible, but those readers who cannot cope with any economic theory could skip all but the first and last sections of this chapter without losing the value of subsequent ones, but will have to take my demonstration of the inadequacy of economic theory as a basis for market beliefs on trust!

Chapter 2 traces the powerful influence of market dogmas upon political thought, especially the way that modern liberalism has reverted to an uncritical endorsement of capitalist markets under the old, misleading banner of 'individual freedom'. The chapter shows how modern markets do not have the voluntary, spontaneous character ascribed to them by Hayek and others, and how the glorification of consumers' choice in the market represents only a thin, one-sided version of individual freedom. Its conclusions trace the need for restoring a more balanced liberalism which links individual freedom to social responsibility.

Chapter 3 deals with the inadequacy of economic concepts of welfare and growth which try to dispense with any consideration of how the wealth is distributed and of what it consists. It argues that economic growth is now delivering decreasing or even negative returns in terms of any broader concept of the constituents of human welfare. Alternative tests of welfare are suggested and applied to the evaluation of collective social services.

Chapter 4 deals with the destructive impact of market concepts of profit and efficiency upon the functioning of governments. It shows how the pursuit of minimum government through privatisation and deregulation will not, as is often claimed, produce a more impartial state but one that is more subservient to market pressures and more liable to corruption. It also shows how the indiscriminate adoption of market methods and the politicisation of bureaucracy are having adverse effects upon the equity and accountability of public administration.

The latter part of the book moves to a discussion of possible reforms of the economic system and of the public policies which support it. Chapter 5 prepares the way through analysing, necessarily briefly for such a complex subject, the actual characteristics of the global economy as opposed to the claims made for it.

Chapter 6 summarises and confronts the neo-liberal philosophy of 'free markets' and extreme individualism so as to show its perverse economic, social and political effects, considers some variations such as the 'third way' politics of New Labour in Britain, and ends with a look at the more radical alternatives favoured by environmental and other groups.

The last two chapters deal with the linked issues of economic and political reform. Chapter 7 suggests ways in which the capitalist system might be controlled so as to reduce its adverse social and environmental effects, and proposes some longer-term measures for producing a more equitable and stable market system. Although there is an urgent need for international and regional co-operation, much of the responsibility for establishing a better system still falls upon national states. These states also need to improve their own performance and reduce their entanglement with the dominant powers of global capitalism. These are not easy tasks and Chapter 8 suggests they will not only require new policies and methods, but depend crucially upon a regeneration of democratic concern and participation.

In the two years since this book was started, an increasing flow of books and articles have begun to question and criticise what was regarded, not long ago, as the unassailable position of global capitalism. This criticism has not as yet changed the course of history, since capitalist markets are powerfully entrenched politically as well as economically, but a counter-revolution of ideas has begun which will in time offer the basis for a different kind of economy and society. Reform is impeded by the unpopularity of the state, which once defended social values against adverse market impacts, but is now generally supportive of global capitalism and is left with much of the blame for its ill effects. Reform therefore has to depend upon a widening realisation that it is possible by democratic action to achieve a better balance of power. That enterprise could lead also in turn to efforts to make democracy more effective and responsible than is now the case.

This book is offered as a contribution towards this hoped for counter-revolution of ideas. Its broad approach distinguishes it from other critiques of the market system which have recently appeared. It is directed at students of public and social policy, as well as of economic and political thought, but will also serve as a guide for any intelligent reader who is concerned about the impacts of the market system upon the welfare and security of society and its members.

My warm thanks are due to several individual scholars who kindly read and commented on drafts of the whole book: Max Neutze, Hugh Stretton, Geoffrey Harcourt and Frank Stilwell. I am also grateful for useful advice on individual chapters from John Uhr, Phyllis Colvin, Sir Christopher Foster, Thelma Hunter and Nigel Hall, as well as much help from Diana Self over bringing the book to some actual conclusions. None of these individuals has any responsibility for my opinions. As happened before, my publisher Steven Kennedy improved the book by urging me to enlarge it with more positive conclusions – or at least I hope so!

I am grateful for the facilities provided me as a Visiting Fellow in the Urban Research Program, Research School of Social Sciences, Australian National University. Patrick Troy, Head of the Program, gave me his usual warm support for a project which entails a catholic interpretation of urban research. I am especially grateful to Coralie Cullen who word-processed successive drafts with speed and patience, and for other help from Heather Grant, Penny Hanley, Christine Cannon and Nicholas Brown.

Canberra, 1999   *Peter Self*

1
The Market Dogma

An age can be defined by its ruling beliefs and its dominant culture. The collapse of communism, perhaps less completely realised than was originally thought, has meant the domination of the globe by capitalist market systems and (to a much more limited extent) formally democratic institutions. The 'end of ideology' was too confidently proclaimed by some enthusiasts for these developments and is far from true, as the rise of ethnic or religious nationalism, neo-fascism and various counter-cultural movements demonstrate. What is true is that the ruling ideas in the world have become those of 'free markets' and 'political democracy'.

In the West these two beliefs have been linked historically, although it should be remembered that the original association of market beliefs was with constitutionalism not democracy, which was seen as a threat to the rights of property. In some circles there is now a reversion to this earlier position as the traumatic impacts of global capitalism render majoritarian democracy an uncertain ally to the market system. Usually, however, this association between market and democratic beliefs is viewed as a strong and very desirable one, at least in Western societies and potentially everywhere. Indeed it seems probable that capitalist markets, lacking a convincing moral basis and being strongly inegalitarian, need support from the formally egalitarian values of political democracy to retain legitimacy, but it is also clear that, in terms of effective power and application, capitalism is in much better shape than democracy.

In many non-Western countries, capitalism is forging ahead under strongly authoritarian or dictatorial regimes. Western governments, led by the USA, urge these countries to respect human rights and adopt formally democratic institutions, but they also act quickly to help suppress by force if necessary any alternative national governments or movements, including some with popular or majoritarian support, which seem likely to impede the operation of capitalist markets. Certainly the governments of Western nations would prefer there to be formally democratic institutions everywhere, but their actions often suggest a much stronger attachment to capitalism than democracy.

More generally, assumed market 'imperatives' now play a dominant role in the politics and policies of almost all countries. The political imperative is to equip the national economy to meet the challenge of global market competition and to maintain or restart the engine of economic growth. Market institutions, methods and motivations are seen as the essential means to this end – hence the extensive measures of privatisation and deregulation, although the latter process may be running out of steam as some counter-measures become inescapable (including not only some degree of social and environmental protection, but the need to keep the market system itself tolerably efficient and workable). Hence too the cutting of government budgets and the sacrifice of collective goods in the assumed interest of freeing resources for the more 'efficient' and 'productive' market sector. Hence also the reorganisation of government itself along market lines and utilising market motivations. Finally market concepts and motivations are being extended into ever widening aspects of social life, both theoretically and practically.

In Western countries the vitality and growth of the market system is matched by an apparent decline in the vigour and status of democratic institutions as shown by the evidence on voting turnouts, party membership and activity, expressed attitudes of indifference and alienation, and opinion polls about the reputation or trustworthiness of politicians. Elected governments appear to have become decidedly less popular and to engender more cynicism about their willingness to honour their promises and their ability to achieve stated goals. These outcomes are hardly surprising to the extent that politicians feel obliged or choose to frustrate popular aspirations and to resist social or environmental claims on economic grounds. Since these economic 'requirements' are not openly admitted to constitute strong limitations upon political choice, which (if true) would debase the role of politicians, popular cynicism is hardly surprising. Moreover the effect of increasing economic inequalities must inevitably invest the formal equality of democracy with less political meaning or impact.

To explain the purpose of this chapter, some terms must be clarified. The terms 'capitalist markets' or 'market system' do not refer to a simple homogeneous entity. There are important differences within capitalism itself, especially between the Anglo-American variety, 'Rhenish capitalism' (German and Central European), and the Japanese and East Asian type. These differences get some attention later in the book. In this chapter the main focus is on the theories and beliefs which are used to explain and justify the Anglo-American type of capitalism.

The term 'market system' is also of potentially wide application. It can include not only different varieties of what may be termed 'strong' capitalism (such as we now see operating in global markets) but also versions of modified or localised capitalism as well as of 'market socialism', workers' co-operatives etc. Further there are important questions as to how extensive or pervasive any market system is or should be, how it is maintained and policed, what areas of life are excluded from its influence or domination, what alternative institutions or counter-cultures exist.

Thus this book will be misread if it is seen as an attack upon *all forms* of competitive market system. There are weighty arguments for according a considerable place in any modern society for some such system. Instead the argument is directed against the present form of market capitalism, particularly in its Anglo-American form but also in its dominant global manifestation. It will be contended that this system, far from being the efficient maximiser of wealth which is claimed for it, is having many deleterious effects upon the use or non-use of resources, the creation of wealth and the distribution of welfare. Above all, its influence has overstepped the bounds which are socially and ethically appropriate to any market system and is invading and undermining political and social spheres of life which have been and should be operated according to different standards and values.

The theoretical underpinning of this market imperialism is provided by the economic theories and beliefs which aim to explain and justify the forward march of the current market system. There is a strange paradox here. Not for a long time have economic theories been in such a state of confusion and disarray, yet popularised economic beliefs press on with their supportive and colonising role. There is a big gap between the weak theoretical arguments which can be offered for a dominant market system and the popularised reasons which appear convincing to politicians and media commentators (and of course to business men; but they think less and act more); and there is another big gap between the dogmatic policies advocated by partisan economists and the sophisticated, sceptical theorising of many academic economists.

It is the purpose of this chapter to explore the roots of what I have called 'market dogma'. This chapter looks primarily at the economic theories, still current in the English-speaking world, which purport to explain in general terms how a competitive market system works and it considers the adequacy of their explanations and justifications, moving at its end to the derivation of simple market dogmas. This task entails a threefold distinction between basic economic theories, the market system itself and popularised beliefs or dogmas about the system. The actual market system differs in important respects from the theories which purport to explain it, while the market dogmas represent very simplified and biased derivatives from the theories.

I am well aware of the difficulties or foolhardiness of this initial undertaking. Economic theorising constitutes an enormous body of often very abstruse thought. It has been well said that there is no economic theory which has not been effectively refuted by some other economist. My aim is modest. This is not primarily a book about economic theory, but is concerned with the impact of market dogmas upon politics, government and society generally; but this enterprise properly requires some initial survey of the intellectual roots of these dogmas, however brief and limited, in order to understand their gross inadequacy as a blueprint for how society should be organised. I have tried (with non-economists in mind) to keep the discussion as clear and non-technical as possible, while asking the indulgence of economists (who can of course skip anything too familiar) for any shortcomings.

The basis of market theory

Everybody knows that modern theories of the market started with Adam Smith. Smith, writing when the industrial revolution was beginning to accelerate in England, was the first thinker to envisage a complete market society wherein all 'factors of production' (labour, land and capital) could be bought and sold in the market-place – a striking change from the traditional system of economic organisation that was still prevalent in Smith's time and which included feudal land rights, an extensive subsistence agriculture, regulated craft guilds, government monopolies and controlled interest rates.

Smith's famous 'invisible hand' theory, the element in his thought that is most resonant today, was represented as a natural connection between the self-interest of butchers and bakers in making profits and the good service to their customers which a competitive market compelled them to perform. In Smith's view the increase of wealth was due not just to market competition but to the increasing specialisation of labour, a notion that foreshadowed the growth of 'Fordist' mass production. This belief in the dominant importance of efficient production, irrespective of its effects upon the nature or conditions of work, has a long history in orthodox economic thought.

However, in some respects, judged by later economic standards, Smith was decidedly old-fashioned. He still believed in the Lockean theory that economic value was created by labour. He was concerned with the distribution of wealth between the three classes of workers, landowners and industrialists, an issue which later dropped out of orthodox theories. He was an individualist but not an egoist – he believed that society was held together by mutual bonds of sympathy and would not have understood Mrs Thatcher's dictum that 'there is no such thing as society'.

Ricardo added theories of surplus rent and international trade. Agricultural rent would be nil on marginal land but it would increase with the fertility of the soil, irrespective of any contribution by the landowner – a first understanding of monopoly profit. He also initiated the theory of international trade based upon the relative (not absolute) natural advantage of each country for producing particular commodities; but he assumed as did Smith that (unlike today's situation) capital was largely immobile between countries.

Malthus, unlike Smith, held a gloomy view of economic progress because population would always grow faster than the means of subsistence. He was perhaps the first thinker among economists to debase the respect accorded to elegant mathematical propositions, arguing (without much evidence) that food production grows by only arithmetic additions but population by geometric ratios. Malthus was wrong about Western societies to date, but stripped of their dogmatism his fears seem justified by the rapid growth of world population. (For the classical economists see Roll, 1992 or more briefly Fusfeld, 1986, pp. 1–54.)

These rather eclectic theories of the 'classical' economists were replaced in the late nineteenth century by the 'neo-classical' revolution, which remains today, with various modifications, the basic orthodoxy of Anglo-American economic thinkers (Austrian thinkers represent an alternative but related tradition). The new theories were developed in different ways by Menger in Austria, Jevons in England and Walras in Switzerland and were then solidified in a wide-ranging manner by the Cambridge economist, Alfred Marshall. Marshall's *Principles of Economics* (1890, reprinted in 1980) became an authoritative statement of the new doctrine and its further evolution has produced no equivalent successor, but numerous first-year textbooks still offer the essence of neo-classical thought. Here a brief summary of some central elements of this thinking must suffice.

Neo-classical theory offers a comprehensive and logical if narrow account of the workings of a market economy which is based upon supposedly voluntary exchanges between economic actors, each of whom will secure the best bargain which he can obtain under prevailing conditions. Prices, wages and rents are all set by the market conditions of supply and demand. There is no room here for the theory that prices are set by an objective standard of the cost of labour; instead they are set by the interaction of the buyer's and seller's subjective expectations of the 'utility' (satisfaction) which each will get from the transaction. Nor is there room for the concern of the classical economists with the distribution of wealth between the main classes. The theory is ruthlessly individualist, each participant considering only his own interest with the resources and skills that he possesses.

The theory makes some strong and unrealistic assumptions. One is perfect competition, meaning that no producer on his own can set or influence the price of his product. In a full version, sometimes still used in theoretical exercises, this proviso requires an infinity of producers; a little more realistically it requires at least that no producer has more than a tiny share of the market for his goods and cannot influence their price. In practice the frequent existence of economies of scale gives advantages to large firms which vitiate the theory of competition. Another unrealistic requirement is perfect information, now revived as 'rational expectations'. A more realistic fall-back position here is Hayek's (1949), which is that the market price system, though not fully informed, conveys more relevant information for making rational economic decisions than could any alternative system such as government planning, although computers have much increased the information that could be made available for the latter purpose.

Neo-classical theory makes extensive use of the concept of 'marginalism', meaning that each actor will organise his market transactions rationally up to the point where he can achieve no further gain. Thus a rational housewife will organise her purchases (within the limits of her budget) so that she gains (or, to be accurate, expects to gain) equal satisfaction from the last unit of each item purchased. A rational producer will go on selling goods up to the point where profit on any further sale would vanish. A rational worker (presuming he has the option) will work longer hours up to the point where leisure becomes more valuable to him or her than more pay.

Neo-classical economics is based upon 'micro-theory', that is the behaviour and interactions of individuals or households and (by extension) firms. 'Macro-theory', the description of a total economy, was supposed to be taken care of by the same principles. It was assumed that if all markets 'cleared' and all factors of production received their appropriate price, a general equilibrium would be reached where all available resources would be fully utilised. If therefore unemployment existed, the reason must be that wages were too high for the labour market to clear – a familiar idea that is again in circulation. The idea that there might be collective aspects of market behaviour which vitiated general equilibrium did not have much salience before the Keynesian era.

The original neo-classical thinkers carried over into their theories the philosophical baggage of the Utilitarians. Just as these viewed 'mankind as under the governance of two sovereign masters, pain and pleasure' (Bentham), so did the economists assume that consumers would constantly strive to maximise their expected 'utility'; a shadowy concept supposed to underlie their preferences but unable itself to be measured. 'Utility' really explained nothing, unless one could swallow the idea that market price somehow measured the pleasure that an individual received – or expected to receive – from some good (Robinson, 1964, p. 48).

Later theorists have tried to drop this baggage (although it still crops up) and substitute the notion of 'revealed preference'; but this substitution does not explain any better than 'utility' why people prefer some things more than others. Individual preferences in the neo-classical world are 'exogenous', that is they are assumed to represent a free choice, and social or other influences upon the formation of preferences are excluded. People just prefer what they prefer. The shade of utility lingers on, however, in economists' tendency to divide experience into pain (costs) and pleasure (benefits). Work is a pain, and consumption, a pleasure – a curious belief when many people in fact get much of their pleasure from their work.

Theory and reality

How does neo-classical theory fare as a guide to reality on empirical tests? The answer seems to be that it fails rather badly, not only in relation to the existing market system but to any probable one.

The first point, already noted, is that conditions of perfect competition and information do not in fact exist in anything like the rigorous terms postulated by the theory. Competition in the real world is vitiated by the existence of monopoly, oligopoly and price cartels, as well as the introduction of branded products which are not closely comparable with similar products (as the manufacturers, perhaps with some exaggeration, themselves claim). Of course some markets are more competitive than others, and it might still be claimed that the theory holds *to the extent that* competition prevails. Unfortunately even this claim is very dubious. The theory of 'second best' points out that, if any of its basic assumptions are vitiated, the conclusions of the theory will not necessarily hold; for example, moves by one country to liberalise trade may not bring that country the expected gains from the theory of comparative advantage if free trade does not hold generally in the world. The likely outcome is indeterminate, depending upon a variety of factors (Lipsey and Lancaster, 1956). Similarly there has been much theorising about the nature of oligopoly, but oligopoly has not been fitted into or squared with the neo-classical framework.

Secondly, the concept of general equilibrium is misleading. Even if this concept can be satisfactorily defined, it will never be reached in practice since in the meantime events have moved on. It will take time for markets to work through to full equilibrium, but the neo-classical theory recognises that an equilibrium point holds only for a given set of consumers' tastes and available technology. As tastes and technology change (and the drive of actual capitalist systems is towards rapid change), so the positions of market equilibrium alter. Hence the theory of equilibrium is consistent with continuous instability rather than the spontaneous harmonisation of all resources which it seems to imply.

The Arrow–Debreu theory of general equilibrium which has recently been revived gets round this problem by assuming the existence of markets in all future events including inventions which have not yet occurred! This mechanistic device removes the uncertainty which is actually a central element of the capitalist system and which provides the opportunity for entrepreneurship itself. Yet this extraordinary mathematic model is still widely taught in universities as a formal demonstration of the truth of the 'invisible hand' – that the pursuit of individual greed will produce a social optimum. As some of its more eminent interpreters themselves say, what the theory actually shows is how little relevance its extreme assumptions have to actual economic life (Harcourt, 1997).

A third criticism follows. The theory offers only periodic snapshots of markets in supposed or potential equilibrium: it does not explain how the economy moves from one state to another. In particular it says nothing about technology and little about entrepreneurship (the capitalist of neo-classical thought is an automaton). These deficiencies of neo-classical thought have been filled in by other economists who have developed theories of trade cycles, waves of technological innovation, and the role of entrepreneurs in 'creative destruction' and innovation. All these theories, however, point to the difficulties of predicting economic behaviour under conditions of uncertainty and innovation. Again the role of money is hard to fit into market theory (and was largely ignored in neo-classical thought) since it is a socially managed institution. Even under the sway of the gold standard, the circulation and uses of money introduced another element of uncertainty into a supposedly self-adjusting system.

Finally the neo-classical assumptions about motivations are not empirically accurate. The theory that market actors are all 'rational egoists' seeking to maximise their gains will not hold. It may be true, as Chicago economists claim, that there is much more selfishness than altruism in the world so that it is safer to make the former assumption. However the distinction made between self-interest and altruism is much too crude. Social norms of co-operation play a necessary part in economic life, particularly within firms, and they have a strong role in some capitalist systems such as the Japanese.

The assumption of rationality, in the sense of the individual maximising his economic gain, seems to be equally inadequate. Consumers do not actually plan their purchases with the systematic rationality assumed by economists. They are often too ignorant, indifferent or erratic to behave in this manner. Moreover, many individuals have other goals and interests in life which conflict with a one-eyed pursuit of maximum economic gain. Herbert Simon (1957) made the point that in the real world individuals do not maximise their possible gains but 'satisfice' – settle for what is good enough; but economists stay with the unreal postulate of maximisation because it suits their equations. What can be conceded, however, is that a competitive market system does provide ample opportunities for the consistent pursuit of self-interest. As the market sphere has expanded in its range, variety and complexity, so consumers have become better informed and more interested in market opportunities and bargains.

From theory to prescription

What is the logical status of neo-classical theory? Its early exponents tended to suppose it represented laws of nature, akin to those of classical mechanics; but this is a false analogy. 'Classical mechanics is constitutive of nature (it seeks to discern the intrinsic order hidden in the properties of the system) but economic theory is "constructed logic"' (Bell, 1981, p. 77). It is an 'as if' model of how resources *would* be allocated *if* individuals maximised their 'utilities' rationally *under* the very stringent conditions of universal competitive markets. To suppose otherwise is false 'scientism' – an imputation of mechanical universal laws to human behaviour. With the scientific switch to the indeterminacies of quantum mechanics, any analogy with physics becomes even less relevant today.

Economic theory cannot really purport, as some people suppose it does, to lay down basic principles of human behaviour. It is not true historically – pre-industrial societies made a very limited use of market exchange and resources were mainly allocated according to social rules or the exercise of political and military power (Polanyi, 1944). It abstracts completely from sociology – the variable social influences which affect market behaviour and individual preferences are simply ignored. It abstracts also from institutional and political factors, although it is clear that changes in the political system have a considerable impact upon the operation of markets.

Economists meet many criticisms by arguing that it does not matter if their assumptions seem extreme or unrealistic if a theory successfully predicts actual behaviour. As Blaug says, economists are reluctant to make detailed tests, preferring to rely upon selective evidence to back up their deductions. The most compelling test is the Popperian one of falsification, which is the methodology of the natural sciences, but this test is rarely applied systematically (Blaug, 1992). Admittedly, empirical testing is very difficult, because of the problem of staging a controlled experiment in human behaviour and because of the many *ceteris paribus* assumptions (of holding other factors constant) which the theories require.

However, some elementary economic 'laws' do seem to predict behaviour fairly well and to give economics (in the eyes of many) a kind of scientific status not possessed by other social sciences. The reason seems to be that, even without assuming maximising behaviour, individuals have an obvious tendency to respond to price signals, and given the massive number of market transactions, uniform tendencies are likely to appear. For example, if the price of an article falls, and individuals' incomes, tastes, etc. remain unchanged, it is no great triumph to conclude that more of the article will be sold. A very simple assumption of rationality (getting a better bargain when possible) is enough to account for a successful statistical forecast if not offset by other changes. However, even this proposition is not completely true because some people (especially the affluent) seem to value a good *more* highly if it costs more money, which introduces the sociological factor of conspicuous consumption or social emulation. Bernard Shaw put this point with his usual wit by arguing that if churches with their pageantry and drama charged for admission, and theatres with their grim modern plays did not, the churches would soon be full and the theatres empty.

It has been said that the most useful part of economics consists in such elementary propositions, and that many political mistakes occur through ignoring them; for example, if housing rents are controlled, landlords will have little incentive to do repairs, and if food is rationed a 'black market' will develop. However, these propositions represent behavioural tendencies which may be countered by other measures – for example, rents may be regulated according to the condition of the property, and how far a 'black market' develops in rationed foodstuffs depends upon the extent of social acceptance and cohesion. Actual behaviour depends upon sociological and institutional factors which cannot be fully captured by economic logic; and moreover what seems logical at the 'micro' level of individual behaviour may work out quite differently at the 'macro' level of the total economy; for example, higher interest rates encourage individuals to save, but if they deter investment and reduce employment (as is also likely) total incomes will fall and total savings in the society (despite individual motivations) may fall too. One cannot say how the equation will work out without tracking a complex causal chain which is open to argument and dispute.

Neo-classical economics is best understood as a Weberian 'ideal type' theory – not in the sense that it is necessarily desirable, but so as to exhibit systematically the fully realised features and logical limits of a comprehensive system of competitive market exchanges between self-interested individuals. As such it cannot be expected to have more than a limited and variable relevance to actual market systems. There seems no need to object to it as a worthwhile mental exercise for illustrating the full logic of competitive markets based on private ownership. The puzzle comes in because this theory was and is treated as being also as a prescription for a socially and ethically desirable economy. Moreover, since this model envisages the scope of the economy in such very broad and comprehensive terms, it will dominate the whole character and texture of the society – unless the need for some countervailing force is acknowledged, which these economists are reluctant to concede: hence the Messianic imperialism of this economic theory if interpreted normatively.

But why need it be so interpreted? A comparison with the thought of Max Weber, the great German sociologist, is useful here. Weber was originally a professor of economics interested in neo-classical theory and then transferred his conception of 'ideal types' to sociology. Weber's 'ideal type' of bureaucracy mapped the logical limits of the emerging state bureaucracies of his day without being fully true of any actual bureaucracy – and is much less so today. However, Weber did not conclude that his model of bureaucracy was necessarily desirable despite its efficiency as an administrative instrument. Weber in fact became a strong critic of bureaucracy. (See Gerth and Mills, 1947, pp. 51, 61, 77, 128, 196, 244.)

The economic theorists on the other hand seem to have generally believed that their model *was* a desirable one for society to follow. This is equally or even more true of orthodox economists today. However, the whole project of a fully marketised society is open to fundamental questioning. The concept of 'economic man' or rational egoism, unless at least it is qualified and restricted, has a destructive impact upon social co-operation and mutual support. Human labour and the resources of nature (land, minerals, etc.) remain the fundamental materials of economic production. Is it right that the labour of human beings and the resources of nature should be treated as commodities to be bought and sold in the market-place in the same manner as consumer goods? Marxists of course thought emphatically not, and started their alternative tradition to orthodox economics. Basing his view not on Marxism but on historical research into the traumatic cultural impact of the growth of the market system upon working populations, Karl Polanyi showed the traumatic impact of capitalism upon human values (Polanyi, 1944).

The response of economic theorists was to distance themselves from these ethical and social issues in the effort to establish a pure science which made no judgements. As already noted, the classical economists were deeply concerned with the distribution of wealth between the principal economic classes, but the neo-classical school ignored classes (while Marxism reified them) and concentrated exclusively upon what were supposed to be the purely voluntary and independent choices of individuals. Thus issues of social conflict and power get excluded from orthodox economic thought.

The ethical issue of the distribution of wealth was also sidelined by treating all income as an appropriate return to some factor of production. In the case of land, Ricardo had demonstrated that landlords earned a surplus value through sitting on the more fertile or accessible land. A much larger surplus still arises from the development value of land caused not by any landlord's efforts but by the growth of population and urbanisation, and in modern times this common element of value has been fully exploited and turned into a major source of private and corporate wealth. It is very difficult to portray this income as in any meaningful sense 'earned' by its recipients, rather than as the result of accident, good fortune and shrewd speculation; for this reason one of the founders of neo-classical economics, Walras, advocated the nationalisation of land (and also of durable capital goods). So obvious is this point that, in line with Ricardo, a significant school of land economists developed who believed in land taxation as the most equitable and efficient way of financing public services (for a recent example see Day, 1995); but the impeccable logic of these thinkers has failed to prevent (except in a few countries and particular situations) the assimilation of land values into the closely intertwined private accumulation of assets. In accepting this outcome, orthodox economics develops into an ideology of private acquisition rather than a logic of markets.

Interest and profit also posed problems of justification. Interest was generally seen as a reward for abstinence through postponing the pleasures of consumption to a future or uncertain date; but it was an unfortunate fact that the main beneficiaries from this abstinence (the rich) had the least need to make the sacrifice. Profit could be seen as a reward for taking risks, but this was doubtfully adequate for justifying its often substantial size. Neo-classical thinkers, with their mechanical laws, gave a weak account of entrepreneurship. The Austrians by contrast gave more weight to conditions of uncertainty and personal initiative in their theory of markets (Kirzner, 1981). In the same spirit Schumpeter viewed entrepreneurial profit as the result of rearranging production (by new combinations of factors or by utilising new inventions and techniques) in such a way as accurately to anticipate a potential market demand; the rare qualities needed for such enterprise could earn a temporarily high profit which in theory would be wiped out when competitors caught up (Schumpeter, 1949, pp. 128–56); but it is questionable how far Schumpeter's justification of entrepreneurship holds under modern conditions of financial manipulation and speculation.

Some of the earlier neo-classical theorists were concerned about ethical issues. Marshall was a social reformer who believed optimistically that the new principles of economics would favour the workers; he supported legislation to improve their lot, although worrying later about the effects of the growing power of trade unions upon Britain's economic competitiveness. His successor at Cambridge, Pigou, was a pioneer of welfare economics, which in its original form stressed the many ways in which market transactions produced indirect social costs and benefits (known as 'externalities') (Hutchison, 1981, pp. 51–70). However, even reformist economists regarded state interventions to improve social welfare as necessary exceptions to the principles which they promulgated.

Revisionist theories

It is now necessary to bring this short history of economic theory up to date. The biggest technical problem of neo-classical theory in its own terms was the relationship between micro theory (the behaviour of individuals and firms) and macro theory (the performance of the national economy). It was assumed that if resources were efficiently used at the micro level then they would be fully utilised and employed at the macro level as well. This was the loose and optimistic construction put on Adam Smith's 'invisible hand'. There were, as already noted, problems about the determination of general equilibrium, and Marshall, for example, primarily concerned himself with the operation of partial markets rather than a total system. Beyond this it was a question of faith and trust in the universal applicability of assumed economic 'laws'.

However, the total economy refused to behave to economic fiat. In the industrial pioneer Britain and in the USA which was fast overtaking it, there were trade cycles of increasing severity from 1850 onwards and unemployment fluctuated wildly, eventually rising in the early 1930s to over 15 per cent in Britain and over 20 per cent in the USA (Ormerod, 1995, charts pp. 165, 166). In some older industrial areas almost half of the male labour force were out of work, at a time when there was also little paid employment for women. To some observers the great depression of the inter-war years signalled a death verdict upon received economic theory along with its orthodox prescriptions of cutting government expenditure and deflating the economy to combat depression.

Keynes offered the best known (but not the only) new explanation of the causes of this situation, together with some remedies for alleviating it. Keynes was a liberal, not a radical, and his aim was to save capitalism by eliminating the curse of large-scale unemployment. His general theory argued that full employment was a special not a general case of the workings of the economy. His reasons were that markets did not operate in the theoretically prescribed way. Wages were 'sticky'; they were influenced (hardly surprisingly) by social expectations and beliefs about fairness, so that they did not move upwards in a boom or downwards in a depression to the extent necessary to clear the labour market. However, his main explanation of unemployment was that the rate of interest did not fulfil its supposed function of balancing savings and investment at a level which would see all resources effectively employed.

Investment was crucial because it produced a 'multiplier' effect upon total demand and employment, since workers employed in producing investment goods would also increase the demand for consumption goods. However, falls in the rate of interest would not necessarily cause capitalists to invest, or to invest sufficiently, because other considerations – uncertainty and lack of confidence in future demand for their new products – could be more important. Conversely, savers, because of a 'liquidity preference' for hoarding their money when interest rates were low but expected to rise, would not necessarily make their savings available for investment (Keynes, 1936).

This theory of underinvestment and underconsumption offered a bold and plausible account of the causes of economic depression. After the Second World War, Keynesian ideas were eagerly seized upon in English-speaking countries (less so else-where) as a solvent for preventing any return to unemployment and depression which was viewed as politically disastrous. Keynesian-ism was actually not really applied in his own recommended way, which put a heavy stress upon public control or co-ordination of new investment (he mentioned a figure of 75 per cent of its volume) to ensure that it continued at a steady rate and on a long-term basis (Skidelsky, 1988). Instead 'Keynesian' demand man-agement worked through the government manipulating its fiscal and budgetary policies so as to ensure a high enough effective demand to sustain full employment (with regional variations where necessary). In Britain these policies followed a frustrating 'stop–go' cycle of government interventions under balance of payments constraints, but their main objective was achieved at a cost of mild but rising inflation.

In retrospect it seems clear that the long economic boom which followed the war was due to other causes beside 'Keynesian' pol-icies. These causes included the needs of post-war reconstruction, generous American aid to Western Europe and defeated coun-tries (motivated by the need to keep a common front against com-munism), the cold war armaments and space race (especially in the USA) and a large expansion of world trade. However, Keynesian policies were also important for maintaining general prosperity, because they provided early checks against minor recessions and increased the confidence of investors that the boom would go on indefinitely – that there would be no return to pre-war conditions and experience (Bleaney, 1985, pp. 92–130). Keynesianism also supported a large expansion of expenditure in the labour-intensive social services.

These halcyon conditions were undermined by the growth of inflation and then, in the 1970s, 'stagflation' (combined inflation and unemployment). Keynes himself had not supposed that his recipes were an adequate or suitable recipe for inflation, but his disciples were more optimistic or blind about the range and effi-cacy of his 'general theory' (Hutchison, 1981, pp. 108–54). Under full employment conditions, the psychological and institutional factors which Keynes rightly saw as vitiating orthodox theory, operate in different directions. The experience of full employ-ment and the expectation of continuing inflation exerts an up-ward pressure upon wages and prices.

The only obvious way to counter this pressure while maintaining full employment was some type of corporatist agreement between government, employers and trade unions for restricting the increase of wages and prices and for dividing the fruits of economic growth on some agreed basis. A system of this type was introduced in Sweden and several other European countries and emulated more weakly elsewhere. In the USA this concept was politically abhorrent and impracticable. In Britain the leadership of both main political parties would have liked (in the 1966–74 period) to have introduced an effective incomes and prices policy, but opposition within each party blocked it. Instead the Labour government of the 1970s made a 'social contract' with the unions promising adequate social policies (the 'social wage') in return for wage restraint. Late in the day the Australian Labor government operated a similar 'Accord' with the unions between 1983 and 1996. These measures broke down under resentment within the unions at having to bear the costs of economic 'restructuring' and the failure of increased profit margins to stimulate enough private investment to reduce unemployment (see Self, 1985, pp. 108–38).

The onset of inflation and stagflation discredited Keynesian theories in the eyes of many economists, although others kept their loyalty, and substantial schools of neo-Keynesians and post-Keynesians continue to exist. It seems clear that Keynes provided some perceptive insights into the workings of the economy and some relevant recipes for improving it in particular situations, but he did not propound a satisfactory general theory which would hold for all situations or phases of development. In a sense this conclusion is hardly surprising. Keynes put a heavy weight upon partly sociological factors such as 'sticky wages', 'liquidity preference' and 'uncertain expectations', but such factors are variable and difficult to fit into a comprehensive economic theory, which is why orthodox economists do not like them. (The fact that Keynes regarded these factors as 'psychological' probably goes back to the belief of economists that they can understand psychology by intuitive introspection but need not bother with sociology.) Thus the new elements which Keynes brought into play are open to different interpretations, but they raise the question of whether a realistic general theory is possible at all.

Influential economic textbooks such as Samuelson's (1964, 6th edn) initially coped with Keynes by simply adding a mechanistic version of his macro-theories to the old orthodox theory, producing the 'neo-classical synthesis'. A principal result of the Keynesian experience, however, seems to be to question the whole idea of this synthesis, or the union of old 'micro' with new 'macro' theories. The prescriptions for 'micro efficiency', which are pressed so vigorously today by orthodox economists, seem often to have perverse effects upon employment, investment and other aspects of 'macro' welfare, so that both types of theory need to be linked (if they can be) to a more complex and uncertain world than orthodox economists conceive.

The problems of Keynesianism led to a vigorous counter-attack from the neo-classical camp. Revived versions of old theories of 'monetarism' and a new statement of 'rational expectations' followed each other in quick succession. Keynesianism had regarded money as more the servant than the master of economic policy, and as responding to, not controlling, the level of economic activity. Milton Friedman invoked the classical quantity theory of money to argue that changes in the quantity and velocity of money circulating through the economy were the prime determinants of inflation and deflation. He even claimed that the great depression of the 1930s in America was due to banking failures and mistaken policies by the Federal Reserve Board. Consequently the correct policy for a central bank was to hold the money supply steady and increase it only in line with spontaneous growth within the economy, but not on any account to force that growth as Keynesians wanted. This theory fitted in neatly with the neo-classical concept of a natural equilibrium by reverting to the old idea that, granted a steady money supply, free market forces would clear the labour market at a 'natural level of unemployment' which the government could not better.

Monetarism as a policy prescription was put to the test under the Reagan and the Thatcher governments in the USA and Britain. The Federal Reserve Board (formally independent of the President) sharply reduced the money supply and caused a costly deflation, which was then quickly reversed by the unintended Keynesian effect of Reagan's big budgetary deficits. Friedman believed that a tough monetary policy, though temporarily unpleasant, would bring down unemployment to its 'natural rate' within two or three years. The Thatcher government of the 1980s came 'as close to testing this bold prediction as any policy ever can', but the result was failure as unemployment never fell below 8 per cent during the next ten years and for half the time exceeded 10 per cent (Blaug, 1992, p. 201).

Monetarism is a complex theory, not least in Friedman's different versions (Blaug, 1992, pp. 192–6). As a practical policy it encounters the technical problems of choosing between several different indicators of the money supply and of predicting the velocity of money through the economy which actually varies a great deal, particularly since financial deregulation (Ormerod, 1995, pp. 95–7). Central banks such as the Bundesbank and the Federal Reserve Board use the theory selectively in their measures to combat inflation. It is not an adequate theory of the causes of inflation and deflation and its supposed cure for unemployment depends upon the validity of the principles of free market economics.

'Rational expectations' is a much more extreme, artificial and curious theory. It started out from the observation that in certain circumstances market players could anticipate government interventions and vitiate their intentions, as already suggested in the case of anticipated inflation. From here one could proceed to the idea that the market will always out-guess the government's intentions. Even as a speculation this seems rather far-fetched since politics often appears unpredictable and the relationship between government and market (over budgetary intentions, for example) can also be seen as a type of two-sided strategic game. It also seems a bit strange that free market economists who frequently complain about government interventions should also now claim that the market can negate them by anticipation.

However, the full theory of rational expectations, as introduced by J. F. Muth (1961), posits that all rational actors will correctly anticipate and discount future economic developments except natural or political events that cannot reasonably be foreseen. Most individuals cannot possibly be expected to do this, but the theory claims that a fully informed representative market observer (for information of this kind is plainly a valuable commodity) will manage to do so. In empirical terms these assertions seem breathtaking; indeed there is no evidence that they are remotely true. The record of expert economic forecasters, the individuals who would seem to come closest to the 'informed observer', shows both a lack of consensus among them and wide margins of error – in fact sometimes they perform worse than some crude rule of thumb (for examples, see Ormerod, 1994, pp. 105, 109–10). This is perhaps not surprising when one reflects that economic 'macro' theorising is itself in disarray – there are numerous theories or beliefs about the relationships between different economic factors. The amazing thing is that at this stage of development some economists should come up with this reassertion in absolute terms of the old neo-classical assumption of perfect information.

A reason may be that the increasing evidence about *uncertainty* (not certainty) in economic expectations, together with the perceived significance of sociological and political factors, has led old-style economists to barricade themselves within their traditional dogmas. Some even argue that 'rational expectations' does not depend upon empirical evidence, but is intuitively given to the enlightened economist as a logical part of the economic behaviour of individuals who (apparently) do not even know they are being rational. Another explanation is that the theory offers these economists the excuse for a yet more elaborate mathematical game. But we need to remember that such theories are still taken seriously when they serve to close an endangered ideological circle of belief.

The crisis of economic theory

Is economic theory in crisis? It seems to be. We can start by summarising the problems already discussed about orthodox neo-classical thought.

(*a*) As positive science, this theory makes unreal assumptions about motivations, competition and information. Despite efforts to rehabilitate these assumptions, they are not empirically true (or only very partially so) of the real world. In addition, through focusing on exchange relations according to a narrow economic methodology, the theory ignores political and sociological aspects of economic behaviour. It assumes a largely spontaneous self-regulating system, but that assumption can be strongly challenged (in Chapter 2).

(*b*) As normative prescription, the theory exalts 'rational egoism' or 'atomistic individualism'. It is true that market exchanges have an instrumental or impersonal character which can be justified up to a point, provided the exchanges take place according to equitable laws and conventions – that there is a genuine 'business morality'. However, the continuous stress upon competition overlooks the value of co-operative norms which actually play a considerable part in some capitalist systems not under the sway of Anglo-American economic beliefs. Moreover, the belief in rational egoism has bad effects when market practices are carried over into widening spheres of political and social life – when boundaries are not set to the market realm.

(c) On both positive and normative grounds, there is a dangerous gap between micro- and macro-theories. Most economists show a good deal of agreement on micro-economic concepts and issues, but are divided on the big 'macro' issues of how the economy works and how to deal with inflation, unemployment, economic growth, etc. (Hutchison, 1981, p. 263). Some hold that 'micro' economic reforms, which work by cutting costs and maximising profits, are unable to ensure adequate levels of stability and efficiency for the economy as a whole, while others suppose that a ruthless enough dose of 'micro' reform – provided it produces really effective competition – will also eventually solve the 'macro' problems – insofar as they are soluble. The evidence suggests that the pursuit of micro-efficiency does not add up to macro-welfare and prosperity, a conclusion which squares with the beliefs of other economists (such as the post-Keynesians) that the problem lies not so much in any disjunction between the two levels of the economy as in errors of micro-economic theory itself. Economic prescriptions have lost credibility at the theoretical level, even while they continue to be applied more dogmatically than ever.

(d) There is also concern among some orthodox economists about ethical and social issues which their theories seem to ignore; for example, Stephen Rhoads (1985) worries that economists over-value money and goods, endorse (and themselves reveal in tests) an excessive egoism, underplay group choices and wrongly try to exclude value judgements (Rhoads, ch. 9).

Neo-classical economics has been described as a 'long cul-de-sac' (Stilwell, 1996) and the 'death of economics' (Ormerod, 1994) has been announced. Even a fairly mainstream economist such as Paul Krugman (1990) remits some of America's basic economic problems to sociology or politics. He regards the three main economic problems of that country as low growth in productivity, excessively unequal income distribution, and unemployment (which ought also to include very low-paid jobs in some service industries and in contracted-out manufacturing, the result of letting wages fall to their market level as an alternative to unemployment). However, he thinks that low productivity and the existence of an impoverished 'underclass' should be seen as sociological problems while the maldistribution of incomes represents a political failure. His title, 'the age of diminished expectations', suggests a sociological treatise, which it is not. It is a popularised, sensible account of economic issues which clears away some mistaken notions but finds no economic solutions for the basic economic problems.

Orthodox economics (itself split between neo-classical and neo-Keynesian or post-Keynesian branches) is today challenged by various forms of alternative economics – 'green', feminist, humanistic, radical, etc. (Lutz and Lux, 1988), as well as a gradual revival of the Marxist tradition. These alternative versions often introduce sociological elements into their theories, as well as proposing different normative foundations for them. Other questioning of orthodox economics has come from the institutionalist school, who have effectively demonstrated how the character and evolution of particular institutions (such as the business corporation) have a considerable impact upon how economies actually work.

By contrast, Kristol (1981, pp. 201–18) claims that it is impossible to develop any autonomous sphere of economic theory beyond the range of capitalist market economics; in his view, widening the subject means returning economics to a branch of political philosophy, as it was with Plato and Aristotle and indeed most thinkers before Adam Smith. He may be right in the sense that it is very difficult to formulate encompassing social theories and that economics could only be an element in such theories. On the other hand, the breakdown of the social sciences into largely autonomous subjects such as economics, politics, sociology, etc., with little communication between them even among experts, has been a disaster for our understanding of human behaviour and indeed for the pursuit of wisdom – the only ironic exception to this specialisation being the imperialism of economic methodology in moving into other fields at the very time it is in disarray in its own sphere. This invasion of other social sciences by economics is probably due to the widening spread of market practices and the normative beliefs which accompany them and leads to a neglect of other aspects of human behaviour, not just the narrowly economic. Hence a return to a more modest brand of economic thought within a broader social framework would have strong advantages.

But if orthodox economic theory is in such bad shape, why do its theories continue to be so politically influential? Why this paradox?

Orthodox economics appears to claim a normative status, however inappropriate that status may be to an 'ideal type' theory. Indeed economics is unique among the social sciences in having a strongly prescriptive bent, in claiming to know the right answers. Of course politicians do not necessarily follow or even understand economic theories; but there is no doubt that they are much influenced by economic advice that claims, often misleadingly, to be based upon those theories.

On the other hand, many economic thinkers agree that their methodology does have a basis in political values. Schumpeter recognised the influence of political ideology on the methods of economic thought. Myrdal (1953) held that economics is an instrumental science to be applied to ends which are politically determined. Lionel Robbins (1935) viewed economics as a science of means for allocating scarce resources between multiple ends; but Robbins was also clear that market exchange theory showed how resources ought to be allocated. A respected and hardly radical analyst of economic methodology such as Hutchison observes that all methodological prescriptions are inevitably based on some kind of ethical or political presuppositions or purposes (Hutchison, 1981, p. 298). Blaug (1992) stresses the resistance of economists to adequate empirical tests. He argues that economists have a 'hard core' of beliefs which they will protect vigorously by adjusting less central or auxiliary hypotheses when they are worsted in debate. For this reason much of the debate between monetarists and Keynesians was confused and unproductive, but it did eventually manage to get the protagonists to withdraw from their more extreme positions. Some little progress was made towards the goal of empirical testing (Blaug, 1992, pp. 192–205).

Heilbroner and Milberg (1995) argue that critical turning points in economic thought come from a mixture of ideology or 'vision' with the consolidation of analytic techniques. Critical points which consolidated economic thought (but sowed the seeds for further controversy) were provided by Smith, J. S. Mill, Marshall and Keynes; but today there is no successor because vision is blurred. The political and ideological vision of these key thinkers is clear enough. Smith fused market theory with liberal politics; J. S. Mill fused market theory with utilitarianism; Marshall consolidated neo-classical thinking with some measure of social reform; Keynes, more specifically than the others, fused capitalism with state intervention and planning. For a time Friedman seemed the theorist who could reforge a link between market theory and 'new right' politics, but his theory (though tried) was not sufficiently comprehensive or effective. This has left the new right dependent on inadequate economic theories to support market dogmas, but the latter have a remarkable staying power which remains to be explained.

It seems clear that much of the influence of neo-classical economics comes from its consonance with powerful business and political interests, currently in the ascendance in the modern world. Its formal logical coherence gives it an intellectual appeal and, as Blaug says, helps it to fight off awkward evidence by withdrawing into deeper theoretical trenches. It is difficult for non-economists to appreciate the value assumptions which underlie orthodox economic thought, especially as these are only rarely acknowledged by the economists themselves.

There appears to be a widening gap between the worlds of theoretical economists and economic advisers. Many 'academic' economists engage in abstruse mathematical exercises, done (according to Sir John Hicks) because they are an attractive intellectual game (quoted in Hutchison, 1981, p. 266). In contrast with the lack of agreement on big issues among the theoreticians, and their complex arguments, economic advisers have become increasingly partisan and often slipshod and superficial (see Deane, 1989, pp. 169–94). It seems that economists often base their economic beliefs on their political beliefs rather than vice versa. This more partisan and dogmatic style of economic advice is probably the corollary of the growth of a more activist style of politics with its downgrading of measured bureaucratic advice and increasing use of advisers who share or cater to dominant political beliefs and prejudices. The dominance of 'new right' politicians and 'think tanks' in English-speaking countries has also narrowed the market for economic advice. These developments have given a new lease of life to cut-down, modernised versions of neo-classical thinking, thereby reducing also the quality and variety of the economic advice relayed to governments. There is at a fundamental level a crisis in or of economic thought, but political bottles are still being filled with old economic wine.

The generation of market dogmas

We come finally in this chapter to a discussion of market dogmas. These dogmas constitute cut-down, simplified and action-orientated views of reality. They are not available in any coherent or authoritative body of writings but form the staple beliefs of many politicians, advisers and media commentators. They are based loosely upon orthodox (neo-classical) theories, but in simplifying they often misinterpret or exaggerate those theories. They ignore a lot of empirical evidence about the actual behaviour of capitalist markets and make claims within a narrow framework of reasoning. But they have a lot of political influence. A brief list of market dogmas might read as follows.

(*a*) 'The "free market" and market-led growth are the principal and overwhelmingly the most important sources of wealth.' Wealth here clearly refers to the production and sale of marketed goods and services, subject to individuals' capacity to buy them. But are all marketed goods equally valuable (or sometimes valuable at all) as sources of wealth? How far does their distribution matter? What, anyhow, do we mean by wealth and are there other major sources of wealth besides the market? These issues will be confronted in Chapter 3.

(*b*) 'Large incentives are necessary to market efficiency.' Almost every economic writer assumes the need for a very substantial trade-off between the claims of 'equity' and 'efficiency' (Okun, 1975), but the necessary extent of that trade-off is far from empirically clear. It is exaggerated in economic theory because of the heavy stress upon the monetary inducements required to stimulate 'economic man', and is still more exaggerated when used, as it often is, to justify the enormous differentials of incomes in modern market societies. Economic incentives appear to be more culturally determined than necessitated by some economic rule. Not so long ago top earners in Sweden paid over 90 per cent in taxes without any discernible adverse effects upon the good economic and export performance of Sweden at that time. Economic differentials today are far wider than in the post-war years when economic growth was higher than now. The enormous incomes and ancillary benefits (share options, etc.) paid today to company directors and executives seems mainly due to their political leverage on the distribution of profits (see next chapter), and to a global escalation of top monetary rewards caused by the fact or fear of 'brain drains' to countries like the USA where rewards are still higher.

(c) 'The wealth created by free markets will trickle down from the successful to benefit all members of society.' This proposition is sometimes justified by the argument that mass living standards in Western countries have risen substantially (though with many hiccups) over the last two centuries. It is not clear, however, how much of this rise was due to improvements in technology, education and other factors which might have occurred anyway under different economic systems; nor can one assume that rises in real money incomes equate with improvements in quality of life, since capitalist markets convert everything they can into monetary terms.

Recent experience in Western countries certainly gives no comfort to the 'trickle down' belief. The market liberalisation policies pursued in Britain and the USA since 1980, and in Australia and New Zealand rather later, have resulted in very large increases in economic inequality and in a growth of absolute poverty, which contrasts with the trend towards less inequality and poverty in the previous decades of stronger government intervention in the market. In Britain the income of the richest fifth of the population rose from four to seven times that of the poorest fifth between 1977 and 1991; in the USA the same ratio of richest to poorest rose from 7.5 times in 1969 to 11 times in 1992 (*The Economist*, 1996, p. 13). Changes in the position of the top rich and the bottom poor were still more striking, with the top tenth in Britain gaining almost 60 per cent more income and the poorest losing almost 20 per cent between 1979 and 1991 (Hills, 1996, p. 106). This rise in absolute poverty, which also occurred in the USA, is especially significant because it shows not trickle down but trickle up! The main causes of rising inequality in English-speaking countries seem to be market deregulation, unemployment and weakened labour protection (*The Economist*, 1996, pp. 14–15). Reverting to historical experience, it seems most doubtful whether 'trickle down' could have worked as much as it did (or probably at all) if it had not been supported increasingly by trade unions and welfare measures and by periods of full employment and war when egalitarianism was stronger.

(*d*) 'The market is intrinsically more efficient than government.' Efficient for what? one must ask. If the term refers to satisfying the particular preferences of individuals, subject to their income, then the market has a clear headstart over government which is geared to some form of collective choice; but collective choices, besides being indispensable for some vital 'public goods', can have other advantages relating to social cohesion, economic security and environmental protection which the market cannot satisfy as well or sometimes at all. These considerations are developed further in Chapters 3 and 6.

(*e*) 'To gain greater "efficiency", government should be redesigned according to market methods and incentives.' This proposition is at best very much of a partial truth. It can certainly be argued that governments, lacking market disciplines, have historically been lax over the costs they incur in relation to the benefits they produce. However, the wholesale adoption of market methods (or what are taken to be such) can have – and is having – some very serious effects upon the integrity, impartiality and accountability of government operations which hinge on different values from those of the market. Ultimately there are severe effects on the political process and the viability of democracy. This subject is explored in Chapter 4.

These various market dogmas (and there are others) rest ultimately upon the hoary figure of economic man (economic woman is rarely mentioned). The old doctrine of a natural harmony among individuals each pursuing his or her rational self-interest still has a lot of potency. This stress upon individual self-interest, while necessary and acceptable within limits, becomes destructive and dangerous when it ignores the complementary need for social co-operation and mutual support. The acquisitive instinct which it celebrates leads on to the steady expansion of the market into socially inappropriate spheres which then quickly get consolidated into the total capitalist system. It becomes still more destructive when treated as a suitable yardstick for political life and carried over into many aspects of social life. These points too will need to be further considered in subsequent chapters.

Despite their exaltation of 'economic man', it should be noted that these market dogmas are weakly grounded even in orthodox economic theory. Neo-classical economics is a theory of efficient allocation of resources according to individual preferences. It says nothing about the content of those preferences and is not committed to the doctrine of economic growth as a necessary goal. The theory does not legitimate the desirability of maximising output; if individuals prefer more leisure to more work, for example, that is a reasonable individual preference. The theory does not require that government be organised along market lines where it is performing different functions. Even the bias to economic incentives is conditional, because the incentives only need to be sufficient to ensure effective competition and in the neo-classical world profits would shrink to a modest level through the force of competition. In the real world financial rewards can become much greater than the theory authorises because of imperfect competition and the difficulty of judging (especially within large organisations) the economic value of individual contributions, especially at senior levels, so that political leverage and social conventions are influential over settling who gets what.

All the same, there is still considerable political support for or at least acquiescence in the capitalist market system. This is particularly true in America. Schotter (1990), who has some strong criticisms of the social effects of 'atomic individualism', nonetheless notes that Americans retain highly individualist beliefs and that even poorer people regard the system as intrinsically fair, and he notes how deeply embedded these ideas are in American culture and rhetoric (Schotter, pp. 151–61). The appeal of the system is the possibility of personal success and self-enrichment. President Reagan put this point crudely when he argued: 'what I want to see above all is that this country remains a country where someone can always get rich' (quoted in Bellah *et al.*, 1991, p. 87). In other countries there is less ideology of this type, but it is significant and perhaps remarkable that Labour (Labor) Parties in Britain, New Zealand and Australia have all switched to supporting most of the features of the present market system under the impetus of what their leaders perceive as either economic necessity or political pragmatism. Whatever the inadequacy of economic theories or dogmas, politics in the last twenty years – especially but not exclusively in English-speaking countries – has moved strongly in a pro-market direction.

Against this fact must be set the equal fact of increasing anxiety or disillusionment with the actual impact of the market economy. Partly this is a result of the disappointment of established expectations – for example 60 per cent of American workers have suffered a period of decline in real wages (Thurow, 1996), contrary to the previous record of rising prosperity. Partly it is due to pervasive anxiety and uncertainty caused by unemployment and the frequent redundancies due to deindustrialisation, rationalisation of services and other traumatic shifts in local and national economies. Partly it is caused by specific concerns about environmental degradation, deteriorating 'quality of life' and the advent of a low-paid female labour market. These developments, sometimes summarised as the 'cruel economy', might be expected to create a strong political momentum for reform of the market system and in due course they will do so. Part of the explanation for delayed reaction is that these sources of opposition lack unity and the support of a coherent set of beliefs, whereas supporters of the existing system are strongly entrenched and well financed in business, politics and the media; but another important fact is that most of the hostility and criticism is directed against politicians and governments, who get blamed for failing to manage economies more successfully and have themselves often contributed strongly to these adverse results through basing their policies upon a crude acceptance of market dogmas.

Another important factor is the growth of global markets. Free trade is another market dogma which gets the support of almost all orthodox economists. Free trade is also supposed to be the essential condition for the further pursuit of economic growth. Globalisation and its dogmas are further explored in Chapter 5. At the level of national politics, however, the ruling assumptions remain that global markets are an inescapable fact, that salvation lies through global advances in free trade and conventional economic growth, that the first necessity for any national economy is to adjust to the exigencies of global competition, and that all other considerations must be subordinated to their need. Strong consequences are drawn from this position. Thus it is supposedly necessary to cut public expenditure in order to free more resources for the market sector, to attract foreign investment with tax and other concessions and to avoid an exodus of the 'hot money' which flows around the world nightly in vast quantities in search of quick profit – a search also influenced by market beliefs about the political 'reliability' of individual countries. A further belief is that it is essential to press on with 'micro-economic reforms' aimed at shedding labour and cutting production costs, although the relationship between these reforms and general prosperity is doubtful – the effect is simply assumed to be beneficial. In this new world it is also assumed that the sources of new investment do not much matter, although in practice dependence upon foreign capital still makes a nation more vulnerable to international economic depressions or monetary crises (see further in Chapter 5).

These pressures of global competition go a long way to explain the compliance of political leaders with the apparent requirements of the capitalist market system. In some respects the leaders seem to swallow current dogmas – for example, over the need to curtail public investment and privatise or outsource public services to a greater extent than global market competition actually requires. One reason for this is that the market's time perspective is a short one, whereas government policies need time to take effect. Public policies which improve the environment and social services, or increase social harmony by preventing poverty, will in the long run probably also make a country more attractive economically, but these aims can be defeated by short-term calculations within the volatile and ubiquitous market system.

This comprehensive endorsement of a humanly contrived and institutionally backed system amounts to a form of economic determinism which is the mirror-image of the Marxism now eliminated by the orthodox from serious consideration. But must the world be so narrowly ruled by uncontrollable events? If a global economy needs to be accepted, must it take its present form? Are there not alternative forms of capitalism or of a reformed market system which might be constructed? Cannot boundaries be set to the imperialism of capitalist markets? Cannot different institutions which cater to other human values and needs be revived or initiated? Is any longer-term vision of human aims possible which can overcome the short-termism and destructive side-effects of current orthodox policies?

These wider questions must be left to the end of the book. Meanwhile, to summarise, this chapter has tried to show how inadequate are orthodox economic theories, and much more so their popularised 'market dogmas', for understanding or justifying the actual economic order which we inhabit. Nonetheless they provide support for political beliefs about the desirability or inevitability of capitalist markets, and these old beliefs are now being strongly reactivated by the apparent 'survival' requirements of living with global capitalism. To understand better the character of current orthodoxies, it is necessary to turn next to a parallel account of the development of political thought.

2
The Corruption of Liberalism

The last chapter argued that economic theory offers very limited justification for the market system even theoretically, let alone as the system actually works. This chapter pursues the same enterprise in relation to political thought. This theme is important because the current revival of a strong faith in 'market forces' rests upon a renewal and indeed an exaggeration of traditional liberal beliefs. We need to consider what basis and justification there is for these beliefs as they are now presented in a fresh and more extreme form.

Liberalism has been central to the development of political thought since the industrial revolution and indeed to the whole enterprise of 'modernity'. It is not a uniform or homogeneous body of ideas since a split occurred in the late nineteenth century between what I will call the 'negative' and the 'positive' liberals. The positive liberals differed from the negative ones in having a more positive view of freedom and equality, and in being prepared to enlist government for these purposes. The negative liberals stayed with a strong faith in the beneficence of capitalist markets and an equally strong distrust of government action beyond the necessity for a few basic laws and services. The positive liberals made a large contribution to the development of the welfare state, the negative liberals are again in the saddle today.

The liberal tradition in Europe (but not in America where it had no rival) was flanked on one side by the continuing existence of an aristocratic conservatism and on the other by the growth of socialism. However liberalism spilt over into these other two political movements and in its two contrasting versions has had a considerable influence upon and within both of them. In this sense liberalism is central to the development of modern political thought. Modern conservatism and democratic socialism are in many respects the heirs of contrasting liberal political beliefs.

By liberal thought and tradition I am not referring to the beliefs of modern parties termed Liberal, although some mention will be made of the evolution of political parties. Much less does 'liberal' include the pejorative American sense of left-wing thinkers accused of 'soft' attitudes over issues such as crime, drugs, abortion and welfare, which is a misuse of the liberal tradition. Instead 'liberal thought' refers to the pursuit of a coherent body of thought about political, economic and social relationships between individuals in a society, founded on some basic concept of the worth and entitlements of each individual.

Such a body of thought may be called an 'ideology' on the understanding that it need not be completely closed to evidence and argument, even if inclined to be strongly resistant to any undercutting of its core beliefs. An ideology in this modified sense is also linked with material interests, but not necessarily or absolutely so. If a set of beliefs is completely dogmatic or a mere rationalisation of interests, there could be no point in rational argument or of evidence such as this book tries to produce; and that conclusion would be a death blow to a central core of the liberal tradition, which is belief in the value of rational debate and the progress of knowledge and mutual understanding.

The philosophic basis or grounds of liberal thought cannot get adequate attention here as that is a vast subject; but it is possible to discuss and evaluate operative beliefs (as many thinkers have done) without having to defend some ultimate philosophic justification for them. Indeed efforts in that direction seem often to end in an unresolved mire of philosophic scepticism (Gray, 1989, p. 234). However, some attention to the philosophic basis of liberalism will be helpful, especially in the last section of this chapter.

The liberal tradition

Liberalism is basically an individualist tradition. It celebrates the rights and responsibilities of individuals. Its strong attachment to individual freedom stresses the right of individuals to choose and make their own lives and to take responsibility for the outcomes. It also endorses equality in the sense of the equal moral worth of all individuals and their entitlement to respect and consideration.

As a child of the Enlightenment, liberalism has always had a strong belief in the value of human reason and in the possibility of human progress.

These lead ideas had, from the beginning, both political and economic applications. Constitutionalism was and remains the first and least controversial achievement of liberal thought. Monarchical power, feudal privileges in land and offices, and arbitrary government were the original enemies. In their place was put constitutional government, meaning the rule of law, an independent judiciary, representative assemblies and civil rights. In this sphere liberalism made enduring contributions which retain great value to this day: freedom of opinion, freedom of assembly for peaceful purposes, freedom of worship, freedom from arbitrary imprisonment.

In the economic sphere, the individual freedoms stressed were the right to own and inherit property, to choose one's own occupation, and to profit from one's own abilities – 'the career open to talents'. Once again the existence of feudal privileges and of state 'mercantilist' monopolies were enemies to be overcome. John Locke pioneered the concept of property and inheritance as natural (intrinsic) rights, based on the proposition that an individual had the right to any land or resources with which he had 'mixed his own labour' and to pass it on to his heirs. Adam Smith developed a more fully fledged theory of how the individual pursuit of self-improvement and gain would yield appropriate rewards and would generate economic progress through a competitive market economy. The long progress of the individual from 'status' (a position determined by the social system or heredity) to 'contract' (a position determined by negotiation or bargaining) mirrored the development of the market system and is being further accelerated today.

Political democracy was a more contested outcome of liberalism. There were, as there are again today, fears that a democratic majority would undermine the rights of property and seek a substantial redistribution of wealth. There were doubts about the fitness of the populace to choose its representatives. However, the logic of liberalism, its concepts of individual liberty and equality, pointed towards political democracy. In Britain it came about by many slow stages, and not until 1928, after the attempted suppression of a strong suffragette movement and the First World

War, was full adult suffrage conceded. In other English-speaking countries the process was rather quicker.

To appreciate the force of early liberalism, one must remember how closely it was associated with a dominant social ethic. Adam Smith believed that society was held together by strong bonds of social sympathy and he was critical of many aspects of commercial life. The purpose of wealth-getting was to assist the pursuit of worthier objectives and the promotion of a cultivated way of life. Despite the liberals' objections to artificial privileges, the existence of social classes was taken for granted. Such social solidarity as existed was based upon a widespread belief in the virtues of hard work and thrift and the possibility of progress. The precepts of religion were a powerful influence on individual and family life, enjoining sober and respectable behaviour.

The earlier capitalists were themselves imbued, as in Weber's and Tawney's well-known accounts, with a strong 'puritan ethic'; and the same values were fed to the workers by strong religious movements (Methodism and other nonconformist sects). These teachings might reach only the 'respectable poor' amid masses living in squalor but they kept open the idea of the possibility of progress to better things. If 'economic laws' were necessary for this purpose, they had to be accepted. Thus the driving force in society was a belief in long-term progress based upon hard work and thrift – a belief very much less in evidence today.

The squalor and dislocation produced in Britain by the industrial revolution was so great that progress was, anyhow, slow. Agricultural capitalism, promoted by the Enclosure Acts, and a rising birth rate had driven vast numbers into the growing industrial towns, where they and their children toiled for extraordinarily long hours in mines, mills and workshops, and lived in insanitary slums. Whatever economic laws might say, some degree of public intervention – whether on grounds of compassion or from enlightened self-interest as a protection against diseases or riots – seemed necessary in order to improve the appalling health and working conditions of the poor; and interventions duly came in a rising tide of health and factory legislation, later moving on to education, housing and slum clearance. As this process gathered steam, a major cleavage opened up within liberal thought.

The liberal cleavage

John Stuart Mill stood at the liberal crossroads. A Utilitarian, he was unhappy with the narrow concept of happiness in terms of pleasure and pain held by Bentham and his father, James Mill. He viewed happiness as the autonomous pursuit of a worthwhile and cultivated life and he cherished individuality and the development of personality in women as much as in men. His attachment to the development of democracy was qualified by his anxiety about the ignorance of the majority and he feared the tyranny of public opinion. Mill therefore was a strong defender of personal liberty in social life, as many liberals are today.

Mill consolidated much of the work of the classical economists, setting out the principles of a market economy, but he became increasingly unhappy with the actual workings of that economy. It seemed inequitable that 'reward, instead of being proportional to the labour and abstinence of the individual, is almost in inverse ratio to it' (Mill, 1983). The excessive wealth of the rich was not helpful but inimical to liberty and the poor had no opportunity to enjoy liberty. Mill therefore advocated a stiff inheritance tax and a guaranteed basic income. He also thought that capitalism was too conflictual and that workers should participate in the running of their firms (Gray, 1989, pp. 1–9). Mill still believed in the truth of market principles, but he also anticipated the 'positive liberals' in his later quest for setting political and moral limits to their operation.

After Mill, British liberalism split down the middle (Freeden, 1996, pp. 139–316). In contrast to Mill's later writings, the 'negative liberals' were greatly alarmed by the growth of social legislation. Holding a 'negative' view of freedom as meaning simply the absence of direct coercion, they believed (as their successors do today) that the market system was fully consistent with liberty but the growth of government a serious threat to it. Herbert Spencer in *The Man versus the State* (1884) (Spencer, 1969) argued that each particular public intervention (such as limiting the hours worked by children in the mines) might seem sensible and desirable, but cumulatively these many acts would result in a dominant collectivism which would undermine the capacity and responsibility of individuals for self-improvement. Like Marx, though for a very different reason, Spencer saw the withering of the state as the route to human liberty and progress. In its place Spencer put a false Darwinian analogy of the inevitability of a struggle among individuals to survive and prosper in a competitive economy. Spencer's books were best-sellers in America.

The 'positive liberals' turned in the opposite direction. For these thinkers the absence of direct coercion was a very inadequate idea of freedom. Individuals could be formally free and yet, caught in the toils of the market system, have little or no opportunity to develop their capacities or lead worthwhile lives. Positive liberty was linked with the possession of personal autonomy and the scope, dear to Victorians but largely absent today, for moral improvement. To enjoy positive freedom, it was necessary to have an adequate minimum of resources and opportunities, particularly of an educational kind. If the opportunities were there, individuals would respond by developing their skills and interests in a positive and beneficial way.

Leading thinkers in this school were T. H. Green, J. A. Hobson and L. T. Hobhouse. They and their disciples had an enormous influence on British life and public policies, and also overseas, especially in Australia and New Zealand. They, especially Green, promoted the development of public education, including liberal adult education through the Workers Educational Association and later through universities, which introduced many workers without formal education to social and political issues and enjoyment of the arts. (Many local councillors and union organisers and some MPs got their education this way.) They pioneered the development of systematic social and community work, including the 'settlement houses' in east London and other deprived areas. They stirred the conscience of the upper classes and appealed to many leading educationalists and politicians (Balliol and other Oxford Colleges were strongly under their influence for a long time). They also influenced the last stage of British colonialism, when liberal administrators were keen to 'work themselves out of a job' by preparing the locals for self-government (Vincent and Plant, 1984).

T. H. Green preached a version of Hegel's 'idealist theory of the State', a view which is very unfashionable today. However, the essence of his thought can also be captured more modestly from his view of the role of the state as 'removing obstacles to the good life'. The positive liberals were strongly opposed to doctrines of class conflict or Marxism; they wanted a unified nation and a moralised capitalism; and they sought to connect liberty to equality through the balancing role of the state and through encouraging the masses to participate actively in the civic and political life of the community.

In the early years of the twentieth century, pushed along by reforming Liberal governments, the positive liberals saw their aims being achieved by the growth of public education, the beginnings of social security and unemployment relief, and a strengthening of the role of trade unions. Events were moving fast away from the Spencerian vision. The high point of positive liberalism as a separate political doctrine was L. T. Hobhouse's *Liberalism* written in 1911. He stressed the social factors involved in the creation of wealth and, while accepting liberal values in the social and constitutional spheres, he argued that his version of 'economic liberalism' 'seeks to do justice to the social and individual factors in industry alike' (Hobhouse, 1964, p. 108). Hence the case for minimum wages and an effective system of social security, although there should still be reliance upon individual thrift above the basic level. A strong internationalist, Hobhouse looked forward to a future of peace and progress just before these dreams were shattered by the First World War and the subsequent collapse of the Liberal Party in England.

The bridge to democratic socialism

The political history of the liberal legacy in Britain can briefly be told. The Liberal Party collapsed under internal conflicts and the rise of the Labour Party which, under the bias of the electoral system to only two main parties, replaced the Liberals as the alternative to the Conservatives. Thereupon many 'negative liberals' migrated to the Conservatives, who were still dominated by a tradition of aristocratic pragmatism and paternalism. Although the Conservatives became increasingly the party of business and employers, their traditions were not favourable to the ideas of 'limited government' and 'free markets'; and during and after the Second World War they moved pragmatically towards a considerable endorsement of the welfare state. The negative liberals had to wait for success until the election of Mrs Thatcher as leader and her victory in the 1979 election.

Meanwhile many 'positive liberals' gravitated into the Labour Party. There then occurred a gradual fusion of beliefs that was of great importance for the development of modern political thought. Initially the positive liberals had been strongly opposed to socialism, because of its linkage with class conflict and with state ownership of the means of production, and which contrasted with the unified and moralised society in which they believed. However the Labour Party gradually shed these Marxist associations, first repudiating its belief in comprehensive public ownership and later reducing its links with the trade union movement. Labour also became more individualist and less collectivist in its aims. Consequently the obstacles for a fusion of thought between positive liberalism and democratic socialism largely dissolved.

In any event both doctrines could unite in advocacy of some form of 'welfare state', which for Labour became increasingly more important than public ownership. In many respects the creation of the post-1945 welfare state in Britain represented the logical culmination of the reforms initiated by the Liberals early in the century. Through its social security provisions, its comprehensive health service and its large public housing programme, it offered in principle, although not fully in practice, the basic material security for all that the positive liberals had long wanted. Where it did not seem to do so well was in providing opportunities for the 'moral autonomy' which the positive liberals valued so highly. The post-war expansion of education services had disappointing results from this liberal standpoint, because it failed to ignite any wide enthusiasm for education as a form of personal development and enjoyment. On the other hand, there was no doubt that most individuals now had much more opportunity than before to live the kind of life they chose.

The post-war development of the welfare state seemed at the time to deliver a permanent defeat to the negative liberals. A new balance between government and market – with a stronger role for the first and a more controlled one for the second – seemed firmly established and confirmed by its coincidence with economic growth and full employment. When Hayek published *The Road to Serfdom* in 1944, he seemed to be preaching a lost cause, made no better by his awesome warnings about tyranny to the people of a mature democracy. Fifty years later his support for 'free markets' and 'limited government' has become the new political orthodoxy.

This is not the place to describe in detail how the modern theories of 'negative liberalism' (or in more extreme form, libertarianism) were hatched and spread (see Cockett, 1983). The intellectual gurus of the movement were the pro-market theorists such as Hayek and Friedman, and the public choice economists, such as Buchanan, Tullock, Olsen, Niskanen and others, who argued that governments were inefficient compared with markets over meeting individual wants and were prone to political and bureaucratic failures (see Self, 1993). These academic ideas were spread and politicised through a growing number of right-wing 'think tanks', well financed by business, which in turn influenced leading politicians and their advisers. When it came to actual policies, the influence of think tanks and academics declined and the more extreme 'libertarian' recipes got rejected, but a new ruling orthodoxy had been established politically. Cockett concludes his account by saying (p. 331): 'far from it being the "End of History", we are now at the point when the counter-revolution against economic liberalism will start, and the Hayekian campaign of intellectual persuasion provides the modern model of how to effect the next intellectual counter-revolution'.

This account has built upon the history of British political thought, but similar conflicts of belief have occurred in other Western countries. The liberal tradition on the continent of Europe was just as strong, but there was less bias towards an exclusive individualism and more recognition from the start of the need to locate individual liberty within a supportive and constraining social framework. These linkages were potently expressed in the French revolutionary slogan of 'liberty, equality and fraternity'. Liberalism sought to articulate all three values equally, although there was naturally argument about their relationship. Belief in the possibility of rational universal law supported the allocation of clear duties as well as rights to individuals. These traditions meant that, while some thinkers did argue for maximum commercial freedom, the liberal tradition in Germany and France was fairly supportive of a positive role for the state in the advancement of basic economic rights and opportunities (Freeden, 1996, pp. 210–25).

The conflict of beliefs in continental Europe occurred more between conservatism and socialism than within the bounds of liberalism. Religion featured much more in the conflict of ideas than in Britain, because of the religious links of conservative parties like the Christian Democrats, and the anti-clerical bias of liberal rationalism shared often by labour. However the conversion of Catholic parties to a belief in the rights of labour linked with the pragmatic moderation of Socialist parties to establish a broad political basis for the creation of welfare states on stronger, more comprehensive lines than in Britain. Simultaneously the influence of market economic theory has grown stronger, but for the most part falls well short of the negative liberalism of Thatcherism, which has little historic resonance on the continent.

In America, as Hartz (1955) says, negative liberalism (or 'Lockean liberalism' as he calls it) carried all before it. There was no feudal aristocracy to contain it on the right flank and no growth of class-conscious socialism to threaten from the left. Helped by the abundant natural riches of a vast new land, protected by the deliberate checks and balances of the constitution, the growth of capitalism forged ahead, and for long government remained small and was regarded critically as a source of political spoils and party machines. In the late nineteenth century strong conflicts did arise in some industries between capital and labour, and (more politically salient) between farmers and the big banking and railroad monopolies. The Progressives achieved some control over monopoly with the Sherman Anti-Trust Act, but this measure still left the door open for the growth of big business and oligopolies. On the whole, big capitalism successfully co-opted its smaller brethren into a peculiarly American faith in 'democratic capitalism'.

Not until the stock market crash of 1929 and subsequent depression of the 1930s was this belief in 'negative liberalism' effectively questioned. Roosevelt's New Deal for the first time introduced considerable government intervention to help the weaker groups in society. They were peculiarly American measures, pragmatic and experimental, but in an eclectic manner they introduced or reflected some of the ideas of positive liberalism and (more weakly) democratic socialism. The process continued after the Second World War with Truman's 'Fair Deal' and, more radically, Kennedy's and Johnson's 'War On Poverty'. With their apparent failure to remove poverty, the reform momentum began to run out of steam and was overtaken by the same powerful revival of 'negative liberalism', backed by well-financed think tanks, as happened in Britain. The election of President Reagan returned America to its traditional brand of negative liberalism, although the term 'conservatism' was now preferred, and indicated a greater distrust of any reformist or radical movement which might threaten capitalist interests.

This brief history of liberal thought provides the basis for examining the theories advanced by the new apostles of market freedom. There is an obvious problem of nomenclature here. I have called these advocates 'negative liberals' because of their espousal of a negative view of freedom and its connection with the earlier liberal split. However, the term may not be generally recognised, especially as these advocates are now generally identified with conservatism and the 'new right'. Hayek argues that his position (and that of other members of this school) is not a conservative one, since the main principle of conservatism is to oppose change whereas his brand of liberalism welcomes the changes which would result from a full application of its competitive market principles. Conservatism has tendencies towards paternalism, authoritarianism and nationalism, whereas Hayek's liberalism opposes these attitudes and believes instead in the 'spontaneous evolution' of the market system (Hayek, 1960, pp. 397–414). Hayek is certainly a negative liberal very akin to Herbert Spencer, but he does not share the old liberal belief in reason and progress because he trusts completely in the development of uncontrolled market forces.

It is often said that the disciples of these thinkers have won the political argument in the West. But have they truly won it at the level of rational argument and evidence? It is time now to consider some of the key propositions which form the basis of modern negative or market liberalism.

The politics of the market

Hayek's central contention is that markets constitute a spontaneous, impersonal and largely self-regulating system, whereas government actions, when they go beyond a limited number of general laws, soon become arbitrary and destructive of personal liberty and initiative. Leaving the second proposition for later discussion I here consider the first one.

How spontaneous is the market system? Hayek stresses that the knowledge of each individual is necessarily limited and he has little sympathy with the extreme claims of 'rational expectations'; but he argues that prices in competitive markets, which evolve spontaneously as the outcome of numerous individual decisions to buy or sell, represent an enormously valuable source of condensed information. They provide a much more rational and consistent basis for individual economic decisions than could any form of planned allocation of resources. There is force in this concept of the usefulness of prices in competitive markets, but the issue does not end there.

Hayek concedes that rewards in the market-place are not proportionate to individual merit or desert. They are due to all sorts of factors – innate skills, inheritance, luck or good fortune as well as hard work. Indeed a man may work hard and long and still get little reward. But Hayek believes that the income which an individual receives in the market-place should be the value placed on his services by their purchaser, since any other principle would bring in controversial and arbitrary tests of merit or need (Hayek, 1949).

But is this an adequate picture of how capitalist markets operate? Hayek and most orthodox economists never mention power or politics in connection with markets, save sometimes for deploring political lobbying by market interests; and the system itself is seen as a smooth-running machine, motivated by rational bargains struck between willing and formally equal actors. One does not have to be a Marxist to see that this is a very inadequate description. It is true that a properly policed market system does not allow for the exercise of any direct coercion, although physical coercion and violence on both sides has and still does occur in labour disputes. But if not coercion then at least power, or what may be termed market power, is prevalent throughout the system.

Its most obvious relevance lies in the relation between capital and labour. These vary greatly by time, place and circumstance, but generally a worker has considerably weaker bargaining power than his or her potential employer. The worker, particularly one with few skills, may have little opportunity of obtaining a job save on the terms offered him. The employer can usually find an alternative worker on similar terms or in the extreme can postpone or cancel some intended investment. This disproportionate relationship is the explanation for the tolerance eventually conceded, not without a hard and long struggle, towards the growth of trade unions as a means of redressing the balance of market power.

The arrival of full employment much reduced this inequality of market power, but also eroded sympathy for trade unions through perceived cases of abuses of union power. The return of substantial unemployment has shifted the relationship backwards, helped along by more stringent laws over the formation and behaviour of unions and their declining membership in the face of unemployment and deindustrialisation. There is no need to posit an explicit capitalist 'conspiracy' to see that 'a reserve army of unemployed' strengthens the hands of employers (Kalecki, 1990) – certainly this situation seems to have a favourable not an adverse effect upon share prices. Contrary to orthodox economic textbooks (which, however, can never properly explain why capital earns a particular return), it is surely not unreasonable to suggest that the share of profits in total income is influenced by these bargaining relationships, and is not just the necessary and correct price of capital within a spontaneous market system.

Moreover the exercise of market power can be seen throughout the economic system. The terms of trade between agriculture and most forms of primary production on the one hand and that of manufactured goods on the other are highly unequal. This result would not be present in a perfectly competitive world, but such does not exist. There are millions or billions of primary producers in the world, mostly very poor, whereas many industrial markets are dominated by a few big firms or conglomerates, and competition is pursued more by salesmanship and the use of brand names than by the intense price competition that occurs in agriculture. Agricultural subsidies represent a possible compensation for this inequality of bargaining power, but they largely go to big farmers or companies (agribusiness) who do not need them, and are not available in the many poor countries which rely on the export of primary products.

Market theory explains the growth of large firms in terms of a rational pursuit of economic efficiency. A firm grows through achieving economies of scale or through integrating production with the supply of materials and/or distribution. All this may be true but another factor is the advantage of strong market power. A big firm has the resources and staying power to squeeze out smaller or new competitors – for example, by reducing its prices for a time until the opposition is defeated, as can be observed in 'wars' between supermarket chains and small retailers. It can buy up and for a time monopolise new inventions or prevent their use elsewhere. The modern growth of big 'conglomerates' is much influenced by financial considerations of diversifying risks, minimising tax and exchange liabilities, and maximising potential asset prices. These considerations have a limited relationship with industrial efficiency and an obvious one with market power based upon great resources and information.

Large firms have greater market power than small firms. Today many small businesses work as contractors or suppliers to large firms. The literature on 'transaction cost analysis' (Williamson, 1985) explains how and when it will be advantageous for a big firm to make such arrangements. Sometimes this is done to get gains from efficient specialisation, but another reason (less mentioned in the textbooks) can be the advantage of drawing upon cheaper sources of labour, since a big firm is often more liable to trade union pressure. Small firms live in a more competitive environment and are more dependent (sometimes wholly dependent) upon keeping their contracts, whereas the big firm has more scope to shop elsewhere or provide the service internally.

Many small businesses are dependent upon franchises provided by large companies, such as development companies, oil companies and so on. An important factor here is the large number of individuals with only modest or little capital who are keen to be 'independent' and run their own business. Thus a property-owning company drawing income from the rents paid by small retailers (rents which actually mainly accrue, as noted earlier, from socially created development values) is in a strong bargaining position vis-à-vis its tenants. It has large reserves to cushion any dispute over rent and there will probably be some other individual willing to take the risk of paying a higher rent to establish his 'independence'. In times of unemployment, many small businesses – shops, motels, garages, restaurants, taxis, etc. – become overcrowded with hopeful individuals, some with capital enough to be moderately independent but many with a precarious dependence upon the decisions of controlling firms or landlords.

Another example of market power or politics is the ability of the directors of firms and their top executives to award themselves enormous increases in salary, bonuses, share options, etc. These big self-rewards do not seem even to correlate with levels of profit (Dahl, 1985, p. 109). Shareholders sometimes protest angrily about this at company meetings but a once-a-year meeting is too infrequent to hold directors effectively to account. These big rewards are usually justified by arguing that they are needed to keep executives with a high level of financial and managerial skills; but the same individuals have the ability to bid up the price of their skills within a system where they occupy a pivotal position.

Further there is the important question of equality under the law. Capitalist markets are not spontaneous in another sense. They depend crucially upon appropriate laws of property, contract, taxation and at least some regulation (in practice quite a lot) to prevent commercial malpractice and other abuses. Hayek admits – indeed stresses – the necessity of this legal framework and concedes 'that how well the market will function depends on the character of the particular rules', but passes over the issue as too complicated and perhaps best left to lawyers, which means that the market again escapes critical scrutiny (Hayek, 1960, pp. 229–30). Actually the subject raises too important political and economic issues to be left to lawyers. The big market players have superior legal resources in drawing up contracts with smaller players. In an Australian shopping mall, for example, the individual shop proprietors often provide in total more capital than the company which owns the whole project, but that company has a central co-ordinating role and is the usual winner from contracts which often are not adequately understood by the small shop-keepers (*Finding a Balance*, 1998). This is one example of a widespread situation. Equitable laws of contract would give protection to the weaker participants in market negotiations.

The politics of markets has been treated here as an internal phenomenon, but it is also more obviously present in the directly political activities of firms, industry associations, trade unions, etc., who contribute to party funds, lobby government, pay representatives to help their interests and so on. The largest part of this money and lobbying comes from large firms or multinationals, and in the USA especially this expenditure has escalated rapidly in the last decade.

In addition, business interests have a powerful influence upon government without any lobbying. So long as new investment and jobs depend primarily upon the decisions of capitalists, the government has to preserve conditions favourable and acceptable to business. Hence the political influence of consumer groups, labour unions or environmental advocates, while sufficient to achieve some victories, is always subject to this tacit but strong limitation, which becomes still stronger in times of recession (Lindblom, 1977).

There has been no coherent theoretical account of the economy which analyses the concept of market power. J. K. Galbraith (1957) came close to providing one with his concept of 'countervailing power' in capitalist economies. He argued that the growth of large oligopolistic firms in industrial production would lead to a similar concentration in distribution, and that where the market did not 'balance itself' in this way, government would step in. Hence agricultural subsidies would compensate for the weak bargaining position of farmers; trade unions would be legally favoured to redress the balance between capital and labour; workers would be helped with minimum wages and social security; and so on. Galbraith's theory had some relevance to the situation when he was writing, but today governments have largely given up this balancing role insofar as they ever performed it. However the market can never itself produce a 'level playing field' or justify the description of a spontaneous system. It has its own politics, internal and external.

Liberty and the state

The issue which divided the soul of liberalism was over the desirability of policies which introduced alternative principles (such as individual need) to those of the market and which required the creation of a substantial collective sphere of social responsibility and action. These were the aims of the positive liberals and also of democratic socialists and they ushered in the creation of the 'welfare state'. This position is completely rejected by negative or market liberals. Hayek was an influential advocate for the market cause because he combined an extreme and undiscriminating admiration for competitive markets with passionate fears about the evil consequences of state action based upon ideas of social justice or equality.

Hayek and the negative liberals are certainly right on one point. The modern state, with its enormous potential resources for coercion, control and surveillance, is capable of becoming a comprehensive tyranny. There is all too much evidence this century of the existence of such states, ranging from the defeated Fascist and Communist totalitarian regimes to the numerous contemporary military or one-party dictatorships that protect themselves by brutal repression and torture. Communist Russia would have been a less terrible place if it had had some protective tradition of constitutional government and civil rights and had not been ruled by so cruel and paranoiac a dictator as Stalin; but it would still have remained a comprehensive warning of the destruction of liberty which results from the complete concentration of political and economic power in the same set of rulers. So it would seem wise and expedient in the name of liberty to aim always at a considerable separation and dispersal of political and economic power, whatever precise form that may take.

One should also recognise another side to historical experience. The rise of Fascism in Italy and Germany between the wars, and its appearance at that time in France and Britain, owed a great deal to the failing of capitalism to provide adequate jobs, and in Germany to the experience of runaway inflation. The same phenomena are reappearing today. The rise of quasi-fascist parties in Germany, France and elsewhere is clearly related to the growth of unemployment and economic insecurity. Just as Hitler targeted the Jews as scapegoats for Germany's economic problems, so today do these 'nationalist' parties target immigrants or other ethnic minorities as the cause of their economic problems (even in self-proclaimed 'multi-cultural' Australia, there is a current campaign against immigration). It is all too easy to divert the frustrations of ordinary people with the workings of an economy which they do not understand and are told they must accept, into anger at identifiable groups competing with them for scarce jobs, housing, etc. These political developments also show how illusory is the existence of a mobile world economy, since for many actual or potential migrants the world is not becoming more open but still more closed (it is capital and goods that are mobile). The market system then also endangers political liberty and toleration if its intrinsic instability and inequality get out of control.

Hayek's own personal experience of totalitarianism naturally coloured his views. In *The Road to Serfdom* (1944) he saw the movement in Britain towards government planning and public ownership as likely to end in a form of tyranny. Later he modified this opinion and conceded that, with Labour's retreat from the doctrine of public ownership, the danger had become less. However he still saw the growth of the welfare state as inimical to liberty.

In *The Constitution of Liberty* (1960) Hayek argues that the pursuit of social justice is a mirage. The redistribution of income – which he assumes to be the main aim of the welfare state – is bound to end in arbitrary and inconsistent political decisions, because there is no principle of need, desert or merit which can provide a generally acceptable or consistent principle for income redistribution. Hayek and the others are certainly right in arguing that there is no such comprehensive principle and some socialist zealots have falsely assumed that there is one. But is this the end of the matter?

Comprehensive social justice is impossible, but how about more modest and incremental measures guided not only by a concept of justice but by the positive liberal principle of helping disadvantaged individuals to use their theoretical freedom in a meaningful way? Economists do not like to distinguish between individual demands and needs, but (as the next chapter will argue more fully) most people recognise that all individuals have certain basic biological and material needs, even if these cannot be closely defined, whose deprivation blocks the pursuit of a worthwhile life. On top of this, many individuals in the modern world occupy an environment which is extremely adverse for the development of their talents, skills and knowledge. Efforts to help these individuals do not require any comprehensive principle of income redistribution. Moreover, given the increasing inequalities of the market system, any steps which reduce those inequalities hardly amount to a dogmatic intent to establish some rule of absolute equality.

At what point do public measures threaten individual liberty, short of the extreme libertarian claim that all such measures do so? In Hayek's view, using the powers of government 'to ensure a more even or just distribution of goods' means using the power of government 'to ensure that particular people get particular things' which 'leads back to socialism and its coercive and essentially arbitrary methods' (1960, pp. 259–60). This loose chain of argument is far from convincing. Social legislation in a democracy does not proceed like a royal dispensation of gifts to 'particular people', but through general laws specifying basic entitlements; and Hayek raises no objection to the making of general laws so long as they operate impartially and without intention to benefit or discriminate between particular individuals. However, Hayek sees the expansion of public social services as leading easily to excessive administrative discretion and policy-making by bureaucratic experts (ibid, pp. 234–52). This is a familiar complaint about the growth of public services, more a matter of detailed administration than general principle since (as Hayek also argues) it is quite possible to frame laws which limit administrative discretion and are capable of judicial review. One may also wonder whether public services are actually better run today when the 'bureaucratic experts' have been pushed by politicians into a back seat. In fact the descent of government into 'essentially arbitrary method' seems much more likely to come about through political and bureaucratic degeneration than through the range of its social legislation. The growth of social legislation in the twentieth century coincided in most Western countries with good standards of bureaucratic integrity and impartiality, despite (or partly because of) the very complexity of the rule book. This was certainly so when compared with previous periods, and with the present one in which the reduction of collective social responsibilities and the cult of privatisation is leading to a definite decline in the integrity and competence of bureaucracies (see further in Chapter 4).

Hayek's basic objection to social security is that it was originally seen 'as an efficient method of providing for the specially needy' (ibid, p. 289) and that under this false cover it has been developed into a comprehensive plan for income redistribution. This statement is not historically accurate since, as Baldwin (1990) says, social security appealed to a majority of people including the middle class as a protection against economic insecurity. Income redistribution is not so much the object as the natural result of an equitable scheme. Hayek, reverting again to market principles, argues that compulsory insurance should preserve market differentials in its costs and benefits; and that public welfare should be confined to the poor and given only on proof of need (Hayek, 1960, p. 293). But why should there not be some collective arrangement for reducing economic insecurity which operates upon a more egalitarian principle than the market? Such a scheme will do no more than modify market inequalities and does not amount to any utopian pursuit of equality for its own sake.

Precisely the same arguments apply to Hayek's wish (on grounds of preserving market differentials) to replace progressive with proportional taxation (ibid, pp. 206–23). Taxation of income beyond a certain point may be inexpedient and perhaps inequitable, but wisely applied it does not injure the exercise of personal liberty nearly as much as impoverishment and the absence of elementary opportunities. Ironically, too, Hayek's advocacy of means-tested welfare payments 'on proof of need' violates his own principle of the rule of general laws much more strongly than does a comprehensive scheme of social security, because it introduces considerable and uncontrolled administrative discretion. This became obvious in Britain when the Conservative government partly replaced statutory entitlements with a limited 'emergency fund' to be doled out to those poor people judged most in need.

Hayek's thought has been covered at some length because he was the most influential and eloquent thinker who contributed to the political victories of the negative liberals, but he was not the most extreme one. He could even say that 'the range and variety of government action that is, at least in principle, reconcilable with a free system is thus considerable' (ibid, p. 231), including public works, town planning, the promotion of the arts and culture and many other activities provided they were not monopolies – although it did not follow that such activities were desirable (a pragmatic issue). Hayek also followed J. S. Mill in advocating the decentralisation of these functions to elected local government wherever possible – which accords with the 'principle of subsidiarity' advocated by the Catholic Church and now the European Union. The arguments by Hayek in favour of democratic decentralisation and limitations upon administrative discretion constitute valid criticisms of the over-bureaucratisation of the welfare state and could find a place within a broader 'constitution of liberty' than Hayek's mainly negative design.

However, Hayek is typical of modern 'negative liberals' in virtually rejecting the concern with social justice of some classical liberals such as J. S. Mill whom he otherwise admired (he edited some of Mill's letters). Mill, like Adam Smith, stressed social sympathy as a crucial bond and linked it with the utilitarian principle of giving equal weight to the happiness of all individuals. He regarded the 'entire history of social improvement' as consisting in the rejection of discriminatory and unequal principles which ceased to be defensible on grounds of social utility, and he saw this same process as culminating in the abolition of distinctions based upon colour, race and sex (Mill and Bentham, 1987, p. 337). In another context Mill saw this same beneficial process working to reduce the privileges of property and wealth, which were as prominent in his time as in ours, through changes in social rules and institutions.

Little of Mill's generous enthusiasm for popular education and reform survives among the modern negative liberals. Their interest in institutional reform has been simply to free market forces. Hayek seems unwilling to allow any room for considerations of social justice which might conflict with the self-interested motivations of the market. It seems a poor outlook after over a century of claimed economic growth, and represents a serious decline from the more balanced view of liberalism which Mill held a century ago.

Negative liberals also often appeal to Isaiah Berlin's (1969) well-known contrast between negative and positive liberty. Berlin gives primacy to negative liberty – meaning the absence of external restraints upon an individual's freedom to act as she chooses – over positive liberty – meaning improvements in the opportunities available for using her freedom more effectively – although he attaches value to both meanings of liberty. Berlin follows earlier liberal tradition in accepting that the coercive power of the state is the strongest threat to negative liberty, although he accepts that it can also act to enhance positive liberty.

However, in the second edition of his essay (1969) Berlin recognises that 'the bloodstained story of economic individualism' has led to 'brutal violations of negative liberty' and that 'the case for intervention, by the state or other effective agencies, to secure conditions for positive, and at least a minimum degree of negative liberty, for individuals, is overwhelmingly strong' (pp. xlv–xlvi).

Berlin further explains that at the time he first wrote his essay it was reasonable to assume that capitalism had been tamed and controlled and that future dangers would come from the growth of a too-mighty state. These initial assumptions are still less valid today. Thus Berlin does in fact agree that it is not just the state but can also be capitalists who block 'negative liberty' and that the state or 'other effective agencies' should intervene to promote 'positive liberty'.

Property, unlimited

Rights of property are basic for the operation of capitalist markets. Nowhere has the victory of market advocates been more complete and also more distorted than in the exaltation of property rights. An extraordinary feature of our times is the extent to which the claims about private property rights, which once were more cautiously put, have been extended without any limit by negative liberals and especially libertarians.

John Locke is the intellectual father of property rights and the traditional hero (along with Adam Smith) of the negative liberal tradition. Yet Locke's justification of property rights was actually quite limited and cautious, at least by today's standards. Locke made the well-known argument that an individual had a natural right to the fruits of nature with which he had 'mixed his own labour' – his homely illustration was of someone gathering acorns or fruits – and hence a right also to the ownership of land which an individual could cultivate and improve, without depriving anyone since originally there was plenty of land available – and when it ran out in England, there was still plenty in North America (Locke like the colonists did not consider the rights of the Indians, probably because he viewed them as making a poor use of land).

Moreover Locke's claim was restricted to what a man could himself use and enjoy – beyond that it became illegitimate as a 'natural right'. Also every indigent person had a moral entitlement 'to so much out of another's plenty, as will keep him from extreme want, where he has no means to subsist otherwise'. Thus Locke's natural right to property is very limited, especially by the injunction that no one should acquire more goods than he can reasonably enjoy. It is true that Locke goes on to explain that the use of money has changed the situation by enabling individuals to expand their possessions indefinitely, and he argues that 'by a tacit and voluntary consent....Men have agreed to a disproportionate and unequal Possession of the Earth.' He does not seem happy about the invention of money and this rather dogmatic conclusion, because it spoils the simplicity and reasonableness of his main argument (Locke, 1970, p. 188 and pp. 303–20).

One can compare Locke's modest claims with an extreme modern theory such as Nozick's. Nozick (1974) argues that there are two necessary and sufficient justifications for the ownership of property, namely that the property was legitimately acquired in the first place, and from then on is legitimately transferred. This notion of property rights rests upon the idea of contracts freely made in the market-place to buy or sell property. Nozick agrees that a great deal of property (probably most of it) was originally acquired illegitimately and/or transferred by conquest, fraud, etc. He vaguely hopes that some restitution could be made for these original misdeeds, but clearly this is an impossible task, so the theory on his own basis collapses. That fact does not prevent him from spinning out some supposed consequences of the theory – for example, that *if* property is legitimately acquired there need be no limits set to the process, except perhaps for the ownership of a natural monopoly, such as water in a desert.

The strongest impression left by Nozick is his sheer audacity. He offers strong criticisms of alternative theories of property while his own theory is full of holes which he does not attempt to fill. But this audacity seems only to reflect that of the claims now being put forward about the beneficent effects of private property, and even the desirability of extending it to common or natural properties such as water, forests, wilderness areas, open land, etc.

It is claimed that the owner of private property has a clear incentive to make the best use of his land and to conserve its natural assets. Under certain now rare circumstances the proposition can be true. For example, landed gentry in England, confident of handing down their property to future generations of their heirs, often created fine parks of lasting beauty – in the process, it should be added, sometimes removing whole villages to improve their view. However, the modern market economy does not operate in this way, nor is it associated with the same degree of family stability or some sense (however limited) of future trusteeship.

The claims for private property over natural resources are being made at a time when profit calculations are generally short-term and when returns from a long-term investment of any kind are heavily discounted if made at all. If private owners are so thoughtful and farsighted, how to explain the massive soil erosion or devastation of forests which are widely occurring?

Conversely, it is claimed that when resources are held in common, no one has the incentive to look after them properly. Hardin's (1968) 'tragedy of the commons' argued that when any joint owner could run his beasts on common land, each one will reason that adding another beast will profit him but make little difference to the consumption of fodder, so that gradually the whole common deteriorated. But this cautionary tale has little relevance to the modern management of common resources, which is either statutorily controlled (as with British commons) or co-operatively managed by a professional public or voluntary agency.

It is sometimes said, quite correctly, that the management of the Federal national parks and forests in the USA has deteriorated badly. But why has it deteriorated? Originally, under the influence of the conservationist Gifford Pinchot and the initiative of President Theodore Roosevelt, these forests and parks were set up and maintained as models of sound conservation and intelligent recreation. Since then their public managers have come under political pressure from tourist operators, timber companies and cattlemen and have survived by making concessions to these interests which then spoil the character of these national assets. In many countries national parks and forests are still well managed and often associated with scientific and educational purposes which increase their interest. This situation will continue unless they too succumb to the pressures of private acquisition and exploitation.

As I write, the Australian government has just set up a large fund for repairing the extensive soil erosion, salination, fouling of waterways, etc. which has occurred mainly on private lands (although some of it is due to publicly promoted irrigation schemes). This situation is hardly a tribute to the conservation practices of farmers and is an indication that remedies have to be sought, even if they have been too long delayed, through large-scale collective action.

Another result of setting no limits to private acquisition is to hand enormous power to a few individuals. In Australia and

Britain the commercial media (newspapers and TV) is controlled by a few very wealthy individuals. Rupert Murdoch's media empire spans three continents and he also effectively controls the international workings of an entire sport, rugby league football. These individuals have enormous political influence, both through their media ownership and through the pressure they can put on politicians to be allowed legally to expand their empires. Wherever is the rationale or justification for this state of affairs? It is flagrantly contrary to the advocacy of economic competition, often pursued by governments against smaller interests but not where the media is concerned. It is completely contrary to the once noble idea that modern media would provide wonderful opportunities for education, culture and the intelligent dissemination of information – Murdoch reputedly once said that his aim was to entertain not inform as the easiest way of making money. Its ruthless commercialism also has a destructive effect upon the standards of well-established sports, as well as transferring the big events as soon as possible to pay channels.

Back in the 1920s, Veblen (1924, reprinted 1970) argued that the era of individual financial entrepreneurs was over, since they were much less knowledgeable about industrial production than the professional managers of big corporations. The reappearance of very rich financiers and speculators is due to the big profits that can be made from organising takeover bids, speculation in the money market, manipulating tax liabilities and other forms of financial manoeuvres. These individuals sometimes overreach themselves and are eventually convicted (not without great difficulty and expense) of illegal behaviour, but while successful they exercise great economic power and political influence. Some such individuals make generous donations to charities or trusts, but it is difficult to find any rationale for tolerating such unlimited accumulations of individual wealth, by means which seem to amount to a sophisticated form of gambling with the livelihoods of innumerable individuals, sometimes described as *Casino Capitalism* (Strange, 1986).

The corruption of liberalism

Today the creed of negative liberalism, which links faith in the market with a critical attitude towards collective forms of action, has become a politically influential but intellectually thin set of ideas. Its modern exponents can and do draw upon the rich vein of classical liberal thought, but the economic and social conditions which accompanied earlier liberal views have changed drastically. Hayek writes romantically about the market as if it were still a spontaneous self-adjusting system of farmers and small entrepreneurs, not (as it is) a realm of large organisations. Nozick and others attempt to justify unlimited rights to private acquisition, which permit the manipulation of money (about which Locke had some doubts) to become a source of unlimited personal gain.

The moral and social grounds of the earlier liberal thinkers have disintegrated. They lived in a society with strong Christian beliefs (Locke was careful to square all his conclusions with the will of God) and which recognised, even if it often did not practice, firm and indeed strict moral standards in personal and family life. Smith stressed the strong bonds of mutual sympathy which held society together. Moreover the growth of capitalism, even if it brought much misery and exploitation, was itself invested with a moral mission. The doctrine was one of progress – from massive poverty to a respectable sufficiency – by dint of hard work and thrift. With this progress (it was thought) would come the development of education and culture, and the transformation of mere brute existence into the enjoyment of a more autonomous but disciplined style of life.

Modern liberalism has shed most of these beliefs and assumptions. It asserts instead a bare individualism. It can still enunciate an impressive ideal such as: 'the essence is that individuals are self-creating, that no single good defines self-creation, and that taking responsibility for one's own life and making of it what one can is itself part of the good life as understood by liberals' (Ryan, 1993, p. 304). But liberals, together with politicians and society generally, are coy about giving any guidance about what the 'good life' consists in. Santayana describes liberalism as believing that 'no normal religion, science, art or way of happiness can be prescribed' (quoted in Gray, 1989, p. 245). The individual must decide for herself. There are some critical issues over preventing harm to others, such as with pornography, where liberals may accept that children should be protected but adults not prohibited (although it may be difficult to do one without the other). To bring Bentham up to date, 'quantity of pleasure being equal,

pornography is as good as poetry', even if liberals (but not libertarians) may feel unhappy with so crude a view of 'the good life'.
This liberal agnosticism has one big exception – a belief in the
market system as conducive to the personal freedoms that should
be cherished. This viewpoint accepts the value of the market as
an arena for free choice of occupation (subject to jobs being available) and free choice of consumption (subject to income), but it
fails – as do orthodox economists – to see the market as a powerful and expanding social institution with a strong influence on
the behaviour and goals of individuals and on how they do or do
not envisage the pursuit of a 'good life'.

The values of the market-place, promoted by incessant advertising and sponsorship, permeate every corner of social life. Capitalist
markets as an ongoing institution are geared to the continuous
multiplication of individual wants which can yield a profit and
the invasion of new arenas (collective or communal) which can
do the same. Work is seen as the necessary cost (pain) of subsequent consumption (pleasure). The goal of all this activity is
materialistic, not in the sense that it will not supply 'higher goods'
(art or culture) if these are demanded, but in the sense that it
downgrades or seeks to absorb those private sources of interest
and satisfaction – whether at work or leisure – which traditionally
lie outside the market. An individual's social worth gets judged
by the market price he can command and by his level and style of
consumption, and unsuccessful individuals (of which there are
many) feel frustrated or humiliated by the continuous visions of
the 'good life' as envisaged from within the market-place.

'Consumer choice' is the ultimate prize, the bedrock value of
the market system. It is in itself a desirable form of individual
freedom but it gets exaggerated easily into the exemplar of a
meaningful exercise of the individual's choice of lifestyle. The figure of the 'super-shopper' (Boldeman, 1996), choosing between
365 types of toy or 30 versions of ice-cream, can seem more beguiling than the more rewarding but harder exercises of individual liberty, such as strengthening friendships, improving one's
mind or garden, helping others, pursuing a cause. The triviality
and salesmanship of the commercial media has a similar effect.
The physical environment also becomes ugly and standardised
under the weight of market pressures. George Grant (1969,
pp. 23–4) describes how the combination of a dominant market

with modern technology overshadows the exercise of choice: 'differences in the technological state are able to exist only in private activities; how we eat; how we mate; how we practise ceremonies. Some like pizza, some like steaks; some like girls, some like boys; some like synagogue, some like the mass. But we all do it in churches, motels, restaurants indistinguishable from the Atlantic to the Pacific.'

Consumers' choice is a valuable feature of competitive markets but it is still only a limited and rather thin form of individual freedom. To a considerable extent, consumption is or should be concerned with means, not ends. The ends for which goods and assets are required can be many, ranging from the need for enough resources to keep body and soul together, to the wish for a comfortable life for oneself or family, to a desire for luxuries or the means to pursue some (perhaps expensive) interest or hobby, to a wish to help others or pursue a good cause. No doubt most people have a variety of such aims and it can be plausibly argued that the more resources anyone possesses, the wider will be his opportunities to pursue ends. As ordinary opinion recognises, it does not work quite that way. The acquisitive instinct can be stimulated by an obsessive concern with security, a hedonistic wish for luxuries and diversions, a quest for 'conspicuous consumption' as a badge of social superiority, or by the uses of wealth as a potent source of economic, political, sexual or familial power. Such desires, which would widely be regarded as anti-social or pathological, are stimulated in a society dedicated to the pursuit of consumption, so that what should be the means to a responsible use of freedom becomes an end in itself. Instead consumers' choice gets exaggerated into the message to keep selling and buying as fast as you can, every day for 24 hours, or 'the economy' will stagnate.

A number of liberal philosophers now recognise that a general position of moral agnosticism or neutrality is untenable, and that it is necessary for liberals to give some fuller account of the kind of society which they favour and why. William Galston, for example, explains that liberalism requires 'a distinctive concept of the human good' (Galston, 1991, p. 8), which he proceeds to spell out in some detail. A liberal polity, he argues, will rule out public policies based upon theological or moral dogmas, barbarism, nihilism or irrationalism. It will not want to stop individuals from following their private beliefs, provided that they do not intrude upon core public values of tolerance and public respect. So far, Galston's account is fairly conventional. However, he goes on to argue that the state should positively facilitate the opportunities for individuals to make a responsible and worthwhile use of their freedom. It should not compel any individual to act morally or responsibly, but it should at least recognise that some exercises of freedom are more worthy than others and have better social effects (or do less social harm). He argues that a liberal society is not a bare assertion of individual liberty but a joint co-operative project for enabling all its members to share responsibly in the gift of liberty. As equal members of this co-operative project each citizen has a claim, insofar as this is practicable, to the necessary requirements for using liberty in a meaningful way, so that the satisfaction of basic needs (nutrition, medical care, education) ought to have a clear priority upon the allocation of society's resources, including the need for 'access either to adequate remunerative occupations or directly to adequate levels of resources' (pp. 184–5).

The interesting thing about Galston's revisionist liberalism (as of parallel soul-searching by some other liberal philosophers) is that it mirrors quite closely the concept of liberty earlier advanced by the 'positive liberals' such as Green, Hobhouse and Hobson. If liberty itself is viewed as without any moral value, it seems hard to sustain any argument as to why liberty for anyone is a good at all. Once liberty is accepted as a moral value, it is not hard to argue further that individuals should be encouraged to use it for good purposes – for what is liberty's moral worth if there are no such purposes? Hence the principle being advocated is that individuals should be encouraged, but not coerced, to use their liberty positively towards good ends.

It may be that the problem of how to specify good ends, cannot be resolved within liberalism itself. It has to draw upon older conceptions of goodness derived from Christian humanism and the value of community, and it is true that many of the positive liberals did draw upon such sources. The liberal stress upon individual liberty may be too strong to admit any parallel conception of the good of the community to balance it. Be that as it may, it is clear that more liberals are beginning to recognise the inadequacy of negative liberalism as a doctrine and its socially destructive tendencies, and as this happens the image of the market as a model of rational individual choice will lose its lustre.

Positive liberalism

At this point then the positive liberals re-enter the stage. One may smile at their earnest belief in the moral improvement of the masses. This attitude is too patronising and a lot too optimistic for modern tastes. All the same, their concept of 'moral improvement' is a great deal more appealing than any attempt at a forced march back to traditional family values. Their notion of moral improvement meant primarily opportunities for the individual to develop her capacities, intelligence and knowledge, not just or primarily for the utilitarian aim of getting a better-paid job (which is overwhelmingly the aim of modern education), but to enhance her appreciation of art, nature and books, and to equip her better for the rights and responsibilities of citizenship. The concept may be a modified Aristotelian one – a vision of the desirable ends of a human being – but compared with alternative visions currently propagated as to how we should live, is it really any the worse for that? (see Nussbaum, 1990).

There are three reasons why those beliefs of the positive liberals are again salient today. First, we are supposedly entering an age of greater leisure. The growth of productivity should be increasing the amount of time available to all outside of paid work, although the actual dynamics of the market are producing a mixture of extremely busy and idle individuals. The unemployed and the growing cohorts of the retired have ample leisure, and this leisure could be more widely and fairly distributed. So the fruitful, intelligent and socially constructive use of leisure time is a feasible and worthwhile goal. Second, the immersion of the market system in a ruthless dynamic of productivity and a materialist ethic of consumption makes alternative visions of a desirable lifestyle very valuable. Third, the extent of political apathy and alienation marks out the promotion of a more active and reflective citizenship as an urgent requirement if democracy is to survive.

It may be argued that many of the developments here recommended are actually happening in liberal societies, such as the growth of non-material values; communities offering alternative lifestyles; environmental concerns; mass attendance at cultural events. All this is true, but these interests mainly engage the affluent part of the population, especially the large numbers of retired who currently can afford cultural and travel opportunities on a scale unknown to history. However a large section of the working population, whom the positive liberals had in mind seem untouched by these events and live lives that are often more culturally impoverished than in Green's time when many ordinary people at least knew the Bible and Shakespeare. Part of the reason for this situation is that the cultural bias of the state has come to reflect, not balance, that of the market and that the mass media audiences get no cultural food.

The state does give support to the arts, the theatre and sometimes the film industry, subject to the erratic and often strong pressures for budgetary economy; but the largest gifts from the state (and often commercial sponsors as well) go to 'prestige' institutions such as a royal opera house or national theatre. Support for regional or 'back-street' culture is pretty meagre. States have retreated from support for liberal adult education, concentrating instead upon technical and vocational education. Some states protect beautiful national parks though on a small budget; but the municipal parks which are much more valuable for the poor or immobile are running down for lack of maintenance. In allocating television licences, states have the power to restrict the volume of advertising and to insist upon reasonable standards of quality and public information; but they use this authority very weakly or hardly at all. The public broadcasting systems (where they exist) have been the main vehicle for intelligent information and debate on public affairs and for showing events of national significance to a wide audience; but this civic and cultural function has been eroded by budget cuts, political dislike of critical opinion and the 'battle of the ratings' which pulls their performances towards that of their better-funded commercial rivals. The state also sponsors sporting events but mainly for nationalistic reasons; so that a viewer of the Olympics is saturated with the performance of the national worthies and gets little chance to admire athletic prowess for its intrinsic skill and beauty.

All these features of state patronage of culture can be explained in terms of political bias towards the middle-class and affluent, an interest in national prestige and sometimes a wish to appear neutral on controversial issues; but taken together they amount to a rejection of any responsibility for enhancing the opportunities available to less privileged people – the exact opposite of what the 'positive liberals' hoped for. The situation is as bad or worse in relation to what were once described as vices or now as 'addictive habits'. It has for long been a social principle of public finance to tax merit 'bads', such as drinking, smoking and gambling, and assist merit 'goods' such as education and culture. There is nothing wrong with the principle, which at least recognises that some choices of a 'good life' are preferable to others, but it can and has led to political reluctance to support any measures (such as prohibition of advertising) against an 'addictive habit' which is bringing in a large public revenue. Much worse, however, is the state's own direct participation in gambling, which is now a vast growth industry and the source of innumerable bankruptcies, suicides and family breakdowns. In Australia, the state governments vie with each other in the promotion of vast glossy casinos, simultaneously (and ironically) setting aside a small sum towards the cure of compulsive gambling. In Britain the Conservative government used its chain of post offices to introduce a national lottery, insisted it be run by a profit-making company, and offered rotten odds to the punters (predominantly lower-income) in order to make payments to charities (largely middle-class). In one blow it reversed T. H. Green's hopes by exploiting the poor and encouraging them in an 'addictive habit'.

The claims put by the positive liberals went much further than the promotion of cultural and educational opportunities for all members of society and not just the affluent. They wanted a framework of social entitlements which essentially held that those who were successful in the market contest had a responsibility towards those who were not. Since the right to acquire wealth was protected by and dependent upon a constitutional and legal framework, they reasoned that this right should entail some reciprocal obligation; if, on the other hand, society was assumed to have no binding force and to consist only of isolated individuals, why should a particular market system expect the full protection of the law? These arguments are at least as pertinent today as when they were first made.

There is one important respect in which the reformed liberals of today take a much weaker and more equivocal stand than the positive liberals did earlier this century. The positive liberals were not afraid to enlist the powers of the state to promote their conception of a basic measure of equality for individuals in their access to resources and opportunities. The state would act as a redistributive mechanism for sharing resources more fairly and for offering desirable opportunities to the less privileged, although they did also have hopes for some contribution to these ends from a reformed or moralised capitalism; and they were prepared to allocate resources to these ends on a clear basis of progressive taxation. Modern liberal revisionists are more hazy about what action is needed and by whom. Galston, in his otherwise persuasive book, seems almost to suppose that the right principles are already widely held within American society and only need a certain fine tuning (1991, p. 184). No hint here of the extreme inequalities and the squalid deprivations of the ghettos which would have appalled a Hobson or a Hobhouse; and while the excessive sway of market values is lamented, there is no clear articulation of an alternative society. This statement is not true of all neo-liberal writers; Beiner, for example, openly advocates democratic socialism as congruent with the best liberal values, and links his advocacy with the argument that socialism will make citizens take democracy more seriously than is possible under the unequal practices bred by the present market system (Beiner, 1992).

In the early part of this century the state could be viewed by progressives as a suitable *deus ex machina* for achieving their ideals. Today the state is regarded much more dubiously or cynically, while its capacity for effective action seems to be undermined by the respect still given to the ascendancy of the market. One cannot expect today's breed of 'positive liberals', or social democrats either, to have the same trust in political beneficence as their more dewy-eyed and inexperienced predecessors. Yet what other mechanism than political action, in some form or other, is available for countering the power of the market and achieving the fairer, more balanced and more positive concepts of society which the reformers want? This is a question that must necessarily engage us in the latter part of this book.

T. H. Marshall (1963) thought that the twentieth century would see the completion of the rights of citizenship through adding economic rights to constitutional and political ones. He was wrong, but is his vision doomed to failure in the future? Certainly the quest will have to be pursued in somewhat different ways from the proposals of the positive liberals and will engage new social issues and political alignments, but the point here is that some of the basic principles for this future programme can be derived from within the liberal tradition itself. By contrast, the claims of the negative or market liberals, despite their current political influence, represent a new and more extreme version of an ideology which has been historically tested and failed.

3
The Erosion of Welfare

What is welfare? Sometimes the concept is viewed narrowly as meaning provision of public support in cash or services for the poor and needy at some basic level of subsistence. As used here, welfare is much broader than that definition. It refers to the well-being and prosperity of society generally. Its primary stress is upon material welfare and the general standard of living, including such collective goods as clean air, clean water, sanitation and protection from infectious diseases. It can be extended in the manner of the 'positive liberals' to include the provision of opportunities – in education, culture and recreation – for the enrichment of individual life and the development of personality; but it will be up to individuals what use if any they make of such opportunities. More broadly still, the welfare of a society can include such notions as respect for law, peaceful resolution of disputes, social harmony and the acceptance of mutual rights and obligations.

The pursuit of welfare cannot dictate to individuals what use they make of their lives, nor can it necessarily produce or guarantee individual happiness. Poor societies often seem to be at least as conducive to individual happiness as rich ones, due to the strength of kinship and community groups, and the absence of the stress associated with the pursuit of individual betterment and status. But where there is a lack of the basic material requisites of life, such as adequate nutrition or a clean water supply, this is an obvious source of misery and it undermines health and shortens life. Moreover poorer societies certainly want, and understandably so, to raise their standards of living. The cutting edge of development is reached when the pursuit of material welfare undercuts the less tangible but no less real social elements of welfare – sometimes described today by economists as 'social capital'.

The pursuit of welfare in modern Western societies is dominated by economic concepts, especially the importance or necessity of economic growth. Consequently it will be necessary first to take a critical look at the subject of welfare economics which provides the supposed theoretical basis for these political beliefs. Economic beliefs about welfare can then be contrasted with alternative social beliefs which introduce considerations about human needs and social harmony – subjects which are largely absent in the orthodox economic account of welfare.

The curious history of welfare economics

Orthodox economics is completely individualistic. It assumes that the welfare of any society consists only in the welfare of all the individuals who comprise it. It does not deny of course that each person's pursuit of welfare will affect and impinge upon the welfare of others. What it denies is that there are any 'irreducibly social goods' (Taylor, 1990), meaning properties of society as a whole which cannot be attributed to particular individuals. Whether this is so or not can be left aside for the moment.

On this basis the simplest (but now discredited) economic concept of the welfare of a society is the sum of the individual 'utilities' of all its members. The historical origin of this concept, as of the notion of 'utility' itself, lies in the Benthamite 'felicific calculus' which attempted to add together the net satisfactions (balance of pleasure over pain) received by each individual. However this Utilitarian principle of the 'greatest happiness of the greatest number' had a disturbing egalitarian implication. If, as Bentham said, each person was to count for one and no more than one (which economists like democrats usually accept), does it not follow that a poor person will gain more 'utility' than a rich person from the same additional unit of income? Does not a hungry person get more satisfaction out of a square meal than a rich one from another helping of caviar? Does not the same conclusion follow from the 'law' of the diminishing utility of income – that money too brings proportionally less satisfaction as one gets more of it?

Bentham himself accepted these implications, saying 'the more remote from equality are the shares (of welfare between individuals) ... the less is the sum of felicity produced by those shares' (Bentham, 1943, vol. 2, p. 27). Earlier welfare economists were disposed to accept the egalitarian logic of Utilitarianism. Pigou stated that a transfer of income from a relatively rich to a relatively poor man 'of similar temperament' would increase the aggregate sum of utility (total welfare) 'since it enables more intense wants to be satisfied at the expense of less intense wants'. The phrase 'of similar temperament' was put in to meet the then fashionable view that the rich had more taste and discernment than the poor, which increased the former's satisfaction. Pigou later argued that transfers of money to the poor would also in time improve their tastes (quoted in Lutz and Lux, 1988, pp. 132–3).

An influential counter-argument against these egalitarian implications of welfare economics came from Robbins, influenced by Pareto. Robbins (1935) claimed that it was not empirically possible to compare the 'utilities' of individuals since we could not see into their minds and their experiences. Hence the rich man *might* be getting more satisfaction from his caviar than the poor one from his steak. It is a curious argument. It overlooks that in practice comparisons between the needs or welfare of individuals are made all the time by parents and teachers, in workplaces and in politics. Are all these comparisons faulty for lack of evidence? It may be true enough that in any particular case we cannot say for sure what pleasure or satisfaction an individual is getting. But are there not any biological laws? Do we not know that persistent hunger or any other serious deprivation is harmful to health and wellbeing? And is not welfare anyhow more to do with states of wellbeing and personal development than with transitory pleasures and pains?

Nonetheless, mainstream welfare economics proceeded to rule out interpersonal comparisons of 'utility', and with it the aggregation of individual utilities into a social welfare calculus. Instead the 'ordinal revolution' in economics offered a changed definition of welfare. It was now postulated that an individual increased her welfare when she showed by her behaviour that she preferred A to B. This concept of welfare gain was derived from the model of a perfect market system, which assumes that all transactions are voluntary ones which will not occur unless all parties expect to gain (or at least no one will lose) from the outcome. Preference orderings now became the key to the economic concept of welfare.

Preserving the Robbins rule about the subjectivity of personal satisfaction, it was now held that there would be a net gain in social
welfare when at least one individual improved her position (in
terms of her preferences) and no other individual suffered a loss.

This famous 'Pareto principle' (after the Italian sociologist, Vil-
fredo Pareto) sounds at first sight unexceptional. Who can object
to someone gaining something and no one losing? It is not nearly
so simple. First, an initial welfare gain may lead to a subsequent
loss – how is this to be included in the equation? Secondly, there
are many possible gains of welfare along the 'Pareto frontier'
which will have different distributional effects. Some of these
possible gains will benefit the relatively rich and others the relatively poor, but it would seem that the former are more likely to
occur in a predominantly market economy. Thus the Pareto principle is consistent with an increase of relative inequality, but it is
not consistent with any measure to help the poor if that injures
the initial position of a single rich person. The principle is thus
profoundly conservative; it fully endorses the existing distribution of assets.

The Pareto principle requires that any change in welfare
should be acceptable to all those affected by it. This means that
adequate compensation must be paid to anyone injuriously affected before a welfare gain can occur; and 'adequate' here refers to
the person's own estimation of her loss. The complete impractic-
ality of this idea was illustrated when some householders, asked
what monetary compensation they required to quit their homes
willingly to make way for an airport, answered that no sum
would suffice. One 'infinity' answer wrecked that whole cost–
benefit exercise (Self, 1975, p. 83). Of course, in practice, schemes
like roads, airports, reservoirs and the rest will not be held up
indefinitely while affected individuals demand enormous sums
or refuse to move. What is needed in such a situation is not Pareto
or any economic principle, but some reasonably fair decision rule,
such as compensating individuals sufficiently to resettle or restart
their business in another location.

Economic attempts to make the Pareto principle workable end
up by destroying the principle. The Hicks–Kaldor (Kaldor, 1939)
amendment suggested that a social welfare gain could be said to
occur if the winners *could have* compensated the losers even if *they
did not actually do so!* This formula still encounters the problem of

what compensation to assume and, since none is paid, it destroys the basis of the Pareto principle. It represents a particularly ugly economic attempt to define welfare without any reference to its distribution. Pareto himself was wiser than that. Essentially he was trying to show that there were circumstances in which one could claim unambiguously the existence of a welfare gain; but the conditions for this are extraordinarily stringent, requiring both acceptance of the market choices of consumers as an adequate test of welfare and a unanimous acceptance of the change by all those affected (Blaug, 1992, p. 128). It is curious that welfare economists should have made a hero of Pareto since he himself had a very modest view of the scope of his theory, holding that most welfare judgements fail his economics test and must be made on ethical grounds (Schumpeter, 1952, p. 131).

Robbins himself modified his earlier position. He conceded that it was quite legitimate and even desirable to apply some principle of equality to the distribution of welfare; but this principle had to be an ethical and political one and had nothing to do with economics. This conclusion still left economics in a shadowy world of subjective experience which seemed to derive from the old philosophic belief that an individual can know nothing about the world beyond his own sensations. It treated economics as a matter of abstract logic, since if economists cannot know anything about other people's experiences, they cannot engage with real world issues.

A different side to welfare economics stems from the distinctions between private and social cost introduced by Marshall and Pigou. Many market transactions and also government decisions have indirect effects upon third parties (sometimes substantial ones) which may be adverse or beneficial. Obvious examples are pollution (an indirect cost to others) or education and training schemes (an indirect benefit through creating a more efficient workforce or better educated citizens). Welfare economists do not stop at such obvious examples, plotting a wide range of other indirect effects, such as the traffic congestion resulting from the preference of too many citizens to drive their cars into the city centre. Indeed the welfare economists' world is full of 'externalities', as these indirect effects are called, although they ignore many of them in their actual models.

Originally termed 'social cost–benefit', cost–benefit analysis represents in principle a welcome extension of economics to cover aspects of welfare which it otherwise neglects. For example, it brings in the effects of road accidents upon the costs of hospital provision and the future earnings of those injured. Cost–benefit analysis is extensively used in the appraisal of public development projects – airports, motorways and so on – in order to bring some of their indirect effects into the accounting. It does this by simulating market prices for these various effects. But there are many snags. What 'externalities' are to be taken into account? How far in space and time is the analysis to be pressed? How are the indirect effects to be measured when they have no direct market price (yet market price is the ultimate criterion being used)?

Cost–benefit analysts have many ingenious answers to these problems, but the difficulty is that the wider they cast their net and the more honest they are in admitting the uncertainty of their figures, the more indeterminate become their answers. Hence a strong tendency to simplify. A good example is the cost–benefit appraisal of road projects where the analysis is usually confined to two factors: the expected reduction (if any) in accident costs and the time savings of drivers. The latter is given much the larger share in the equation and time is valued on the basis of the average hourly earnings of the driver (for business travel) and some artificial proportion thereof (for leisure travel). These time costs are necessarily arbitrary – indeed some people may even regard time spent upon a jaunt into the countryside as a benefit, not a cost. Further, what account should be taken of the fact that a new road may itself soon become congested? And how about the environmental and amenity effects of road projects? Partly because any attempted economic measurement of these effects has proved so contentious, these further impacts of road projects are left, at any rate in Britain, to a separate environmental appraisal (Colvin, 1985, pp. 76–117; Adams, 1981, pp. 168–91).

Here we encounter welfare economics being used in practical politics. The results are pretty messy (and hardly defensible) in terms of economic theory, but they do widen the framework of economic analysis. However, the basis of cost–benefit analysis in the simulation of market prices excludes distributional issues, although some analysts are unhappy with this situation and may suggest giving 'weights' for different income levels, or producing a 'balance sheet' showing how different groups would be affected by the decision, and leaving politicians to decide. More analysts, especially in America, ignore this problem so that their conclusions are still based on the assumption that 'market testing' (done through notional or 'shadow' prices) is an adequate welfare criterion.

Cost–benefit analysis is also biased towards those factors which can plausibly be quantified, leaving in the minds of some innocents the impression that this data is somehow 'harder' and more reliable than factors which have been excluded or not quantified – although, as in the above example of road appraisal, the latter effects (environmental and social) may well be considered more important for welfare than the time saved by drivers as measured in shadow prices. Indeed the most useful part of a cost–benefit exercise should be to put some issue within a broader framework and introduce a variety of relevant data, much of which need not be measured in economic terms. The final decision is bound to be a matter of political and social judgement, but at least it should be well informed (for a review of cost–benefit analysis, see Self, 1975).

Welfare economics has become an extremely narrow subject, still tied despite its exposure of market failures to market tests, and contradictory to what most people and other disciplines usually understand by welfare. The Robbins principle can be seen as an attempt to keep economics 'scientific' by isolating it from what are seen as political issues about the distribution of wealth; but it leads to the absurd conclusion that the welfare of a society is not affected by whether it consists only of millionaires and beggars or has a more even distribution of wealth.

The Pareto principle is a last-ditch attempt to get out of this cul-de-sac, but it only digs the ditch deeper because its conditions are impracticable and its extremely conservative ethics are unappealing. Thus the theory of welfare economics reaches a dead-end. It need not have done so if it had recognised that statements about welfare are inevitably normative and have to include comparisons and evaluations of welfare in broader terms than those of actual or simulated market behaviour.

However, welfare economics has its more positive side in the analysis of market failures and of differences between private and social cost. It is true that these effects are often difficult to translate into conventional market prices, but they can be mapped and evaluated, partly in economic and partly in other terms. There could be a fruitful partnership here between welfare and institutional economists that would be relevant to ordinary understandings of welfare. Unfortunately the fruitful application of such work has got (for the time being at least) buried under the weight of market dogmas which take a dogmatic view of the virtues of markets and discourage investigation of their wider welfare effects. Even the limited promise of cost–benefit analysis has got distorted by narrow and partisan applications; while privatisation and the use of market tests by government is eliminating welfare economics in favour of the still narrower (but more easily intelligible) test of commercial profit.

The dogma of economic growth

By comparison with these abstruse theories, the subject of economic growth is relatively straightforward. Yet the subject is widely misunderstood. Economic growth is a powerful dogma and its association with social welfare almost taken for granted. Economic growth seems often to be pictured in political discourse as like a flow of water, each drop of which is equally valuable. Such beliefs are quite mistaken.

To start with, it should be pointed out that the assumed correlation between growth and welfare has little basis in orthodox economic theory. Since that theory usually accepts the principle that interpersonal comparisons of wealth are not possible, it is also illegitimate to aggregate the income of individuals into that of a nation and to treat the result as an index of welfare. But if this assumption about comparisons is wrong – as ordinary experiences suggest that it is – economists are still in a quandary. What distribution rules are to be applied to the aggregate to obtain a better measure of human welfare? The usual economic answer is that this issue, if it is to be tackled at all, must be left to politics. Some cost–benefit analysts, as already indicated, suggest rules of distribution to help those politicians who will listen. This is helpful of them – but the fact remains that there are no correct or right rules, and it is a matter of political judgement, based on a wider range of factors than attempts at economic measurement.

These theoretical objections will not dispel political belief in the value of economic growth. For years, statistics of gross domestic product (GDP) have been widely treated as reliable guides to economic welfare, and have become virility symbols of the economic progress – or lack of it – of individual countries when converted to constant prices and expressed as income per head. Economists know that there are all sorts of snags about these figures as indices of welfare, but they continue to have a hypnotic effect upon opinion-makers and politicians. The aim here is not primarily a statistical critique, but to assist understanding of the varied impacts of market growth upon welfare, and in particular the shifts in those impacts which occur over time (and which further vitiate time series).

(*a*) National income statistics cover only goods and services which are priced; they exclude production by households and communities outside the market-place. In poor countries these forms of production account for a much larger share of total output, and of social welfare, than does the market system; but we have no way of knowing their exact scale. In rich countries the market system accounts for a rising volume of total consumption. Many people who once grew their own vegetables now buy them, and more eat out in restaurants instead of cooking their own food. People watch television or go out to entertainments instead of amusing themselves. People play poker machines instead of conversing at home or in a pub. Households are more likely to get new clothes than to mend or darn their old ones. People buy a great variety of gadgets and gimmicks in the search for novelty and are shamed into sending bought greeting cards on 'mothers' day' and other commercially decreed anniversaries. They also frequently change their household equipment and other possessions because goods are no longer designed for a long life – and are often expensive or impossible to repair because models have changed.

These familiar examples of market growth are not meant sarcastically. Individuals regard these activities as improvements in their standard of living and feel unhappy and alienated if they lack the money to participate in the market society. But how far do these activities represent equal increments of welfare? They appear to accord with the economist's welfare criterion of individual preference, since this is what people actually do with their money; but there must be doubts about how those preferences are formed. Whilst producers certainly cannot dictate to consumers, they have ways of boosting consumption such as 'rapid obsolescence' of goods and intensive marketing and sales techniques. Marketing is currently a growth industry, paying high rewards to the successful and becoming as important for profits as production. While no one can push another person into a shop, the old motivation of social emulation, of keeping up with the Joneses, has mass application in a marketised society.

There is also in modern society a positive ethic of consumerism. Governments and opinion makers, even while urging people to save, are also dismayed when retail sales drop. The dynamic of the system, even the self-respect of society, seems to depend upon maintaining market expansion. One feels a duty to shop. With so many influences pressing on consumers in one direction, it is hard to see individual choice as fully autonomous even though formally unconstrained. Some economic behaviour seems better explained by sociology than economic theory, but welfare judgements by economists continue to view all consumer expenditure as equally beneficial to welfare (Lane, 1991; Mishan, 1977).

(*b*) Economic growth statistics take no account of environmental costs. They do not deduct anything for increases in pollution, the loss of natural resources, the destructive effects of acid rain, the decimation of rainforests or (potentially) global warming. These impacts are having and will have a depressive effect upon the standard and quality of life of almost every individual unless they are prevented. With so much written on the subject, there is little need here to labour their importance, even if the extreme warnings of environmentalists are discounted (see Diesendorf and Hamilton, 1997).

These environmental costs do not have a market price. They can still be given some form of monetary evaluation, but such measurements are inevitably inadequate and flexible. How are we to measure the impacts of environmental degradation upon future generations? Not only are these impacts difficult to forecast in any detail (a fact which gives comfort to the advocates of continued growth), but the market rate of discount – now the dominant factor in the viability of long-term projects – values the welfare of future generations at almost nil. Yet we do know by now that the effects will be serious. Thus the answer to environmental problems requires a lot more action than can result from a belated recognition of the 'costs' which growth entails.

It will still be useful to introduce a system of environmental accounting into national and international accounts, as is now being urged, so long as the result is more than a few adjustments to conventional economic statistics. There is an obvious danger that environmental costs, because they cannot be at all accurately plotted in a conventional way, will get undervalued. Ultimately the basic question about environmental concerns is how far their effective treatment is compatible with market growth at all. The orthodox answer, strongly voiced by most politicians and economists, is that the two goals, with perhaps a little adjustment, can be made compatible; but this is a very dubious answer, unless at the least economic growth changes its present character and directions (Dodds, 1997).

(c) A third critique of market growth centres on the concept of 'positional goods' first introduced by Hirsch (1976). As economic activity grows so do problems of crowding and redundancy. Physical crowding increases when too many people clog the roads, beaches, countryside, etc. in order to enjoy second homes, yachting, holidays, etc. Social crowding occurs when individual competition escalates for a limited number of superior positions, so that each person has to devote more effort to acquiring the relevant qualifications (sometimes called the 'diploma disease'). These are examples of the increasing costs of satisfying certain types of individual preference or ambition.

(d) The criterion of economic growth produces a perverse entanglement of benefits with costs. Thus longer journeys to work add to the growth statistics, but for the commuter this is a cost not a benefit. Pollution, far from being a debit to market growth, adds to it when citizens in Tokyo buy oxygen masks; and having done a lot to pollute the environment, the market discovers a profitable new industry in pollution abatement. This new industry is certainly necessary – but the example again shows the contradictory features of economic growth.

(e) Last but not least the pursuit and measurement of economic growth takes no account of how the growth is distributed. Some economists, following Robbins, try to argue that one can divorce the goal of maximising wealth (sometimes called the 'efficiency' principle) from the question of its distribution. As noted earlier, the former purpose is then treated as a legitimate and unambiguous aim of economic policy, the latter allocated to the controversial arena of ethics and politics – but as already pointed out, this formula simply will not wash. Not only is it vitiated by its own premise – the illegitimacy of adding together different individual 'utilities' which cannot be known – but it is flatly contradictory to any more ordinary experience of the meaning of welfare. Economic growth without regard to its distribution can end up with a nightmare of inequality and unmet needs.

These points are intended not just to show the errors of national accounts (and of comparisons between them, which are also distorted by foreign exchange ratios), but to suggest the errors in treating economic growth as an index of human welfare. But, it will be objected, surely this is being too cynical? Has not market growth delivered over time very real improvements in the standard of living? The answer is that – despite the above reservations – it has certainly done so in some periods but is having a less positive effect (if positive at all) under current conditions. Economic growth is not like a stream of water. It has selective and variable effects on welfare.

In the post-war decades after 1945 there was undeniably a sharp rise in the standard of living of the populations of Western countries. Most people – often for the first time – had ample resources for food and clothing, holidays with pay and an increasing ability to buy cars, washing machines, refrigerators and other consumer durables. Their prosperity was also much enhanced by conditions of full employment and government provision of social security and health services. Some of the problems just listed – such as environmental degradation – were already appearing but they were not yet so serious or recognised as such. Since about 1975 or so, the directions of market growth have had a much more ambiguous impact upon human welfare for at least four reasons. They have become more directed towards satisfying the affluent, while many people's standard of life has declined; they have been more concerned with luxuries and superfluities; they have had higher environmental costs; and they have been influenced by ill-digested concepts of market competition. And all these processes appear to be accelerating.

Evidence is now available to support these conclusions. Alternative economic indices have been prepared for some countries which offer a less misleading guide to economic welfare by such corrections as including estimates of household production, deducting some environmental costs and other perverse effects, and making some allowance for changes in distribution (for example, by giving some weighting to the position of the bottom 20 per cent of households). While there can be no one right way of designing this or any other index of economic welfare, the results indicate how misleading is the conventional treatment of economic growth.

For example, one such measurement, the 'genuine progress indicator' (GPI), found that the Australian GPI increased almost as rapidly as the Australian GDP between 1950 and 1977, but since then GDP has continued to rise but the GPI has stagnated. Explanations of the divergence include the high costs of unemployment, the rising costs of environmental pollution, the growth of inequality and failure to maintain investments in the national capital stock (Hamilton and Saddler, 1997).

To further fill out this argument it may be useful to look briefly at some of the growth industries of the last three decades.

Financial services   Measures of deregulation have increased competition (foreign as well as domestic) and have gradually enabled all financial institutions to operate and compete in the same markets, in place of the previous segmented system of commercial banks, merchant banks, savings banks, building societies, etc. – each catering for a particular clientele and operating according to definite rules. The result has been a splurge of financial activity, further boosted by a parallel deregulation of foreign exchange dealings.

In principle the increased variety and competition of services on offer should be beneficial to consumers, but actual results have been much less benign. Most individuals get somewhat lost in the financial jungle and many might well prefer the simpler system which prevailed before, when they could be more certain where their money was safe, where to turn for a housing loan, and so on. The new system puts a premium on expert knowledge and advice, but many of the increased number of advisers or consultants have a personal interest in the advice tendered. There have been many cases of even large, well-established banks and other institutions convicted of giving misleading or wrong information to customers. The spectacular losses of Lloyd's of London showed how ruthless some 'insiders' within this once respected institution could be over misleading new recruits to its insurance syndicates. Fraud and illegality have increased and so have the difficulties of regulation, since the financial scene is now so complex and fluid; yet strong regulation is increasingly demanded by angry customers. It is only to be expected that 'insiders' are more likely to benefit from speculation on the stock exchange and the money market than ignorant members of the public.

There must also be doubts about the real extent of competition between financial institutions. They make their profits by borrowing money at one rate and lending it at a higher one. There can be some competition over rates but it is limited by a joint interest in preserving this basic source of comfortable profits. More banks than previously have found themselves with a large accumulation of bad debts, related to the growth of takeover bids and other financial speculations requiring big injections of quick cash; but bad debts can largely be passed on by stages to the banks' ordinary customers and, as was shown by the Federal government's rescue of small savings banks in the USA who had lost $460 billion of their depositors' money, governments seem ready to use taxpayers' money to save banks from their own rash speculations. One must doubt the contribution to human welfare of the enormous efforts and skills devoted to speculation in the money market, while the collapse of Barings Bank due only to the speculations of one staff member showed the enormous problems of accountability building in this deregulated global financial system.

Tourism   Tourism is a major growth industry. Certainly it provides much pleasure and interest for vast numbers, but it also has grave environmental effects. For example, overcrowding on the shores of the Mediterranean has caused extensive beach and sea pollution, which has stimulated tourists to fly very long distances to tropical 'paradises' and reproduce similar problems there. It is now clear that jet travel is a serious source of atmospheric pollution, yet tourism accounts for a high proportion of air travel, including the more damaging long-distance journeys.

The social effects of tourism are also often negative. It brings some jobs and income to poor countries, but the profits on hotel developments frequently go back to a metropolitan centre and much of the food and other requisites are imported. A bad feature is the frequent exclusion of local people from tourist areas and beaches, sometimes by security guards, and most tourists seem to have rather little interest in the local society. There are much worse features such as sex tourism and exploitation. Conversely, of course, many people's lives and interests are enriched by travel. All that is being suggested here is that the contribution of tourism to human welfare diminishes as the numbers and distances travelled increase, pollution grows and social impacts upon local populations become too intensive and one-sided.

The media A third growth industry is the media, especially *television*. Commercial television has a curious institutional structure and logic. Business pays out enormous sums for advertising on television because it is a popular medium suited to quick visual messages, and once the practice is enshrined it seems essential to competition. Commercial TV companies pay large sums to government for a licence which still usually leaves a handsome profit from advertising. They then arrange their programmes in such a way as to maximise advertising revenue. The public has become so habituated to the system that few people protest at the restless and pervasive impact of advertising upon the enjoyment of programmes and sporting events. Nor do they realise as a rule that they are paying for the programmes through the prices of goods and services. So this curious system has no real relationship to consumers' market choices and produces bogus competition through advertising, much of which has no value as information but constitutes specious 'image building'.

As noted earlier, governments have the opportunity to influence the quality of television by operating a public, non-commercial system and by attaching conditions to companies' licences (about quantity of advertising, range of programmes, etc.); but unless these powers are firmly exercised, commercial television will tend strongly towards catering for the lowest common denominator of taste and entertainment. Indeed more is sometimes spent on producing a short, sophisticated advertisement than on a whole programme. Oligopoly in the form of a few dominant owners or companies adds to the lack of variety and to philistinism.

Admittedly, the introduction of pay television by cable or satellite is bringing increased diversity of offerings. But there are costs here too. The digging up of roads to install cables or the hanging of large new cables under existing power lines has angered local residents and councils in many cities, and the new technology adds to the perception of increasing electro-magnetic pollution. Then the specialisation of channels is bought at the expense of reducing the access of non-paying viewers to events of wide or national significance, such as big sporting events. It also leads the big media owners to change the whole structure of established sports such as rugby league in order to capture the best teams and players for exclusive television performances, thereby also killing much local interest and participation in the sport. This outcome of sheer market power has no basis in the choices of public and players. Essentially a new institutional system is being forged which offers specialised viewing (at increased costs) at the expense of a simpler system which pitched its appeal to broader audiences.

It will be said, truly enough, that these examples give an impressionistic account of the relation between growth and welfare, but they serve two purposes. One is to introduce more ordinary social judgements into a description of what is often regarded as a homogeneous and beneficial flow of economic growth. The other purpose is to show how often the economists' account of the rule of individual preference is distorted in practice by the existence of large 'externalities' (such as environmental impacts) and by the actual institutional conditions of competition, which produce some curious outcomes that could hardly be predicted or justified by economic theory. It has been said that the main developments in America today are not fine buildings or meeting-places but golf courses, casinos and prisons. As a golfer I can accept the first one as contributing to welfare, although environmentalists have criticisms, but casinos and prisons are surely mirror images of the impacts of economic growth in a perversely acquisitive society.

Needs, preferences and welfare

An alternative welfare criterion to individual preference is that of individual need. Orthodox economists tend to treat individual needs as if they were preferences and to make them equally subjective, as a matter of personal choice not of physical or psychological urgency or priority. But neither ordinary opinion nor science supports this position. Biology is clear that all individuals have basic physical requirements – such as adequate nutrition, clothing and shelter as well as clean air and water – if they are to survive and maintain health. Biology is in fact much more scientifically based than orthodox economics. Psychology offers a wider interpretation of needs, as in Maslow's (1954) hierarchy of individual needs, which starts with physical survival and rises to forms of self-realisation, as simpler needs are successively satisfied and replaced with more complex ones. Sociology can add understanding of how basic needs are interpreted in particular societies and how preferences are shaped by social conditions.

It is possible to divide needs into three ascending categories. First come basic biological requirements for effective physical functioning. Second come derived needs, that is necessary requirements for participating in the common life of society, such as (in modern societies) a need for education and for access to employment. Finally come 'higher needs', such as Maslow's concept of self-realisation, which can be said to require (for example) a need not only for employment but for a meaningful, worthwhile job which enables an individual to develop her talents and self-esteem and to contribute to the good of society (Lutz and Lux, 1988, pp. 149–50). However, this third sense of need, while it can be assisted or retarded by the opportunities which society offers, goes beyond the material provision of welfare, and requires, besides the possibility of access to suitable opportunities, a positive use of the individual's own capacities and energies.

Concepts of need, even to some extent biological needs, are culturally variable and their applications are bound sometimes to be controversial. Also the idea of need is capable of indefinite expansion and abuse in political argument. There must be doubts whether a comprehensive list of needs, such as Braybrooke (1987) produces, could ever be agreed, although Braybrooke gives many good reasons for distinguishing needs sharply from preferences and for taking needs seriously. However, basic and derived needs have a strong claim to social priority, because of their vital importance for individual health and effective functioning, even if they leave much room for argument in detail.

The concept of need offers a strong principle of welfare, but one whose bounds are hard to set. By contrast the concept of preference offers an apparently clear and uniform yardstick which fails badly in practice as an adequate guide to welfare. The idea that all preferences stand for wants which are equally significant for welfare, so that needs should have no special status or recognition, is hardly plausible. Even orthodox economists agree that other undesirable preferences should be taxed ('merit bads' like gambling, smoking, alcohol), while useful preferences should be encouraged and subsidised (education, culture). Some neo-classical economists such as Marshall and Pigou recognised, as does ordinary opinion, that there is an important distinction to be made between necessities and luxuries or 'superfluities' even if the borderline is blurred. Necessities have an urgency for the relief of pain and distress or for maintaining a tolerable standard of life, while superfluities represent additional, and sometimes transitory or dubious, pleasures. The economic claim that an individual's material wants are unlimited and endless is a form of crass materialism, which reflects the continuous pressures for market expansion rather than some immutable 'law' of human behaviour.

Further, individual preferences are shaped not in some value-free arena but within a market system continually seeking to escalate material wants and subject to considerable distortions in their provision. Some of these distortions figured in the brief descriptions of growth industries. Financial competition suffers from the asymmetry of information between insiders and the public; tourism from the neglect of its substantial environmental costs; and television from weak competition and the perverse effects of advertising to shape programmes and choices.

There is inevitably conflict between the 'needs' and 'preference' criteria for defining social welfare. If a society gave complete priority to meeting a generous listing of individual needs, there would be (even in a fairly affluent society) rather little scope left for the exercise of individual preference. This would represent a strong curtailment of an individual's freedom to select the goods and services which she personally prefers, and in this sense would also curtail her welfare. But in modern market societies it is the criterion of need, not preference, which gets neglected.

Even many orthodox economists accept the case for providing all citizens with minimum income sufficient to meet their basic needs if they choose to do so – and if not, that is their responsibility.

But this recipe, while offering some concession to the needs criterion, is subject to severe limitations. It does nothing to protect the welfare of dependants, especially children, who in the modern world have become the most unfair victims of inadequate welfare services. In the USA in 1993, 23 per cent of children lived below the official poverty line, and in Britain as well as America malnutrition and once-banished diseases have returned to afflict poor families, especially children. Moreover there are basic needs which cannot be met by a minimum income unless it is a very generous one.

Housing is both a basic need and an important source and condition of improvements in human welfare. It can provide opportunities for study, reading, indoor recreation, handiwork, gardening, etc., which raise the quality of life, contribute to household production, and improve the educational and job prospects of the household members (Stretton and Orchard, 1994, pp. 187–94). Given that nutrition and clothing are relatively easier to obtain in advanced societies, although quite often inadequate in practice, housing conditions are probably the most important index of welfare in Western societies. Yet there is more inequality in housing conditions than in any other respect. Many individuals have a large, comfortable home and/or two houses, but many others still live in decrepit, small or crowded accommodation and often pay a high price for it.

Unable realistically to join the majority ranks of owner-occupiers, poorer families rely on public housing or private renting. Under the influence of market dogmas, governments in the USA, UK and Australia have sold off and/or drastically curtailed the supply of public housing and substituted rental subsidies or vouchers; but the supply of low-cost rented housing is small and inelastic, especially in the inner urban areas where many of the poor live, due to high land values and the existence of more profitable alternatives. In the USA, for example, the demand for low-cost rental housing has increased substantially yet the supply has diminished (Lutz and Lux, p. 230). The rising cost of the rental subsidies going to private landlords has in turn led governments to ration or reduce this form of assistance. The final outcome for many poor families is poor housing at a high rent, sometimes up to 50 per cent of their income, which further reduces their capacity to meet other urgent needs.

The housing needs of the poor cannot be adequately met by a minimum income provision, but require a supply of subsidised non-profit rental housing of reasonable quality – which is just what is being reduced as the number of poor increases. In Australia the Industry Commission, the flagship of 'economic rationalism', was actually forced (reluctantly) by the evidence to conclude that subsidised market solutions would not work with low-income housing, and favoured continued direct public provision (Industry Commission, 1993; Coles, 1997). Its advice was ignored by a still more dogmatic government.

People in modern societies have to be increasingly mobile in order to get to work, schools, shops, etc. Hence adequate transport can reasonably be regarded as a derived social need. Just as the explosion of car travel has increased the mobility of motorists, the consequent drastic cuts in public transport have reduced the mobility of anyone without access to a car to a lower level than previously. This is another case like housing where the preferences of the more advantaged have undercut the needs of the less advantaged who have gone backward. This situation can also be pictured as the unintended outcome of inadequately informed preferences, since in getting a car many individuals did not envisage the growth of congestion or the rundown of public transport, which they themselves often value for periodic use or as a standby facility. In this case priority for neglected needs and concern for environmental effects are both strong arguments for creating a more balanced transportation system.

It is also unreasonable in a market society strongly tilted towards the stimulation of immediate wants, to expect poor individuals to be very responsible and farsighted about their own needs and those of their dependants; yet this is just what many rich people, who may not themselves set a good example, do seem to expect. One may also doubt whether the provision of an adequate minimum income is likely to happen if that is the only recognition which basic needs receive. Politics moves by incremental steps and questions of need and equity have to be raised in the context of each relevant policy, not confined to a single attempted solution. Otherwise welfare issues drop out of sight, as extreme market advocates would no doubt like.

The case for the provision of public goods rests not only upon the concept of need and the perversion of some market preferences, but on the workings of democracy. After all, there are important political preferences for public goods which are not based upon paternalism but the exercise of choice through political channels. Admittedly the supply of public goods cannot usually conform so closely with the precise tastes or desires of each individual as can market supply; but public goods have compensating features such as (sometimes) the higher efficiency of a comprehensive public service, affordability and equity, promotion of a sense of collective security and mutual co-operation, and contributions to community and cultural life.

Thus the possible arguments for public goods are varied and multiple, unlike the simple case for market provision with its accompanying limitations. There is no agreement in the literature as to whether public goods are likely to be undersupplied, because individuals want them but strategically disguise their willingness to pay taxes for them, or oversupplied, because of the ambitions of interest groups, bureaucrats or politicians (see Self, 1993, pp. 36–44). The latter has become the dominant economic assumption and joins with a dogmatic coupling of individual preference with market provision to discredit the extent to which public goods may be actually wanted or preferred. A subtle erosion and debasement of the concept of political preference seems to be taking place. Nonetheless the exercise of political choice over the balance between public and market provision is the essential foundation of an equitable, balanced society which values human welfare.

As already argued, conventional economic growth data is a poor guide to welfare because it ignores distribution and non-market sources of consumption, values the provision of necessities and superfluities equally, and contains many perverse items which muddle up costs and benefits. By contrast, social indicators provide a useful guide to a society's level of material welfare and basic need satisfaction. Social indicators for life expectancy, morbidity, mobility, literacy, educational standards, housing standards, the distribution of cars, telephones, refrigerators, etc. offer a more straightforward profile of the welfare of a society than does economic growth data. There can also be indicators of the state of democracy, such as voting data and attitude surveys. There are technical difficulties over collecting some of this data, but its meaning is fairly clear. The whole set of indicators provides only a basis for informed social judgements; but such judgements cannot be avoided. While, as already noted, economic evaluations of welfare can be and are being improved, all such evaluations appear more objective than is really the case because they are presented in the common numeraire of money, behind which lie many assumptions that need an expert to unravel. Too much faith in quantitative data of this kind is one of the deceptions perpetuated by economic imperialism.

While there can be no full agreement on the content of welfare, many people might agree upon some of its constituent elements. These perhaps would include:

- Priority for basic and derived needs up to the point where all members have a reasonable opportunity to participate in the common life of the society. Beyond this point individual preferences would be respected and would largely be met through a market system, subject to the recognition of some important collective needs of society as a whole and the need for major improvements in market functioning.
- A responsible society, giving recognition not only to individual responsibility for one's behaviour and choices, but to social responsibility for meeting basic needs, for care for the environment and for the welfare of future generations, and for restraint in the pursuit of wealth and personal acquisition.
- A society where every individual has a reasonable opportunity of finding a worthwhile occupation suitable to his/her abilities. A worthwhile job is an important source of individual dignity and status, and its absence is a potent source of crime, alienation and personal degeneration. Robert Lane (1991) has shown that, in the most consumption-orientated society in the world, people still get a large part of their satisfaction and happiness from their work.
- The society should aim at social harmony and the avoidance of conflict. This aim is impossible to realise if there are wide differences between rich and poor and between the conditions of life and opportunities experienced by different individuals. Where these differences are stark enough, it becomes hypocritical and insulting to attribute them to failures of individual responsibility or to some immovable culture of poverty. A society with extreme differences is also an ineffective

democracy because participation is limited and unequal. Rousseau may have exaggerated in supposing that only a society of poor and sturdy individuals would cherish liberty and democracy; but a society of extremes is a breeding ground for forced repression, demagoguery and tyranny, and quite contrary to the pursuit of welfare.

Welfare and collective goods

Modern Western societies are the creators of the welfare state, but some of them no longer perform well on this suggested list of welfare principles. Particularly in the English-speaking countries, and especially in the USA, there is dwindling provision for the basic needs of the poorest groups, and everywhere a dominant stress upon individual preferences as mediated through the particular institutions and expanding role of the market system. There is a declining sense of social responsibility for the general welfare of society and for its future. There is substantial and fluctuating unemployment and considerable economic insecurity. There is growing inequality of wealth, of physical conditions, and of individual opportunities and there are signs of increasing social conflict.

These wider issues about society and democracy will be left for later consideration. Here attention will focus upon the striking contrast which has emerged between the treatment of private consumption and collective goods. By collective goods is meant here not the economic concept of a 'pure public good' (one that is technically indivisible and must be made available to everyone or no one), but those goods which have come to be largely provided, free or at low cost, by public authorities. The list includes education, health services, public or non-profit housing, social security, basic infrastructure and public works, public utilities and numerous regulatory activities. Many of these goods are not 'pure public goods' since they are allocated to particular individuals, hence in principle could be supplied for profit by the market system. A considerable range of these traditional collective goods has already been privatised. This section is concerned with privatisation where it affects the affordability and equity of these collective goods.

The importance of these collective goods to standards of welfare should be obvious enough. Health, education, housing and social security are basic requirements of individual welfare as well as being essential for the prosperity and effective functioning of a modern society. Adequate infrastructure such as roads, railways, ports, airports, drainage, sewerage, water supply are basic requirements of the economy and of public health, and their distribution is also significant for equity between local areas and for regional development. Public regulation of many kinds is necessary for protecting consumers over food standards, the safety of drugs, the reliability of financial information, etc.; workers about the safety of appliances, hours of work, etc.; the public about the safety of vehicles and the competence of their drivers; while regulation has had to be extended into new activities such as pollution controls. Some collective goods are provided by public agencies for technical reasons (economies of scale, natural monopolies, etc.), but a stronger reason is their importance for individual and social welfare. Collective goods represent a sphere of social responsibility, one with fuzzy edges but a large core, that was marked out for collective decision-making and accountability as opposed to the rule of the market-place.

What is causing the endless string of cuts and economies in the supply of these collective goods? Some politicians claim that the market system is 'more productive' than public services and is the source of 'real jobs', but these statements are absurd and insulting; is the making of plastic dolls a more 'productive' and 'real' job than those of teachers or nurses or welfare workers? Such talk amounts to propaganda for privatisation by trying to label collective goods with a false stigma of being 'public'. Such a transfer may increase 'micro-efficiency', usually by cutting the wage bill, but whether it increases 'productivity' is a more open question, since this must depend on the quality of the service provided. In any event these moves to privatisation, whatever conditions about 'public service obligations' are attached (and often later modified), will usually – with some exceptions – undermine the principles behind collective provision and introduce a powerful new consideration, that of profit, into the production and distribution of the service in question.

A main reason for the decline in collective provision of goods is pressure for budgetary economy, which is also one reason for the political appeal of privatisation (another potent reason is the short-sighted one of raising public revenue by 'selling off the state'). But is it actually the case that Western governments cannot 'afford' to fund a satisfactory level of collective goods? Or that their taxpayers will not let them? Or that it will only be possible to do so with a high rate of conventional economic growth? Or that switches to privatisation will save money and resources? Public finance in modern economies certainly poses some difficult problems, but the intention here is to draw attention to some rather simple facts and principles which place the question of the 'affordability' of public collective services in a more favourable light.

In the average OECD country, government outlays, as a percentage of GDP, rose from 33.1 per cent in 1970 to 45.8 per cent in 1982, declining to 44.0 per cent in 1989. Strenuous budgetary efforts have halted the growth of public expenditure but done little to reverse it. However, a large and increasing proportion of public expenditure consists of transfer payments from taxpayers to the old, sick, handicapped and unemployed. Other transfers are subsidies to industry or agriculture and interest on the national debt. These transfers involve no direct claims upon real resources, and their principal effect is to switch purchasing power to people who usually (if not always) need it and which shield a wide range of individuals against the instability of the market economy. For the average OECD country, transfer payments absorbed 41.5 per cent of total public expenditure in 1968 but over half (53.6 per cent) in 1988. Since English-speaking countries are less generous over entitlements than most European ones, the increase there was not quite so dramatic but still rose from 32 to 40 per cent in the USA (a special reason here being the increase in public debt) and from 41 to 48 per cent in the UK (data from Saunders, 1993, pp. 22 and 27).

The cost of these transfer payments has been rising because (despite cuts in entitlements) the number of unemployed and others below the poverty line has increased and so has the number of retired people drawing public pensions. Gloomy prophets see the 'burden' of the aged increasing substantially in the future; in OECD countries, the proportion of the population over 65 is expected to increase from 12.6 per cent in 1990 to 15.3 per cent in 2010 (*The Economist*, 1992, p. 16), but this issue is often wrongly diagnosed. If there will be too few workers to support dependants, the obvious solution is to take advantage of the fact that many older people would be quite willing to go on working a few years more, now that they live longer in better health, instead of (as is now often the case) being pushed into taking early retirement. We are thus back to the proposition of the 1944 Beveridge Report, that an effective system of social security depends upon the maintenance of adequate levels of employment. The number of aged need not in itself be any burden.

There is a further point. If, instead of public provision, reliance is placed upon private insurance schemes, the cost to each individual for cover will increase, because of their higher risks and administrative costs and their need for profit. Even Hayek (1960, pp. 285–7) agreed in principle that a comprehensive system of social security may be the most efficient, low-cost method of protection against the vicissitudes of illness, unemployment, widowhood and old age. It is also much the fairest method since the dominance of private insurance would leave many people weakly covered against future contingencies and needs or not covered at all. Private insurance has a legitimate role over encouraging savings and providing those who can afford it with additional cover, but not to the extent of denying a basic degree of security to all citizens. What the basic cover should be is a matter for reasoned discussion, and some European countries (but not English-speaking ones) may have pitched their entitlements rather high, but the problem of 'affordability' is not actually so great as to preclude a fairly generous answer – at least if the employment implications are tackled.

Besides transfer payments, governments provide a wide range of services, of which the most costly are defence, education and health. Considering the importance of these services, it is perhaps surprising that in OECD countries total government consumption expenditure averages under a third of total private consumption expenditure and uses up less than a fifth of the annual gross domestic product (*The Economist*, 1992, p. 48). However, health and education budgets (like most public services) are under heavy pressure and there are strong arguments for increasing their funds. The questions are: can any increase be afforded and would privatisation achieve more effective results?

In the case of health services, it is plain that moves to privatisation both increase costs and reduce coverage. Americans spend 11 per cent of national income upon a mixture of privatised medicine and limited public schemes, almost twice what Britons spend (6 per cent), mainly through the national health service; yet life expectancy, infant mortality and other health statistics for the population as a whole are no better in the USA (*The Economist*, 1992, pp. 210–19). Enormous sums are spent by rich Americans on expensive forms of health care, yet about 37 million people lack any health insurance and may be unable to afford a visit to the doctor. It is plain that either a nationally provided service as in Britain, or a comprehensive system of coverage as in Canada, are the best ways of trying to meet individual needs equitably (for health is a basic need) and to contain medical costs (Self, 1993, pp. 135–41).

This is not to deny that there are difficult problems over the financing of comprehensive public health schemes. One familiar problem is that the individual as taxpayer is reluctant to finance the medical services which he may one day urgently need or which are necessary for the seriously or chronically sick. Another problem is the high cost of the expensive operations and organ transplants which medical science increasingly makes possible, but which cannot reasonably be provided in every case – hence contradicting the full principle of priority for basic needs. These problems have led to the queues for elective surgery, to desperate attempts at rationalising medical services and to the informal rationing of expensive treatment by doctors.

Yet there are possible answers. Politicians have failed lamentably to educate the public in medical realities. Given the rising costs it may be reasonable to levy some modest user charges, with rebates for the poor. It may be right to earmark some revenues specifically for health, as with the Australian medicare levy, as this makes more apparent the general connection between costs and benefits. It will be necessary to dissuade old people from expecting expensive operations which at best can only prolong their lives for a short while. More attention has to be given to health prevention and education, and to engaging with the problems of allocating scarce and expensive resources. It is contrary to individual liberty and perhaps to medical innovation to deny those who can afford it access to private treatment, but the aim must be to offer public provision which is good enough for most purposes and for the great majority. That conclusion implies some requirement for increased resources, but this is the only way of satisfying basic health needs for all members of society both fairly and economically.

Education is the public service most likely to receive support even from market advocates. Their case rests upon the importance of education for creating a more capable and technically sophisticated workforce. They may exaggerate the likely demand for such workers and overlook the need to provide suitable training and opportunities in the world for less talented or unambitious children. In any case education is widely regarded as the right of every child and the ladder to future opportunities so it has an egalitarian character, an obligation to educate every child up to the limit of her abilities. Thus the financing of education becomes primarily a public responsibility, however the system is organised, apart from the debatable case for levying charges for some aspects of higher education – a policy which easily undercuts equality of opportunity unless (as with the Australian graduate tax) the charge is paid subsequently when and only if the student achieves a prescribed level of earnings.

There are also many problems with the public education system. It seems to make inadequate use of the vast stores of accumulated knowledge and information techniques now available, which could also reduce costs. It has difficulty in developing education as a source of personal development and self-fulfilment such as the positive liberals wanted. It has to cope with an enormous amount of alienation, conflict and bad behaviour, attributable to poor job prospects, narrow personal orientations and a lack of social purpose. These are defects of society, not faults of education, but sensitive and gifted teachers can help to overcome them by focusing on the individual worth and potential talents of each child. How education can combine recognition of diversity with a principle of equality, how it could be the source of a counter-culture as well as serving necessary economic functions, are key issues of this age. What seems certain is that education will require substantial public finance in any fair and democratic society, if it is to contribute to both economic performance and personal development.

These problems admitted, it remains extraordinary that current political efforts should be so strongly directed at restricting or cutting the collective provision of health and education. These services are necessarily much more labour-intensive than manufacturing and distribution, so the logical and sensible outcome of the drastic labour cuts occurring in those two sectors should be a gradual transfer of labour to the personal services. The economist William Baumol says that if all forms of output are multiplied by three and a half times by 2040, so that they retain the same parities as now, then (because of their labour intensity) expenditure upon health and education will need to rise from 20 to 60 per cent of total national expenditure in the USA! Therefore 'a fiscal illusion underlies that view that consumers as a group cannot afford to pay the rising costs of education, health and other such services' (Baumol, 1993). Baumol's example does not deal with the question of how the money should be raised, but his argument for higher expenditure applies logically to taxpayers wherever public provision is preferable.

The claim that government cannot 'afford' to invest in infrastructure is largely based upon a budgetary illusion. The figures for a budgetary surplus or deficit lump all expenditure together, both capital and current. A firm will usually borrow at least part of its funds for new investment and there is no reason in principle why government should not do the same when investing in economically productive assets such as infrastructure. If capital investment were treated as a separate item, the budget deficits of most Western countries would become surpluses (see *The Economist*, 1992, pp. 132 and 140). Of course prudence is still necessary for governments on capital as well as current accounts, and some are financially too weak to borrow more, but this is not the case with most Western countries.

There are actually strong arguments, both economic and social, for public organisations retaining responsibility for most infrastructure (Neutze, 1995). Governments can borrow more cheaply than private firms. When private firms are given financial responsibility for some major project, as has happened with the Sydney Harbour Tunnel and with a group of large road works in Sydney and Melbourne, the private firms require a substantial risk premium for their contribution. The financial illusion occurs because government incurs no new debt, but instead the firms achieve their eventual profits from agreed user charges for the new facilities, often sweetened by tax concessions. The final cost to the public in user charges and tax concessions will usually be a lot higher than a public scheme (the New South Wales Auditor-General reckoned the extra cost for privatising the Sydney Tunnel at two billion dollars). Insofar as user charges are reasonable (as they sometimes are) they can equally be levied by a public agency. Equity also is relevant here, since private developers will be biased towards meeting the demands of more affluent areas and groups; and cities will sprawl and environmental conditions deteriorate if developers get more freedom to invest where they wish, regardless of effects on the city as a whole.

This brief review reminds the reader of the traditional reasons for entrusting collective services to public agencies. These advantages still remain. Public provision of these collective services, either directly or through a suitable agency, remains not only the fairest but most efficient arrangement (Self, 1993, pp. 141–55). But if this is so, why is the public seemingly so unwilling to vote adequate taxes for these purposes? Some reasons for this situation derive from pressures of the global economy (see Chapter 5), but others stem from developments of political culture and manipulation (see next chapter).

Ways of raising adequate revenue exist if the will is there. Progressive taxation is the fairest method, but its scope has been eroded by political competition over tax reduction, as well as by tax evasion both by the rich and in the informal economy. More use has necessarily to be made of indirect taxation, but such taxation can also be made progressive through differential rates graded from necessities (*nil*) to luxuries (top rates). Hypothecated revenues could be used to establish stronger links between costs and benefits. Some linkage of this kind could rest on a principle of equity; for example, taxation of large houses and second houses could establish a fund for non-profit housing for low-income people in bad housing conditions. User charges could be applied wherever restraint is desirable upon environmental grounds (road traffic or water consumption), subject to suitable relief for low-income groups (e.g., rebates for fuel or water); income from road pricing could be earmarked for improvements in public transport; receipts from an energy tax used to subsidise the heating and housing costs of poor families; and pollution taxes could be linked to environmental repair work and improvements.

Does the financing of collective goods depend upon economic growth? This linkage has been and still is widely assumed. There is an obvious apparent truth in the proposition. Conventional economic growth of any kind contributes to tax revenues. It is for this reason that governments support casinos and lotteries, for example. But the proposition must still be questioned. A sane society would be a more stable one than present societies, more dedicated to the maintenance and where necessary the improvement of basic standards, more concerned with protecting the environment and the future, more directed towards social justice and harmony instead of the endless pursuit of individual gain. Economic development will still be useful for public revenues, but in more selective and discriminating ways.

Economic growth as currently pursued through global market competition seems unlikely to improve the prospects for a welfare society. Its strong tendencies towards more economic inequality, both within and between countries (with some exceptions), will make it harder to meet the basic needs of the underprivileged; and its stress upon personal acquisition is hardly helpful for the social cohesion which welfare policies require. There is little evidence that societies become more generous or prudent with gains in material wealth, where those gains are not widely or generally shared. If conventional economic growth is closely connected with social welfare, it is hard to understand why countries with twice the 'real income' per head of twenty-five years ago, are becoming less generous to those in need. The pursuit of welfare entails questioning the market dogmas which underlie support for global competition as this is now practised and suggesting alternatives. It also suggests strongly the need to reactivate the principle of full employment, both as a major element itself in human welfare and as a potential contributor to other welfare goals. These issues are tackled later.

It must be admitted that present economic and political trends are strongly antithetical to the concept of collective welfare described above. Claus Offe (1984) argues that the principle of meeting basic needs, which was the basis of the welfare state, is in inevitable conflict with the principle of individual gain, which is the basis of the market economy; and that the latter principle will drive out the former one. The process can be pictured as another 'tragedy of the commons'. As public services get dismantled or eroded, and market provision takes over, social co-operation gets weaker and the impulse to a selfish or self-protective form of individualism grows. Colin Ward (1997) gives a striking example. In the English drought of 1975–6, when water was a public service, households willingly co-operated over rationing and sharing available supplies; but in the drought of 1995, they were unco-operative and angry, arguing that a private water company which made large profits ought to guarantee an adequate supply.

But is the triumph of self-interest over co-operation described by Offe due to some intrinsic feature of human nature, or is it due to the dominance of one system over another – to the successful assertion and expansion of the market system? It is the thesis of this book that the latter is the case, and that the revival of belief in social co-operation and mutual responsibilities can only come from a development of countervailing power to the infiltration of the market into the arena of needs and welfare; but it has also to be admitted that the state, once looked to, to provide that counter-vailing power, is in danger of becoming only a weak auxiliary to the growth of the market. This chapter has been concerned with restating the principles appropriate to a society which values human welfare, but it is now necessary to look more closely at the political processes which are eroding this quest.

4
The Destructive Quest for Minimum Government

It is a widely held opinion of our times that governments have become too big in terms of their staffs, functions and expenditure. To some extent this belief is an understandable reaction to the rapid growth of government which took place after the Second World War. It is also plausibly argued that, in a new age of intense international competition and slower economic growth, we can no longer afford such 'big government' and nor are taxpayers willing to pay for it. These considerations provide a simple rationale for efforts to reduce the scale of government wherever that seems reasonable and possible, and to transfer some activities to the market or perhaps to voluntary organisations.

Unfortunately these arguments, which have at least a pragmatic rationale, are accompanied and inflated by some very strange and strong market dogmas. Their basis lies in beliefs that markets are more 'efficient' than government over the provision of most or almost all services, that markets work best with a minimum of regulation, and that consequently the less governments do the better. A further significant argument is that, insofar as government is necessary, it should be remodelled according to the principles of competitive markets. Taken together these dogmas represent a powerful thrust towards some loosely defined goal of minimum government which would work primarily as an auxiliary to the market system and would reflect the market's image.

These dogmas may seem too extreme to get wide acceptance and are perhaps thought to be the opinions only of very right-wing politicians and extreme libertarians; yet they are proving very influential in shaping the agenda of Western governments, especially English-speaking ones. While there are reasonable arguments for changing the scope and methods of government in various ways, this ideological quest is already damaging the competence and integrity of government and with it the capacities and effectiveness of democracy. This crusade is based upon fundamental misunderstandings about the nature and conditions of democratic government, and it has been twisted to assist a mixture of political ambitions and market interests.

This chapter will explore these developments, returning at the end to a consideration of the meaning and feasibility of the concept of 'minimum government'. Before proceeding further it will be useful to take a brief look at some theoretical arguments for culling government drastically. These claims go well beyond the pragmatic case for government economies (which does not necessarily question the value of most of what democratic governments do) into alleged demonstrations that the political process yields very inferior results to the market process.

(*a*) Public choice economists argue that the political process involves many gross distortions of the individual preferences of citizens, which do not occur (or certainly not to the same extent) within a competitive market process. They assume in the tradition of neo-classical economics that all individuals are 'rational egoists' and that they will pursue their private interests in politics or administration as well as in the market-place; but while competitive markets supposedly harmonise the interplay of self-interest, the political arena offers no such natural discipline. While institutional rules can no doubt help to keep the participants honest, these rules can also be manipulated by interested parties. At any rate (they argue) there are plentiful opportunities for interest groups, bureaucrats and politicians, separately or in alliances, to exploit the resources of government for their own private advantage or gain. The electorate may have the power to throw out an unpopular or corrupt government, but it has no means of supervising the political process or of ensuring that its wishes (insofar as there can be a collective wish, which these thinkers doubt) are implemented. The question to ask is how far this description of the political process is a valid one. (For further discussion, see Self, 1993, pp. 1–69.)

(*b*) Market theory argues that government is less 'efficient' than markets over providing services to individuals. 'Efficiency' here has two different meanings. The first one is that market firms, because of competition and the profit motive, make a more effective (less costly) use of given resources than government agencies who lack similar incentives. The second one is that individuals can choose the precise services they require from the market, subject to their income, whereas government provision of services is the result of a complex collective process which leaves them with little or no choice. The question to ask here is how far the different purposes of public services vitiate such comparisons. However, the increasing tendency of governments to treat the users of public services as consumers or customers, not clients or citizens, and to use market techniques of service delivery, shows the influence of this dogma.

(*c*) A third argument derives from the 'overload' debate of the 1970s, when it was claimed by many writers that government had become 'overloaded' and public expenditure inflated by the claims of numerous organised interests. Public choice theory asserts that interest groups are essentially 'rent-seekers', pursuing their own advantage at the public expense. Writers such as Olson (1982) claimed that in the English-speaking democracies, the main barrier to economic growth was the influence of entrenched interests. The argument then goes that a much smaller government, limited in its ability to raise and spend money, preferably through constitutional restrictions, would be less responsive to these group pressures. It would also (it is claimed) be a more impartial government, holding the ring fairly and not yielding to particularist claims (Buchanan, 1986). The questions to ask here are what effects small government has upon the influence of various interests and whether it is likely to be more impartial or the reverse.

These three arguments (which will get more attention as the chapter proceeds) provide intellectual ammunition for the pursuit of minimal government. They also have direct relevance to the actual ways in which governments are being slimmed and reshaped so as to achieve three goals:

- To reduce the size and discretion of public bureaucracies, introduce market tests of their performance and bring them under much stronger political control and leadership. This aim owes an intellectual debt to the public choice critique of bureaucrats as essentially self-serving, as well as other critiques of the traditional model of bureaucracy.

- To privatise public services wherever possible, either by direct sale or through competitive bidding for service delivery; and to infuse remaining public services with market techniques and a 'market philosophy'. This aim owes a lot to blanket endorsement of market theories about the nature of service 'efficiency'.
- To reduce the political pressures upon government and to establish a more limited and impartial type of state. This objective is influenced by 'overload' and public choice theories, but it is less of a realisable aim than the other two, since it is difficult for democratic governments (even if they have the wish) to stifle the political process although they may manipulate it to their own advantage.

The next three sections will deal in turn with the way these goals are being pursued and their effects.

Taming bureaucracy

A principle target of the political advocates of smaller government has been the established bureaucracy. In the last 20 years drastic changes have occurred in the status and functioning of bureaucracy in all the English-speaking countries. In Britain and the USA this process was initiated by two political leaders, Margaret Thatcher and Ronald Reagan, who made no secret of their hostility towards the large bureaucracies over which they presided; but the process has been carried on, more discreetly but in the same direction, by their successors and by politicians in Australia, New Zealand and (more mildly) Canada. Bureaucracies in continental Europe have been less assailed, although new conceptions of the bureaucratic role are having some influence there.

The new measures can be seen as a political reaction to the strong status which Western bureaucracies had acquired, as well as a main element in the pursuit of small government. By 1975 Western bureaucracies had won a considerable degree of autonomy and authority as the result of two prolonged and parallel historical evolutions. One was the hard-fought creation of a merit system, which required all appointments to be made on objective criteria, shielded the process from political patronage and gave bureaucrats lifetime security. The other was the growth in the numbers, influence and discretionary authority of bureaucrats, that arose naturally from the steady accumulation of the functions of the state. Together these developments created a situation of considerable but responsible bureaucratic authority. Most Western bureaucracies acquired a reputation of integrity and impartiality, due to their Weberian features of appointment on merit, security and detachment from any financial interest in their advice or decisions. A strong collegiate code and a stress on informal teamwork existed in most bureaucracies, although less so in the USA. There were less attractive features. Senior bureaucrats were often seen as an insulated class, drawn from a narrow range of social origins and educational institutions, shielded from 'real world' experiences and with conservative attitudes, although many officials did not fit this stereotype – partly because of the recruitment of outsiders and rapid promotion from the ranks during the two world wars. Bureaucrats certainly defended their rights and privileges, and the prestigious administrative class in Britain and the *grand corps* in France were adept at maximising their status and influence. The one British report which sought to inject new life into the administrative class (the Fulton Report of 1968), though formally adopted by the politicians, was effectively stymied by the top bureaucrats (Etzioni-Halevy, 1983, pp. 99–229).

The Whitehall system, created in Britain and exported overseas, offered a theory of how political–bureaucratic relations should work. A top bureaucrat had the right to offer independent even if unpalatable advice to his minister, based upon his experience and knowledge, but once a ministerial decision had been made, the bureaucrat must implement it to the best of his ability. Bureaucrats had a collective duty to assist and co-ordinate government decisions, usually through numerous committees; to process and submit essential information; to convey faithfully the viewpoints of affected interests; and to apply laws without fear or favour. Although somewhat idealised, this concept of a working partnership between politicians and bureaucrats, who followed different career paths with hardly any mobility between them, did produce coherent government in which ministers had the final say. The strength of ethical conventions meant that there were few cases where a bureaucrat needed to resist a ministerial order on grounds of financial impropriety. The snag for the politicians lay in implementation. Whatever the theory said it was all too easy, given a short ministerial life, a clogged agenda and the stress upon co-ordination, for bureaucrats to delay action on ministerial policies which they considered unwise; and such behaviour was probably not infrequent, although the evidence from politicians is inevitably one-sided (on the Whitehall model, see Campbell and Wilson, 1995, pp. 1–71; Barberis, 1996).

In the USA this formalised style of administration, working almost like a chess game, was always regarded as too 'bloodless' for emulation. Instead there was a more variable, uneasy and often conflictual relationship between the political executives appointed by the President and the career bureaucrats who headed the numerous Federal bureaux, the building blocks of the system, and who could often draw on Congressional support (Heclo, 1977). (Reagan's animus was directed against the size more than the performance of the bureaucracy.) In many European countries bureaucrats are more politically partisan than in Britain and more capable of moving into politics. This situation gives them a stronger political leverage than in English-speaking countries and, together with the European stress upon juridical administration, explains their partial insulation from the market-based concepts of administrative reform which are sweeping the English-speaking world.

The agenda for bureaucratic change has been motivated by market dogmas and the desire of political leaders to assert their will. The methods used for reshaping bureaucracy reflect these mixed aims and have hardened into a set of institutional dogmas about how governments should operate, without much attention to their consistency or long-term effects. These methods can be summarised as follows:

- Drastic reductions in the numbers of full-time public servants, brought about by privatisation, contracting-out and continuous political pressure to cut numbers. In the UK by 1996 the permanent staff had been reduced by a third from its 1979 level (from 735,400 to 494,300) and was back at its position in 1939. In the USA, the Reagan Administration cut the Federal civilian bureaucracy from 3.33 to 2.78 per cent of the labour force. These processes have continued (Self, 1993, pp. 159–61).
- Reduction of security. Public servants no longer enjoy lifetime security and rights of appeal against unfair dismissal have been

reduced. Impartial public service commissions, the guardians of
the merit system, have had their powers reduced or transferred;
for example, the Australian Public Service Board was abolished
and its powers reduced to the much weaker reserve powers of a
single Public Service Commissioner. Control over personnel
management has been switched from independent to central
agencies working under political supervision, and senior public
servants are typically appointed on short-term contracts.

- Managerial devolution from central agencies to line departments and again down to hived-off executive agencies, such
  as the more than 100 agencies in Britain which now employ
  over three-quarters of the total civil service. This development
  can be seen as an enhancement, not a reduction of bureaucratic authority, since it is supposed to 'let the managers manage'. However, the heads of departments or agencies now get
  much more freedom over appointments, pay and conditions,
  so that individual public servants have less security and often
  narrower prospects; while the new managerial discretion is
  restricted by tight financial controls.

- Spreading politicisation. Partly this comes about in Westminster systems from an increased use of political advisers and in
  the USA from Reagan's insertion of a further layer of appointed
  political executives over the Federal bureaucracy, who now
  head many bureaux, the traditional bastions of the career civil
  service. Increasing appointments of outsiders (often business
  men) to senior public service jobs and the extensive use of
  outside consultants rather than internal experts have com-
  pressed the functions and influence of the career service.
  Career civil servants, even in Britain, are now more liable to be
  judged by their political attitudes and expected to comply
  unreservedly with political instructions. Also the more
  thoughtful type of public servant, who tried to strike a balance
  between often conflicting goals, is getting replaced by the
  'can-do' official, dedicated to quick implementation as measured often by superficial targets.

- Introduction of financial incentives into the public service,
  such as performance pay and short-term contracts for top officials, which reduce their security but offer bonuses for satisfactory performance. Wide use of financial targets to govern
  the performance of devolved agencies.

Clearly many influences can be seen at work in this new set of bureaucratic rules. One obvious element is pressure to cut the size and cost of government. Another is to increase the power of political leaders. A third is to stimulate a more flexible and decentralised style of management in place of previous beliefs in the importance of co-ordination and control. These elements are often dumped together within a supposedly coherent doctrine of the 'new public management', but they do not really cohere very well.

This treatment of bureaucracy can also be seen as one element within a comprehensive restructuring of government along market lines. Key elements here include privatisation; the purchaser–provider split and competition over service delivery; financial incentives and targets; and managerial devolution on similar lines to the use by a big firm of subsidiary companies or operating divisions while keeping strategic planning at the centre.

The market model is assumed to assist the quest for smaller government, but it seems to have been pursued with more ideological fervour than sense. In particular there seems to have been little attention to the suitability of this model for political–bureaucratic relations, or to its effects upon those traditional values of bureaucracy which continue to have much importance for the effective working of democracy. Some likely effects can be discerned.

All observers agree that senior public servants have become much less able or willing to give independent advice to ministers (Plowden, 1994; Campbell and Wilson, 1995). The fact that top officials now hold office on short-term contracts naturally makes them more reluctant to risk their jobs or their performance pay by offering critical advice, and reduces their concern with the durable effects of administrative decisions. Foster and Plowden (1996, p. 22) put this point strongly in the case of Britain: 'Experience suggests that the activity of advising Ministers requires a permanent elite of high intellectual ability . . . A government which instead relies on a narrowly drawn band of dependant and like-minded cronies will sooner or later regret it.'

The widest danger is the loss of bureaucratic integrity over such matters as due process, dealing impartially with interest groups, and administering the laws without fear or favour. These are long strived for, essential features of modern democratic administration, which have no parallel within business because they relate to the special legal status and powers of government. These administrative ideals have never been completely realised and a tension has always existed between the wishes of political leaders and the principles of fair administration. These principles are only safe to the extent that they are well protected by laws and strong conventions which politicians generally respect. In Westminster systems, which lack strong administrative laws, they depend upon conventions which are becoming undermined.

Some cases from Britain which could be replicated elsewhere, show the loss in bureaucratic integrity. Officials have been required to doctor statistics of unemployment, poverty and other matters (Foster and Plowden, p. 199). In the Westland case, officials spread malicious rumours about each other's ministers (Campbell and Wilson, pp. 273–4). In the Scott inquiry, foreign office officials were found to have lied to Parliament about the sale of arms to Iraq (ibid, pp. 281–3). The head of the civil service, Sir Robert Armstrong, admitted in the Spycatcher case to being 'economical with the truth'. Sometimes the situation has been too much for a civil servant's conscience. One official, Clive Ponting, was sacked for revealing that Parliament had been given a false account of the sinking of the Belgrano in the Falklands war and was prosecuted (unsuccessfully) under the Official Secrets Act (ibid, p. 258). Much more moderately, a departmental head has the right to request a written Ministerial instruction, reported to the Public Accounts Committee, before complying with an order he considers financially improper. In a rare case of this kind, Sir Timothy Lankester, head of the Overseas Development Administration, objected that a proposed loan to Malaysia was a wrong use of foreign aid and his view was upheld by the Public Accounts Committee and later vindicated in the courts; but it can hardly have been coincidence that a few years later he was squeezed out of the civil service (Foster and Plowden, pp. 232–4).

These cases have sparked off attempts to define the rights and duties of civil servants more closely (Hennessy, 1988, pp. 182–208) and led to the introduction of codes of practice for both civil servants and ministers (the Nolan Rules), which could logically evolve into what Britain has always lacked, a proper system of constitutional and administrative law. But administrative practices in Britain have already changed to the point where two academic observers have declared that the Whitehall model is now dead (Campbell and Wilson, 1995). That model may have produced too much administrative privilege and political frustration, and have been in need of some reform, but is the model that is replacing it consistent with equitable and competent administration?

Another way of looking at this issue is to question more closely market analogies. A favourite defence of the new treatment of bureaucracy is the principal–agent theory. This theory, based upon a contractual view of relationships, argues that the principal (the minister) needs to guard himself against the opportunism of his agent (the senior bureaucrat) through having a dominant say in the latter's appointment and holding him accountable for results. This theory, consciously applied in New Zealand and influential elsewhere, has been used to justify placing senior public service appointments on a basis of short-term contracts which include financial incentives and penalties linked to targets set by the minister. In this way the minister can control the actions of his agent (the bureaucrat) by rewarding him if he follows instructions faithfully and by terminating his contract if he does not. This device is now widely employed in Westminster-type systems.

This arrangement may be seen as a corrective to situations where bureaucrats were not responsive enough to political directions, but it goes much too far in the opposite direction. It is surely wrong to see bureaucrats as simply the 'agents' of political leaders. They are responsible for equitable and effective administration and it has taken a century of hard struggle to detach this role from political patronage of appointments and intervention in the application of the laws. Equally the minister himself can be considered an 'agent' of parliament or ultimately of the electorate; but the means of enforcing that relationship are limited and become still more limited if the minister appropriates a wide administrative discretion. Democracy requires a balance of power throughout the system, with appropriate roles for the electorate, parliament, political leaders and bureaucracy. These relationships cannot be captured by so crude a theory as principal–agent and will deteriorate if too much irresponsible power accrues to political leaders.

The new treatment of bureaucracy can find no real justification even from the public choice theory which has been used to justify it. Niskanen's (1971) critique of the empire-building bureaucrat was music to the ears of Mrs Thatcher, who urged her Cabinet to read it. Niskanen's account was erroneous on many counts (see Self, 1993, pp. 33–4), but in any case his target seems to have disappeared and been replaced by the official in a central agency who obediently controls and eliminates other bureaucrats (Dunleavy, 1991). Moreover, public choice theory cannot trust politicians any more than bureaucrats, because it assumes that politicians will also seek their own personal advantage by whatever means are at hand – for example, by rewarding supporters or possible allies through patronage or helpful decisions. Reverting to principal–agent theory, the politician generally has more opportunity than the bureaucrat to exploit their relationship for private or partisan ends (Perrow, 1986, pp. 14–16). Thus, if we were to accept public choice theory, the curbing of bureaucratic excesses through political domination can only lead to still worse political excesses.

Bureaucracy has never been very popular and offers an easy target for criticism. There is an inevitable tension between the multiplication of rules to preserve equal treatment for equal cases and the humanist itch for discretion in hard cases. The need for political accountability and the fear of political blame easily drives bureaucrats into defensive attitudes and complicated procedures. Hierarchical control gets overstressed and innovation dampened. It may also be true that by the 1970s public service delivery had become inadequately responsive to the more diverse needs and expectations of the public. Insofar as the 'new public management' manages to shake up these practices and create a more responsive and innovative bureaucracy, it will have some value; but unfortunately the new management doctrine has been launched in a climate of political assaults on the public service which has shaped its actual practices and is producing a negative effect upon bureaucratic performance.

Before this assault, had bureaucracy become so unpopular as is now alleged by its critics? Guy Peters's *The Politics of Bureaucracy* (1978), written just before right-wing governments started to dismantle bureaucracy, gives little ground for this belief. He notes that public opinion was generally supportive of the value of bureaucracy in Western societies, although more ambivalent in the USA. Quite contrary to public choice beliefs, he notes (p. 88) that 'purposive' (goal achievement) or 'solidary' (collective ethos) motivations were as or more important than financial incentives for bureaucrats. He agrees that the expansion of public programmes had left administrative agencies with more power to set their own agenda, but concludes that bureaucracy as a whole, divided internally, was politically directionless. He even rashly predicted that, with rising affluence, people may feel that 'goods and services produced through the political process may be superior to those privately produced' with 'less questioning of the actual costs and benefits of public programmes'. Here he proved wildly wrong, not so much because of the supposed unpopularity of bureaucracy, as from pressures to cut taxes in a period of low economic growth and the strident attacks upon government by a resurgent market liberalism.

The privatisation dogma

Privatisation can be pursued pragmatically or as an ideological dogma. The pragmatic justification for privatisation is the gain from economic competition, but it has been pushed on ideological grounds into activities where competition is weak or non-existent and where counter-arguments exist which have received too little consideration.

The history of privatisation offers an interesting parallel with the previous history of the reverse process, the nationalisation of privately run industries. Nationalisation expanded after 1945 and led in most Western countries (but not the USA) to the public ownership of a wide range of industries, including gas, electricity, railways, water, coal, iron and steel and shipbuilding, as well as government participation in other industries such as automobiles and oil. The technical rationale for these nationalisations was often the advantage of co-ordinated management of a natural monopoly, and the nationalisations of gas, electricity and railways by the Labour government in Britain were all based upon expert reports arguing for public ownership on the grounds of efficiency; in the case of coal, a further argument was the dismal history of labour relations. However ideology also played an important part with the argument that the state should take over the 'commanding heights of the economy' in the interest of full employment and economic planning. This belief was later perceived to have been largely irrelevant for the actual way the economy was managed; but in later nationalisations ideological beliefs seem to have outlasted economic and technical reasoning, and the same evolution can be observed in privatisation policy although with a more powerful momentum.

Privatisation takes two main forms (although there are variants) – the wholesale disposal of nationalised industries or other public assets to the private sector, and the use of competitive bidding ('contracting-out') for the delivery of public services. These two devices raise different issues.

The main argument for privatising whole industries is that of 'micro-efficiency', but often the vaunted goal of economic competition is not genuinely achieved. In some cases a weak degree of competition can only be achieved at the cost of duplicating or disrupting a co-ordinated network of pipes, cables, wires or transport routes, as happens with the laying of cables by rival telecommunication companies. Co-ordinated networks are valuable assets, for example in public transport. Thus the fragmentation of British rail among a large number of private operators means that co-ordinated services and fares – an important factor in getting people to use public transport – are much harder to achieve. In the cases of telephones and electricity, technical innovation has made competition feasible, but it is rather artificial and the price reductions in these services owe a great deal more to technological advance than to 'competition'.

In other cases where competition would be feasible, a public corporation has been sold as a single entity. This happened with British Airways, which kept the advantage of government-negotiated landing rights and a dominant position in the British aviation industry, although smaller players were keen to get in on the act. In Australia the government actually lumped two public corporations together (Qantas and Australian Airlines) into a single sale. In these cases it can be argued that the pressures of international competition require large, dominant national airlines, but it cannot be argued that the result is more competition. There sometimes seems to be an idea that two players are enough to achieve competition; for example, electricity generation in Britain was divided between two new firms whereas British Gas was sold off as a monopoly.

Competition aside, it is claimed that the quest for profit makes private firms more efficient over the use of resources. This result, where it occurs, seems due to the greater willingness and ability of private firms to cut labour costs. An adequate comparison should take account of the side-effects of drastic cuts in the labour force. In the real world as opposed to a mechanistic economic theory, one likely effect is to increase unemployment, especially among older workers who lack the skills or resilience to find new jobs. The consequent costs are socialised – paid for from the welfare budget – while the human effects (simply ignored in conventional economic analysis) consist in a loss of pride and purpose among workers suddenly made redundant. While some redundancies have to be accepted, privatisation adds a ruthless edge to the process. Also the consequent increase in profits and reduction in the wage bill adds further to economic inequality and erodes the modifying influence of the public service on top incomes. A more unequal distribution of income can also adversely affect the state of the national economy by reducing effective demand.

Privatisation often has an adverse effect on environmental goals. Privatised utilities such as gas and electricity are subject to price regulation per unit sold, which gives them a strong incentive to maximise consumption. The American company which bought into electricity distribution in the Australian State of Victoria did so with the specific idea of achieving a big increase in consumption. Such aims are quite contrary to the strong environmental need to restrain energy consumption. Privatised utilities naturally oppose introduction of a carbon tax and make this desirable measure very much harder to implement than under public ownership. Another example is that, in order to privatise the British electricity industry, the government agreed to take over the considerable costs and problems of decommissioning nuclear power plants, but it no longer has electricity profits to finance this difficult task.

A further point is that governments usually get too low a price (often much too low) for the assets they sell. This had been shown to be true of nearly all the British privatisations. One reason is that the government wants to make sure that there is a strong demand for the shares in the new company. Another reason is that bureaucrats typically lack the expertise and probably (given political keenness to sell) the motivation to press for a tough bargain, while external financial advisers are hardly disinterested. A more respectable reason is the political decision to sell shares at a discount to employees and small investors, which links with the political preference for a low initial price so as to encourage the growth of a 'share-holding society'. A further factor may be market doubts about the possible impact of regulation, and yet another was political zeal (such as Mrs Thatcher's) to shed publicly owned firms as fast as possible while the political opportunity was there. At all events the results have been that most flotations were heavily oversubscribed and traded immediately at a large profit (Self, 1993, pp. 93–104). The fiscal illusion of budgetary devices has obscured the public loss from privatisations, but one analyst concludes that 'in many cases the sale price is around 50 per cent of the present value of the stream of earnings foregone' and that the UK's large budget deficit in 1993 'may be traced, in large measure, to the effects of privatisation' (Quiggin, 1994, pp. 30–1).

It is not true that private firms are necessarily more efficient in a technical or micro-economic sense. The evidence is mixed and by no means one-way (for evidence, see Stretton and Orchard, 1994, pp. 80–122). It is true that some nationalised industries required big public subsidies, largely because of political pressure to hold down prices and avoid strikes, coupled with a risk-averse attitude by management who feared the unpopularity of industrial action or any service breakdown. However this outcome was not inevitable, as can be seen from the efforts that governments have made to prepare industries for privatisation by injecting capital, writing off debts and slimming the labour force. Ironically much of the trauma and pain of reconstruction was experienced by some industries before privatisation. 'The death of the theory of public incompetence' should have occurred when in Britain 'a public owner turned Western Europe's least profitable steel producer into its most profitable' (Stretton and Orchard, p. 96). These processes of reform through 'corporatisation' could have been left intact without exposing these industries to the further and unnecessary trauma of privatisation, which seems to have been driven by ideology or the wish for easy revenue.

A main effect of privatisation is not to increase the volume of competition – sometimes it is the reverse – but to launch nationalised domestic industries into the global arena. There may be more intense competition, but it will take place between global corporations, conglomerates and strategic alliances of giant firms. This is not of course competition in the orthodox economic sense. Whether or not it serves to reduce prices, it certainly undercuts the capacity of nation states to promote employment, protect standards and raise adequate tax revenue.

The contract state

'Contractorisation', an ugly word for a disjointed process, is the other leg of privatisation policy. Public authorities have always contracted out many operations to private firms, frequently in the case of public works and often for such standardised local services as garbage collection and street cleaning. There seems nothing wrong with this pragmatic approach which can also be used to counter inefficiency in a public workforce or corruption in the town hall.

The new doctrine of privatisation replaces this pragmatism with a strong principle. It believes in a clear split between the function of the 'purchaser' (a government body) which specifies the service it requires, and the 'provider', the agency chosen to provide the service in question. It postulates competitive bidding for the service contract. The public agency already providing the service may be allowed to bid against commercial firms (or sometimes voluntary bodies), but sometimes political dogma has decreed that only private firms can compete for some contracts.

The purchaser–provider split seems clearer and neater than is actually the case. The process entails difficult decisions about the terms of the contract, the nature and quality of the service required, the reliability of the contractor, the political repercussions, etc. Contracting is a complex process which is not cheap. It relies upon a legal document, and the sanctions against default can be difficult or costly to enforce. If these difficulties can be overcome, competitive bidding should enable a public agency to deliver a given service at lower cost (or, in theory at least, to achieve a better service for the same cost). If an in-house agency is allowed to bid, outside competition will compel it to improve the efficiency of its operations.

The system works best with standardised services which can be clearly specified, but encounters many difficulties with services where results depend upon professional skills and sensitive relationships which cannot be bought but need to be carefully nurtured. The 'purchaser' is locked into a purely commercial relationship with the 'provider', which blocks out the partnership, monitoring and exchange of information that are vital for the intelligent administration of a sensitive public service such as health or education. In such cases contracting-out can have a depressive effect upon the quality of service without any formal breach of contract, while the costs of proper contracting and monitoring rise.

'Contractorisation' has been pursued with extraordinary zeal. In Britain it was first compulsorily introduced for local government, then all central departments and agencies were submitted to two rounds of 'market testing' to find services that must be either privatised or contracted-out. One dogmatic element is 'strategic outsourcing' where a decision is made to transfer a function *en bloc* to the market sector, as has happened with information technology in Australia (with consequent fears for the effects on the local computer industry). Also in Australia, the Department of Finance is setting the pace by 'outsourcing' most of its functions, including recruitment, industrial relations, occupational health and safety, and internal audit (*Canberra Times*, 28 May 1997, p. 2).

Ironically, governments seem to be pushing this process to an extent that would not be acceptable to a business corporation. 'Transaction cost analysis' deals with issues about when to keep a function 'in house' and when to contract it out to a supplier (Williamson, 1985; Perrow, 1986). One usual conclusion is that core functions, which are central to the purpose of the organisation or which are liable to changing requirements, should be kept within the organisation. However, some governments are keen to contract out what would seem to be core functions, such as legal services, information services and policy analysis. To take policy advice, sometimes an external opinion can be useful, but market consultants are not specialists in complex issues of the public interest. Inspection of their reports suggests how often they are employed primarily to lend credibility to ministerial wishes or pet projects.

In Australia the Attorney-General's department has outsourced most legal services and leaves departments to get legal advice from wherever they choose. (There is even talk of contracting out advice on constitutional issues!) This seems an extraordinary decision. One would have thought that there needed to be at least some consistency in the legal decisions of public agencies; they are not private firms competing for profit but embodiments of the ultimately coercive powers of the state requiring careful attention to equity and effectiveness. Contracting-out can be utilised for corrupt political purposes. In Victoria (Australia) the Auditor-General found evidence of corruption in the award of contracts and the Premier (Mr Kennet) responded by moving to contract out the A-G's work to consultants (*Canberra Times*, 15 May 1997, p. 5). As a servant of parliament, the Auditor-General clearly needs his own staff to investigate the probity and efficiency of government transactions, and external consultants appointed by political decision can hardly be expected to have the same zeal or accumulated knowledge. This use of contracting undermines the integrity of government and parliamentary accountability.

Contractorisation poses a serious problem of accountability which has still to be resolved. Ministers have justified the new system by claiming that it will deliver better and prompter services to consumers. This has been backed up by documents such as the British 'citizens' charter' of individual rights in public services; but how can contractors be made accountable for results beyond their strictly legal obligations (which are also often difficult to monitor and enforce)? It is even doubtful as to how far Auditor-Generals and parliamentary committees will be able to monitor the efficiency of contracted-out services because of commercial confidentiality, even though they are spending public money. In particular, great caution is needed over contracting out social services which surely are core functions because of their political sensitivity – yet this is happening widely. The irony is that the minister who usually initiated the process cannot easily be called to account for the outcome. Any blame will fall upon the local government or executive agency who made the contract, usually under political demand or pressure.

Another warning from transaction cost analysis is the need to guard against opportunism by contractors. A firm may put in a low bid in order to secure a contract and when it runs out no feasible alternative supplier may be available. Many substantial cost increases have occurred from the variations firms were able to make to their original contracts (Foster and Plowden, 1996, p. 108).

Privatisation in both its main forms entails difficult issues of regulation. In Britain each privatised utility is obliged to observe some 'public service obligations' and is supervised by a small regulatory agency appointed by the minister. The chief function of the agency is to protect consumers by specifying maximum prices. This control can be used to require a firm to remedy specified service deficiencies – as when British Telecom was required, as one condition of a price increase, to repair the many neglected public phone boxes. These public obligations are often subsidised (as in the case of rail services) on the grounds that commercial firms are legitimately concerned only with profit and any social obligations should be publicly paid for. There may be increasing political reluctance to find the money to pay to private firms for these purposes. It seems that the regulators have no ability to consider issues of equity between different classes of user or problems of poverty, unless obligations have been legally specified and (usually) paid for publicly. Nor as a rule can regulators consider the environmental consequences of the utilities' behaviour – another subject which could cut across commercial considerations and is therefore out of bounds. However, environmental concerns were sufficiently strong in the case of water for the British government to introduce (somewhat reluctantly) a national environmental body which can give directions to the privatised companies, and which are then reflected in the decisions of the price controller; but this complex juggling also suggests how much simpler for environmental ends would be public ownership.

Within these limits regulators do have some power over prices. However, their resources are minuscule compared with those of the privatised utilities, upon whom they must depend for most of their information; and they are politically appointed and ultimately dependent upon political support for taking any punitive action. OFWAT, the British regulatory agency for water, was unable to prevent the water companies from appropriating into profits a large part of the price increase specifically permitted for purposes of capital investment. The ability of privatised utilities to accumulate large profits (partly as the result of the low acquisition price) justified the new Labour government in 1996 imposing a special levy upon their accumulated profits to be used for labour market policies. This action also showed the limits of regulation for controlling profits.

It would be too strong to prophesy that the regulatory agencies will be 'captured' by their industries, as happened with the older regulatory commissions in the USA (who possessed a broader but vaguer remit); but it does seem that their effective powers will continue to be very limited, unless some reforming government is prepared to take on the privatised utilities with more vigour than a single intervention. Conversely, a government friendly to or dependent upon strong market interests could reduce regulation to a cipher.

As already noted, the purchaser–provider split is not a simple concept but introduces important constitutional and political issues about the new relationships. Even advocates of privatisation such as Foster and Plowden agree that, as the market sector invades public provision, social goals such as the state's role as a good employer and its support for equality of opportunity will become much harder to maintain. Traditional public ethics will get absorbed into business practices. Opportunities for corruption will grow and 'separation (of functions) must be expected to result in more fraud' (Foster and Plowden, pp. 123–4). Much waste as well as corruption will occur if the contractors are allowed virtually to determine and monitor their own contracts, as happened in the USA with the Environmental Protection Agency's responsibility for cleaning up toxic waste dumps (ibid, p. 115). Another problem is that the wide appointive powers and influence of ministers give scope for political favouritism in the award of contracts. A converse problem is that a new government will find its hands tied by a multitude of contracts made by its predecessor.

In the 'hollowed-out state', as this new system is sometimes called, a new code of constitutional and administrative law is much needed to regulate these relationships. However, new laws cannot resolve everything and culture is probably more significant than law for maintaining public service integrity. Traditional public service ethics have been damaged by the dismantling of bureaucracies and in all English-speaking governments their morale has plummeted. This situation has led US Federal agencies to set up ethics offices. These developments are a bad basis for the inauguration of a complex system of contractual relationships under which the protection of public interest will not be easy. Far from a 'hollowed-out' state having (as its political advocates suppose) *less* need for bureaucracy, it will require – if it is to work tolerably at all – a bureaucracy with high standards of competence and integrity together with adequate legal or constitutional safeguards.

These arguments are not intended to discredit all cases of privatisation. The previous system hardly warranted a blanket endorsement and left much room for improvement. Some nationalised industries have no doubt been privatised for defensible reasons, and competitive bidding for public services can yield economies without loss of quality, provided there is the prospect of genuine competition and the process is well managed. Unfortunately though, privatisation has been pursued with excessive haste and dogma and with scant regard to wider and longer consequences. Many public assets have been sold off cheaply and, once privatisation seemed politically respectable, used as a quick means of raising revenue; but what will happen when all the assets have gone? If the state is 'hollowed-out' by extensive contracting and outsourcing, it will increasingly be absorbed into the workings and standards of the market and lose its ability to act in an independent and impartial manner.

The myth of impartiality

One claim often made about the pursuit of small government, with its correlations of fewer functions and lower expenditure, is that such a state will be more independent and impartial in its treatment of diverse and conflicting interests. The argument here is the public choice one, that, in the previous post-war era, the state was ripped off by 'greedy' and 'rent-seeking' interest groups, culminating in the problem of 'overload' – overloaded demands producing overload government.

It is worth taking a glance back at the theory of political pluralism which enjoyed much support in this earlier period. In principle pluralism took a favourable view of interest groups. The theory went that in a democracy every individual had a variety of interests or beliefs which could be separately conveyed through organised groups. This diversity of interests encouraged moderation and compromise. Moreover it was the function of political parties or the legislature to integrate and reconcile these diverse interests, to adjudicate upon their claims and to modify or reject them when necessary from a broader perspective. The whole process was a fairly benign one of 'muddling through' or 'disjointed incrementalism' which would produce reasonably acceptable public policies.

Of course this halcyon political theory was some distance from reality. Many political scientists showed that interest groups were very unequal in their resources and influence, due to such factors as size, money, education, ability to employ sanctions and political linkages. Hence there were plenty of demonstrations, especially in relation to the USA, of how the resources of government had been appropriated for the benefit of some well-organised private interest. These critiques did not imply a blanket condemnation of all interest groups, since pluralism when working in a more balanced way had beneficial and democratic aspects.

A special critique of pluralism is that 'intensive' interest groups, which seek some advantage for a relatively small group (such as an industry wanting a tariff or subsidy), have an intrinsic advantage over diffuse groups, such as taxpayers and consumers. This is because there can be political profit from helping a concentrated interest, whereas the consequent cost spread throughout the nation is unlikely to lose votes (Wilson 1973). The same situation occurs with political favours to marginal electorates. These activities can be seen as an archetypal form of 'rent-seeking'. Pluralist theory itself suggests a possible remedy for this situation through the role of political parties and leaders. If excessive group claims are being conceded, they will eventually need to be wound back to avoid unpopularity among taxpayers and consumers. Although these diffuse groups are weakly organised, it may be possible for political entrepreneurs to mobilise their support – as indeed happened over the championing of taxpayers by leaders such as Thatcher and Reagan. (On pluralism, see Self, 1985, pp. 79–107.)

The generally benign view of the political process held by pluralists has been replaced, as a ruling paradigm, by the hostile theories of public choice. The new doctrine is not content to point to specific examples of 'rent-seeking' behaviour but extends the concept to cover the activities of all interest groups. This comprehensive critique is a poor and undemocratic argument. Many organisations such as environmental and welfare groups are not concerned with their own material interests but with what they see as serious social problems. Sometimes they may be too dogmatic or partisan, but they warrant respect and attention for seeking to put neglected subjects on the political agenda. Among the self-regarding interest groups there are variations of behaviour. Their demands may often be excessive or unreasonable, but they may also recognise that their interests have to be squared with other and wider interests. Their behaviour can alternate between extremism and moderation. Mancur Olson, one of the strongest critics of interest groups, concedes that a group becomes more moderate as its coverage broadens (Olson, 1982), so that a comprehensive trade union such as the Swedish LO will realise that excessive claims have an adverse effect upon its own members.

More basically the public choice position assumes an idealised market system such that any interest group claim will distort the market and divert resources from their appropriate market use. However, the market system works within a political framework which is concerned with other goals and standards apart from those operating in the market. Some interest groups are seeking to remedy what they see as avoidable inequalities, instabilities and failures of the market system. Others are concerned with social or environmental goals which transcend the market. Hence an ambit claim about 'rent-seeking' is simply economic language for condemning the political process. It is the function of a properly functioning democratic process to hear diverse claims and opinions and to judge them, unless one is silly enough to believe that in all matters 'the market knows best'.

What, then, will be the effects of reducing government functions and of privatisation? It will not spell an end to interest group activity, although the Thatcher government did formally distance itself from such activity, avoiding consultation even with professional and voluntary bodies – a stance slightly modified by the Major government. However, these attitudes did not actually mean the exclusion of all interests from political influence but their diversion into personal contacts with the leaders and members of the ruling party which led to the cases of 'sleaze' and corruption that eventually discredited the Conservative government.

A tight rein on public expenditure means stronger competition for public funds. It does not prevent politicians from pursuing their own agenda or favouring particular interests. The weakening of bureaucracy gives political leaders more discretionary power to advance these purposes. Privatisation also gives a unique opportunity to use public assets for political goals or favours. The Thatcher government was able to win easy popularity by selling off millions of council houses cheaply to their tenants and by offering low-priced shares in privatised industries, while the City of London was given a financial bonanza from the privatisation industry.

A more enduring effect of restricted public funds seems to be that the worst affected interests are those of the poor. This is partly due to a familiar point about interest groups – the poor are not organised and their interests depend on the advocacy of welfare organisations. They are also less likely to vote in elections, especially in the USA. When expenditure cuts are being made, there is reluctance to offend large middle-class groups or the 'median voter' who is inevitably middle-class, and discretionary grants to the poor seem an easier target. This policy of the Reagan administration led to a protest by his budget director, David Stockman, that he wanted to attack 'weak claims, not weak claimants' (Self, 1993, p. 90).

It is certainly the intention of many advocates of small government to do just the opposite of the Reagan policy – to cut out the expensive comprehensive public schemes and concentrate resources upon limited, means-tested services for the poor. It is politically doubtful if this goal will be achieved, and if it is it will require large tax rebates to persuade the middle class to switch to privatised systems.

The quality of service provision declines when only the poor get it, because of less public interest or protest, and the absence of any broad political support for maintaining good standards. A market-dominated society is likely to be a meaner one. Thus a smaller state does not hold out much promise of being more impartial as between rich and poor – quite the reverse since the state becomes less willing or able to remedy the increasing inequalities produced by liberated markets.

In a state dominated by the market, the strongest interests become business ones. They want lower taxation and less public expenditure; less regulation or, if there must be some, self-regulation by business; and favourable opportunities for business in and with the public sector. The business lobby is not homogeneous since there are conflicts of interest between big and small business, between different industries and between domestic and international capital. The strongest interests are those of big business and, for the time being at least, international capital supported by the economic dogma of free trade. These developments are not just speculative since they can be clearly observed in the USA. Business-dominated political action committees dominate lobbying in Washington. In 1986 Barry Goldwater (a very right-wing presidential candidate) commented that 'it is not we the people but PACs and moneyed interests who are setting the nation's political agenda' (Lutz and Lux, 1988, p. 216). Since that date, expenditure by private corporations on lobbying has grown rapidly between each Federal election. In Britain a scandal developed over the payment by business interests to MPs for asking helpful questions in Parliament. Instead of the more systematic access for interest groups which used to prevail, the British system has moved to particularist lobbying on the part of individual firms or entrepreneurs (Foster and Plowden, 1996, p. 79).

Another feature of a 'hollowed-out' state is its direct permeation by business executives. Increasing numbers of top jobs in the public service are being filled from this source, in the USA through appointments to the inflated ranks of political executives and in Britain through outside appointments to many of the new executive agencies. In Australia in 1996 the Howard government appointed as head of the public service a business man (known as Max the Axe) who made no secret of his view of government as markedly inferior to business. In Britain, under the Conservative government, the vast number of political appointments to 'quangos' (up to 10,000 a year) were very largely filled from business ranks, especially the top positions. There were few people included from trade unions, local government or the universities. The result looked like a narrow corporatism between politicians and business, only weakly modified by bureaucratic rules or conventions. The Labour government elected in 1997 can be expected at least to modify this structure – it must offer something to its supporters – but its leader has made clear his wish to work with business interests (and not to offend media proprietors).

It would be wrong to see business people in government as always advocates for market interests, although some will be just that. Many of them no doubt try to follow some perception of the public interest as expressed by political leaders, and some respect or even admire the public service. However, the influence of market ideology can only be strengthened by the presence of so many people who have earned their living and their profits from market operations. Alternative goals to that of supporting and enhancing the scope of the market, and liberating its forces, will have a tougher time getting support.

Historical evidence gives no support to the idea that a smaller government will be more impartial. The nearest approach to a 'night watchman state', that of Britain in the early nineteenth century, was strongly partisan. It prohibited trade unions under the Combination Acts and deported some of their organisers as convicts to Australia, but took no action to prevent collusion among employers, although Adam Smith himself had recognised the ubiquity of such collusion. A progressive income tax to finance public services was regarded as unthinkable until the end of the century. More balanced policies and a wider reflection of interests only occurred as the franchise was extended, trade unions organised and the scope of government widened.

The belief that government, whatever its size, can be shielded from political pressures is a myth. Some believers in small government seem genuinely to believe that it is possible to turn the state into an impartial umpire for establishing and enforcing a framework of laws whose main function will be to enable the market to function efficiently and fairly. But this cannot be done: the scope of the market and the meanings of 'efficiency' and 'equity' are contested issues, not to be read off from an economics textbook. If other interests get weaker, market interests get stronger. If government is remodelled in the image of the market, a green light is given to market interests. There are certainly dangers of excessive calls on the public purse from too much interest group activity, but the remedy lies in a better democratic process, not the domination of one strong interest.

The principles of a democratic process cannot be drawn simply from old-fashioned pluralism, although they can adopt elements of that doctrine. There has to be balance in the democratic process, and pluralism puts too much stress upon interests and interest groups. The acceptability of interest groups depends upon the ability of political parties and leaders to discipline the claims of strong interests and to recognise those of neglected ones; while market pressures have helped to activate the interests of taxpayers, they have had an adverse effect upon other generalised interests such as environmentalism and weak ones such as the poor. Another key element is the status of bureaucracy as independent adviser and impartial law-enforcer. Manipulation of these relationships by political leaders keen to replace government with the market is bound to have a destructive effect upon the democratic process.

Towards the corrupt state?

Is the concept of a minimum state feasible? That depends upon the meaning attached to the term. It is certainly imaginable that the functions of the state will be extensively privatised, partly through the relinquishment of functions to the market or sometimes the voluntary sector, partly through competitive tendering or outsourcing. The state's functions in health, education, and social security are all possible candidates for this treatment. The state would continue to provide these services for the poor, possibly delivering them mainly through competitive tenders, while most of the community would rely upon market or co-operative forms of provision. After all, this path is already being trod, and its acceleration could be possible given sufficient political skill and initial inducements. These would take the form of starving the public services of adequate funds, in the name of taxpayers' interest, while offering incentives (such as tax rebates) for individuals to switch to the private sector.

The full effect of this process would be to return the state to its role of about 150 years ago, before the great flow of public programmes had started in education, health and social security (and other functions such as housing and town planning). The comparison is far from an exact one, since in the modern world governments could hardly forgo a continuing involvement with the standards of education and health, and with new issues of rapid technological, economic and social change. However, many advocates of minimum government want to push this vision to the furthest limit possible. In their eyes the result would be a final victory for the principle of 'consumers' choice' over the concept of uniform (or 'regimented') public provision. They also argue that problems of poverty could now be confronted directly, without the need to 'waste resources' by servicing individuals who could pay for themselves. They also may envisage or hope for a renewed flowering of voluntary and co-operative organisations, such as the friendly societies, workers' and consumers' co-operatives and charities for the poor, which provided the principal source of mass welfare before the state took over.

Could public expenditure also be drastically reduced by these measures? That seems more doubtful. A reversion to the Victorian age in this respect faces large obstacles. Even by dry economists, a comprehensive system of education is now accepted as a vital public good, and of much importance for global competition – indeed there is a widespread view that more expenditure on education is needed. While in theory the delivery of education might be privatised, it would seem economically necessary and politically expected that the state should pay a high proportion of the total bill. In the case of health, the high costs of modern medical technology, the wide range of treatments now available and the growth of public expectations make it likely that, however the service is delivered, a substantial cost will fall on the state. With social security, the first obstacle to expenditure cuts is the accumulated weight of individual entitlements which will continue for a long time and cannot be fairly or honestly repudiated, although they might be subtly watered down (hence the paradox, already noted, that despite its professed aims the process of cutting welfare often started with the poor). The other expensive public service, defence, must presumably continue to be a government responsibility and charge.

There will also be increased costs associated with the continuing provision of public services for the poor. Whatever the inducements, many people will not feel able to switch to private health or pensions. There will be more poor to look after if global markets deliver high unemployment, low wages, and job insecurity. If technological advances are allowed to make a proportion of the population unemployable, there will be the same result. For these reasons the costs of fighting crime and drug traffic and perhaps of controlling political protests, are also likely to rise. Simultaneously public revenue will be adversely affected by the substantial tax incentives necessary to woo individuals into privatised services and by economic dogmas (more perhaps than political pressures) about the necessity of low taxation. All these factors could create pressures to minimise the cost of public services for the poor and to tighten eligibility rules, contrary to the supposed original aim of helping the poor by eliminating services for the rich. Even a ruthless political agenda of cutting down government will find it much harder to reduce public expenditure, even with mean standards of provision for the poor.

The third main category of state functions is regulation, but this function seems more likely to increase than diminish in the future. The number of purposes for which some measure of public regulation seems essential is growing. Old purposes of state regulation – such as laws about the sale of food and drugs, factory and working hours, health and safety regulations, etc. – are often amended but rarely abolished, and new or expanded public functions are continually being added. This accretion of functions reflects the rapid pace of technological and economic change, the pressures of urbanisation and mobility, the emergence or recognition of grave new dangers to the future of society, as well as increases in social turbulence and conflict.

One familiar example is environmental regulation which may still be very inadequate but is certainly likely to grow, and which seeks to control pollutants of all kinds, to limit energy consumption, to control the destruction of forests and the poisoning of watercourses, to check the exploitation of natural resources, and to protect wildlife and wilderness areas etc. Other examples of issues requiring regulation include dangerous drugs, genetic engineering, euthanasia, abortion.

Market deregulation is the very substantial counter-example to these trends, but the opportunities for malfeasance within a liberated, extended and unstable market system produce demands for new forms of regulation. This is particularly true of financial services, where hardly a week passes without some financial scandal or evidence that customers have been misled by wrong advice about investment or insurance. The control of monopoly and the principle of fair trading are important and contested issues, which introduce all the questions about differential bargaining power within the market that were raised in Chapter 2.

The process of privatisation itself, as already noted, produces new and difficult issues of regulation. Consumers must at least be given some protection against excessive prices and profits in the case of natural monopolies; and for basic utilities like water or electricity some public services obligations about the availability, quality and safety of supplies have to be laid down and enforced. The importance of regulation takes on a new and critical dimension with the growth of competitive tendering and outsourcing, since the quality and cost of services turns heavily on the efficiency and foresight with which the contracting process is managed.

It is an illusion to suppose that a small government will be less political or involve fewer ideological and controversial issues. This cannot be. The state will still dispose of large resources. It will have continuing responsibility, even if often indirectly, for a wide range of services. It will have widespread regulatory functions even if politicians try to rely as far as they dare upon some concept of industrial or corporate self-regulation. It cannot leave all responsibility for national prosperity and development to the workings of the market. It will still have to respond to natural and social disasters, to social conflicts or breakdown in civil order, and to many unforeseen or traumatic events, and it will of course retain its traditional responsibilities for defence, foreign affairs, international treaties and trade agreements, etc., whose ramifications are still growing.

In theory perhaps there need be no necessary threat to the effective performance of these functions from extensive privatisation. A vital condition for this conclusion would be a continuing capacity by government to devise and apply a very wide range of regulations and contracts in an impartial and effective manner. This formidable task will be very badly handled if left to politicians and their compliant advisers. It needs officials with a high level of competence and integrity, and at the top particularly a commitment to unravelling and pursuing complex issues of public purpose. What is needed for this purpose is a more capable and intelligent bureaucracy than now exists, not a weaker and more dependent one.

But if bureaucracy is fragmented and compliant or servile, politicians will get more opportunity to make patronage appointments and to intervene in particular decisions; and the temptation to bend the rules or make secret deals will be increased by a host of market interests which can profit from public contracts or be affected by public regulations. This primrose path is made easier by the erosion of public service rules and protective devices which, however cumbrous, maintained the standards and ethics of the public service. One of the strongest warnings about the danger of administrative corruption has come ironically from two advocates of privatisation, who point out that high standards of bureaucratic integrity and impartiality must be preserved if the new system is to work effectively (Foster and Plowden, 1996).

To return finally to the issues with which this chapter started, market advocates are fond of saying that political failures are worse than market failures. The comparison is not meaningful because the two types of 'failure' are so different, nor could any amount of political failure remove the dependence of markets upon laws made by the state. One must question too whether the two types of 'failure' have a converse relationship, as public choice thinkers assume, or whether they move together in either a vicious or a virtuous circle. Thus the current quest for minimum government seems more likely to increase than to diminish the 'political failures' listed by public choice theorists, by adding to the opportunities for key actors (especially politicians and some interests) to pursue their private advantage at the public expense; while 'market failures' seem even more certain to worsen, due to the weakened public capacity to regulate an expanded and still more dominant market sphere. The administrative system also becomes less responsive to the democratic process and more open to market interests and favours. The state becomes more partial to particular interests and probably more corrupt. Thus those market advocates who are zealously pressing for 'minimum government' are likely to end up with a state which still spends a great deal of money but which lacks the structure and the integrity to spend it at all wisely or justly.

The whole project of trying to reorganise government administration according to market principles contradicts the distinctive nature of public administration and historical experience about the evolution of the administrative system. Public policy-making is inevitably more complex than business policies, since its objectives and criteria are more diverse and often conflicting. Administrative organisation unavoidably entails striking a balance between conflicting values and goals – between the roles of line and staff, concentration on a single goal versus policy co-ordination, speed versus accountability, economy versus equitable procedures, and so on. It also entails an appropriate balance between the roles and functions of politicians and bureaucrats. Through successive stages of administrative evolution, the nature of these issues became better understood. Under the new ideology public administration is being thrust into a narrow, cut-down framework which puts all its emphasis upon one set of administrative values at the expense of their alternatives (Self, 1997).

The administrative 'reforms' being undertaken are not, as is often claimed or supposed, about means but closely affect the meaning and purposes of democratic government. To view government as merely providing a residual set of services which, for one reason or another and perhaps unfortunately, the market cannot provide adequately or equitably but can still (in principle) deliver efficiently, is to overlook the broader aims and aspirations of a democratic polity which extend beyond particular services and require concerted action across a broad front. It is also to endorse a market concept of efficiency which could erode the performance of public services to the point where the market may indeed seem to many people a preferable or anyhow an inevitable alternative to a devalued public system – which is what the extreme privatisers hope. Instead the real need is to improve public administration's capacity to achieve its distinctive tasks effectively, and to relate its operations better to the aspirations of a more active democracy.

5
The Shock of the Global Economy

This book does not question the proposition that competitive markets have a legitimate place in a good society. The critical questions, however, are how wide and large this place should be and how the market system should be organised. The argument so far has demonstrated the ways in which capitalist markets have expanded their scope and influence to the detriment of other institutions and values, and to the detriment also in some respects of the market system itself. The world is increasingly ruled according to a set of market dogmas which, as Chapter 1 suggested, have a shaky foundation in 'orthodox' economic theory, which itself is only an idealised picture of the tendencies of a fully competitive market system and not an authoritative normative recipe for a good society (as some economists seem to suppose). Chapter 2 suggested how an exaggerated belief in consumers' choice and the right of private acquisition as the meaning of freedom have come to overshadow the more balanced view of personal liberty and social responsibility which had developed within the dominant liberal tradition of Western societies. Chapter 3 showed how concepts of collective social welfare have been perverted by narrow and unconvincing economic arguments. Chapter 4 suggested how the state itself is being turned into a weak imitation and auxiliary of the market system to the grave detriment of a democratic political process and good standards of public administration.

It is now necessary to confront the most palpable modern feature of the dominance of the market system, namely its global scope and character. The ramifications of global markets are too vast to be fully treated here. Instead the aim, in line with the previous chapters, is to analyse the actual trends and behaviour of the global market in order to show how its perverse elements outweigh the benefits claimed for it. In particular the functioning of global markets, which are not themselves democratically accountable (except very indirectly and weakly through international agreements), is impinging strongly upon the exercise of democratic political choice within individual nations – to such an extent that commentators often declare that the people of the world have no choice but to accept the iron 'disciplines' of an economic order which they have not consciously or freely chosen, and of whose implications many people remain unaware. Certainly the political impact of global markets is formidable, but the issue of whether or not it leaves democracies with no political choice must be confronted later.

Theory and reality of free trade

The concept of free trade has always resonated favourably within the Western liberal tradition. It is associated with freedom, peace and prosperity. Freedom is enhanced by the ability of individuals or firms to trade without restrictions with members of other nations (so long as the products traded are not patently harmful). Peaceful trade between nations is a very desirable alternative to war, and its growth has always been supposed to make wars less likely, although trade in armaments and strategic war materials represents a large dent in this assumption. Finally, and most saliently today, free trade is seen as a highly important generator of economic growth. Just as Cobden and Bright argued so eloquently for free trade in nineteenth-century England, so do many modern liberals give a strong priority to further expediting a global freedom of trade, which they regard as a principal cause of the post-1945 economic boom and as the essential basis for continued economic growth.

The traditional economic argument for free trade is that of 'comparative advantage', which states that it will pay every nation to specialise in those products in which it is relatively (not absolutely) more efficient and to trade them for products that it can produce (if at all) with relatively lower efficiency. Although this sounds logical enough, the theory has always been open to criticisms which become stronger under the actual conditions of modern world trade.

- It assumes that exchange rates will operate smoothly to facilitate balanced trade between nations, but exchange rates no longer operate primarily to balance trade, and are governed far more by massive short-term speculative movements of money in search of quick returns.

- It assumed originally (as articulated by Ricardo) that capital would not be exported from one country to another, but would be invested in those domestic industries with the greatest comparative advantage. When capital can flow freely around the world, as is now the case, this condition is completely breached. Adam Smith himself was clear that the 'invisible hand' achieved its beneficial effects in trade only because entrepreneurs in his day had little option but to invest in their own country and not abroad (Smith, 1937, p. 700). This important condition is now completely negated. So the modern enthusiasts for freedom of capital find their patron saint on the other side of the debate, negating thereby one of the conditions of mutually beneficial trade.

- The theory also ignores the transitional or 'structural' costs associated with shifting patterns of trade and investment. When these adjustments are gradual or minor their costs may be modest; but when (as is the modern situation) new imports can arrive from all over the world and capital can be shifted between countries quite easily, the impact of the consequent dislocation is often considerable. A whole local community can and quite often does find its basic livelihood wiped out, with consequent local unemployment, waste of infrastructure, and disruption of local community life. All the care and investment put into a local industry can be destroyed by the fact that the same good can be produced slightly cheaper elsewhere in the wide world.

- The theory claims that the trade relationship will be mutually beneficial. If (as is often now the case) the effect is to shift unemployment from one country to another, this assumption is falsified. Economic models are often used to suggest that any such effect will be only temporary, since cheaper imports will free income to be spent on additional goods or invested; but much of any income savings may also go on imported goods and there may be inadequate domestic investment to take up surplus labour. The free trade case is often bolstered by unrealistic and artificial model building, which does not adequately recognise the institutional and social blockages to successful adaptation or the fact that there is inadequate world demand to sustain full employment.

At the least these considerations suggest that complete mobility of both goods and capital cannot be rationally advocated as a universally desirable goal for all countries. Certainly in principle free trade offers consumers the gain of buying in the cheapest market, but for any given society these advantages may be outweighed by its effects upon employment, the balance of payments and community life. In point of fact, it is usually the economically strongest country (Britain in the nineteenth century and more recently the USA) which gains most from free trade and is its keenest advocate. Many countries have reason to be more cautious about its benefits.

Historically, the case for free trade has always been up against the opposite case for at least some degree (and sometimes a high degree) of national security and autonomy. One traditional reason for protection was the need for a nation to have sufficient resources of materials and foodstuffs to fight or endure a war in which trade was interrupted. Another motive was to protect new domestic industries until at least they were strong enough to compete in the world market – a policy that still appeals to many countries and includes some like Japan who used protection deliberately to build up a leading position in world trade. A third reason was the case for a government retaining enough effective control of its national economy in order to pursue its chosen economic and social policies. Also, since there has never been (and is not today) full competition, governments have a strong motive to use protective measures such as tariffs and quotas as bargaining chips in trade negotiations.

An objective view might conclude that these protectionist arguments have at least as much validity as they ever did. A high degree of protection can be rightly criticised as a failure to utilise the advantages of trade and injurious to consumers; but some measure of protection and internal autonomy to direct a nation's pattern of development is another matter. These considerations could lead to a balanced position on the respective merits of free trade and protection, which would advocate pragmatic policies that were related to the situation of the individual nation. However in current discourse this position is treated as completely outdated. The advocates of free movement of capital and goods carry all before them on the issue of principle, and protectionist measures (although they still occur) are regarded as undesirable deviations from the true economic gospel and due to regrettable 'political' pressures.

This new gospel draws upon the dramatic growth in the volume of trade and drastic changes in its character. World trade has grown much faster than world production, rising from $25 billion in 1938 to $1,915 billion in 1984. Its composition has shifted from the earlier importance of trade in food and raw materials to a dominant position for manufactures and increasingly for services such as advertising, accountancy, consultancy and education. The bulk of this trade takes the form of the exchange of similar products (or parts of those products) between developed economies (Strange, 1988, pp. 166–72).

The new trading system is dominated by large international corporations. The world market share of the top five firms in each industry amounts to nearly 70 per cent for consumer durables, over 50 per cent for the automotive, airline, aerospace, electrical, electronic and steel industries, and over 40 per cent for the oil, personal computer and media industries (*The Economist*, 27 March 1993). It has been estimated that the percentage of world economic output traded between countries rose from just under 9 per cent to just under 19 per cent between 1965 and 1992, and that 70 per cent of world trade is controlled by 500 corporations (Korten, 1995, p. 124). This situation is poles apart from the economic theory of competition and represents a strongly oligopolistic concentration of market power throughout a wide range of large industries.

While trade and monetary liberalisation have enabled capital to move quite freely around the world, labour mobility is still closely constricted by national boundaries. Firms in the advanced economies can take advantage of the enormous reserves of cheap labour available in developing countries, including most recently the vast labour reserves in China, by transferring simpler or more routinised production functions to these new locations, either through direct investment or by contracting out the function to a local firm.

World trade has been developing as a complex jigsaw of interconnected elements. 'Multinational' corporations originally established subsidiary companies in a variety of countries, which replicated the production functions performed for the home market and often included arrangements for local shareholding and inputs of local materials. The newer 'transnational' type of corporation may cut down or eliminate altogether production plants in its home base and assemble its products from parts made in a variety of different national locations. The general effect of these developments is successive transfers of simpler forms of technology to cheaper countries and locations, with the more sophisticated and specialised functions remaining in the home base. Hence arises a core–periphery relationship: the headquarters of a big corporation and its specialised managerial, research and marketing operations remain in its metropolitan base, while many or even all of its production functions are transferred to peripheral locations in the world where costs are lower – sometimes very much lower.

The justification for these developments is that they have contributed greatly to global economic growth and that their further stimulation is an essential condition of continued growth – hence the attempts by world economic leaders and their acolytes to forge a new economic philosophy which justifies these developments in free trade terms and calls for what is seen as their logical culmination. For example, Akio Morita, Chairman of Sony Corporation, has urged world leaders to find the means of lowering *all* economic barriers between North America, Europe and Japan – trade, investment, legal and so forth – in order to create a harmonised world business system with agreed rules and procedures that transcend national boundaries (quoted in Korten, 1995, p. 122). Morita's vision does not stop with the complete integration of the more advanced economies but is intended to embrace the whole globe. His agenda corresponds to strong trends that are already occurring in the world, even if they are still a long way off their logical culmination. This new 'corporate philosophy' (as it is sometimes called) appears to have three main principles:

- Complete freedom of trade, investment, and money (preferably an integrated monetary system). Theoretically there should be complete mobility of labour as well, but that idea at least seems politically impossible. Its logical corollary, however, is possible – namely that wages for given skills and qualifications should tend towards a common world level. That process has already started.

- Unification of government standards and regulations concerning economic, social and environmental issues, so that trade and development occurs throughout the world on the basis of a 'level playing field'.
- Effective legal protection of property and contract rights in all countries so as to give security to traders and investors.

Theoretically, these are supposed to be neutral principles for promoting the global growth of trade and investment. It is easy to see, however, that they are likely to favour the interests of capitalist institutions and to disadvantage other interests and values. In the world as it actually is, with extensive unemployment and a plentiful supply of labour waiting to be utilised, the first principle puts a downward pressure upon wage rates, especially in developed countries. The second principle is liable to be detrimental to countries which have established good standards of social and environmental regulation because of international competition for investment funds. In theory a greater uniformity of the legal framework could include measures to couple the rights of private ownership of capital with some correlative degree of public accountability, but such a step seems unlikely in a politically fragmented world. The result is more likely to be to strengthen the rights of private ownership in countries where it is still subject to some limitations.

These principles are all advanced on the basis that they are essential to global economic growth and disregard the many ways (pointed out in Chapter 3) in which the conventional concept of market-led growth fails tests of human welfare. Yet the final irony is that the argument can be faulted even in its own terms. The Swiss economist Paul Bairoch criticises the belief that protectionism dampens economic growth and free trade promotes it as basically a myth. It can sometimes be true but for many countries and for some periods of modern world history it has not been true (Bairoch, 1993, pp. 16–56). This conclusion is not altogether surprising when one reflects on the benefit of some degree of stability for fruitful economic development which is hard to achieve on a global basis. The apparent importance of world trade for economic growth in the post-1945 period was

greatly helped by the existence of full employment, stable exchange rates and more balanced economies which no longer exist.
The advocates of complete 'globalisation' are desperately struggling to run faster without considering whether they are on the
right track at all.

The new economic order

The new economic gospel gives a highly biased interpretation of
the principle of open economic competition on which it is supposed to rest. The global economic system is not at all a level playing field. It exhibits a complex mixture of economic and political
power. The main elements in the system are the big corporations
which dominate world trade, the international money market,
national governments and international economic organisations.
The big corporations use their bargaining power in relation both
to weaker market competitors or suppliers and to the national
governments, whom they often exceed in resources. In 1980 the
sales of each of the top ten multinationals exceeded the national
income of 87 countries and in 1990 the hundred largest economies in the world includes almost as many companies as nations
(Horsmann and Marshall, 1994, p. 201). They also put direct political pressure on their home government to support their global
interests. The international market for capital is the vital conduit
for the supply of credit to fuel growth, but its continuous search
for maximising profits is also a source of unwise loans, often to
developing countries at high rates of interest. The national governments possess the power to regulate economic activity within
their territory in the interest of their citizens, but have been
increasingly driven (willingly or otherwise) to adjust their policies
to the global pressures of trade and capital flows. The stronger
national governments can also of course exert political and economic pressure upon the weaker ones to promote what they see
as their economic interests. The international economic organisations generally side with the pressures to liberate global economic
forces.

Some points should be noted about this system. While it includes
centres of both economic and political power, no international
political authority exists which can match or regulate the global
range of the business corporations and money markets. Hence

there is a basic weakness in the balance between economic and political interests and goals, and a serious limitation for democracy which can operate only at the national level, apart from the relatively weak influence emanating from the United Nations and its specialised agencies. (However, the European Union is a partial but important exception to this statement.) Next the operation of the global economy is not simply to be explained by power relationships any more than by a purely spontaneous and undirected pattern of economic competition. Both power and competition, both dominant control and mutual advantages, figure in how the system works.

Moreover, while corporations plan their activities purposefully and governments attempt to do the same, the system as a whole is not the product of deliberate planning or purpose. The money market, for example, has evolved in a curious and unplanned way, under the influence of improved communications, growing trade, and ingenious efforts by traders to evade regulations and promote sophisticated new financial products. Even the corporations are driven by factors beyond their control such as the intensified global competition for profit and the threat of takeover. Governments too are jostled off course by often unforeseeable forces, and (from political as well as economic swings or dependencies) have got a weaker capacity than a big corporation to act consistently. All these elements explain why the global economic order is chaotic and unpredictable.

Without being the result of any overall design, but with the support or acquiescence of the most powerful economic and political players, the global economic system has become strongly biased in certain directions. It favours the accumulation of profit and the growth of financial speculation, and it disfavours political attempts to regulate markets in the interest of social and environmental standards or goals. It undermines the workings of democracy at the national and local level through subjecting the exercise of political choice to largely uncontrollable global economic pressures, and it is threatening to destroy the internal cohesion of nations through detaching the interests of the dominant economic class from that of the nation to which they belong. And while world trade is certainly associated with increases in productivity, some global developments (especially in financial markets) are undermining both business integrity and efficient production. These propositions can be illustrated by considering the functioning of business corporations, the money market and states.

Business corporations were once closely regulated by governments in the general interest, but over time they have escaped from public accountability, secured all the privileges of a legal persona including freedom of speech and political activity while being conceded only a limited liability for their debts, and gained almost complete freedom over the deployment of their resources and profits. In the USA competition between the states has enabled a corporation to choose a state with minimum registration requirements or it may base itself in some small, compliant country. A multinational corporation can manipulate its internal relations so as to minimise its tax bills in different countries and to juggle the prices set by its subsidiaries. The world competition for investment funds helps it to externalise some of its overseas costs by persuading foreign governments to offer tax concessions and provide local infrastructure, and by leaving the local authorities to repair environmental damage when it leaves. A corporation can also escape the odium associated with extremely low wages and bad working conditions or the destruction of local habitats in poor countries, by contracting out the operation and denying responsibility. Some large corporations do have a sense of responsibility over these matters; their size and visibility can influence them to behave responsibly in environmental matters, while their interest in long-term investment can produce a greater concern with local stability and prosperity than the search for quick monetary profit; but still, weak regulation, competition with more ruthless firms and new opportunities for profit all weaken these resolves.

As Susan Strange says (1988, p. 86), a big corporation can spend its money in much the same way as the rulers of a state once did – although in democratic societies the politicians have become a lot less lavish and more accountable than the corporate elite. Its controllers are able to award themselves large fees, perks and share options; to spend money on industrial espionage to protect their patents; to advertise widely and to indulge their tastes and improve their images as patrons of the arts, sport and education; to make political donations and engage in political propaganda – sometimes lavishly; and to charge most of these activities against tax liabilities. The erosion of progressive national taxation is one very serious effect of the global reach of corporations. Equally the significance of financial manipulation over taxes, exchange rates, etc. for a corporation's profits has little to do with its productive efficiency.

Money markets have increasingly escaped from effective regulation, first by exploiting international gaps in the regulatory apparatus, which is how the Euro dollar market started, later from national measures of financial deregulation. Monetary movements across the world have grown with enormous rapidity (by a multiple of ten within one decade) and now exceed by far the relatively modest sums required to settle trade accounts and make overseas investments, most of it consisting of 'hot money' in search of maximum short-term profit. This rapid flow of 'hot' money destabilises exchange rates for reasons that have little to do with the long-term prospects of a national economy, and sets off speculative cycles which national governments and banks (even when acting in concert) find difficult or impossible to limit and control. The futures market in currencies and financial 'derivatives' has become enormously large and complex. A defence of this system is that it enables firms to hedge their bets against exchange fluctuations, but small businesses, farmers and individuals are usually unable to protect themselves in this way and suffer accordingly – often severely (Strange, 1986).

The whole edifice of the money market seems vastly top-heavy for sustaining the legitimate functions of trade and investment and represents the creation of a 'self-exciting system' whose growth has become parasitical upon actual production. Its legitimate function of providing credit for business enterprise has got overwhelmed by speculative activity and short-term profit seeking and distanced from the social function which it is supposed to be serving.

The speculative mania of the money market has added to the pressures and temptations on corporations to act in a narrow, ruthless manner. Once there was at least some connection possible between holding a company's shares and approving of its purpose and methods. The growth of mutual funds who compete vigorously for profit margins regardless of where or how the money is made has weakened this connection. The market is also continually stimulated by the speculative possibilities of a successful takeover. In modern economic lore a takeover is supposedly the ultimate weapon for keeping a corporation efficient and on its toes; but it is no secret that many takeovers are inspired by the scope for cutting the cost of labour, selling off assets and other forms of 'reconstruction' that can yield quick profits, and this operation may be financed by heavy short-term borrowing, with the issue of 'junk bonds' a notorious example. The result of a takeover may sometimes be an increase in productive efficiency, although that is far from certain, but takeovers are a constant threat to established corporations which try to balance their duty to their shareholders with a responsible attitude towards their employees, their customers and care for the environment.

David Korten (1995, pp. 212–13, 252–3, 242–3) gives many examples of how 'responsible' corporations such as Stride Rite and Levi Strauss have felt compelled to modify their policies by closing domestic plants and employing very cheap foreign labour in order to keep up with their competitors and forestall the danger of a takeover. He believes that 'the dynamics of this system (global markets) have become so powerful and perverse that it is becoming increasingly difficult for corporate managers to manage in the public interest, no matter how strong their moral values and commitment' (p. 13). Many business executives would like to take a broader view of their responsibilities than the maximisation of profit (and short-run profit at that), but can become ruthless, or be replaced by more ruthless individuals, through the pressures of the system. Admittedly, some private attempts are now being made to promote ethical standards of investment (mainly in the environmental field), but ethical investment still has to compete in profit terms and is limited in the absence of political support.

The executives of large corporations still retain great power to shape their policies, allocate their vast resources and influence key figures in government and finance. As Peter Drucker says, they are dealing with political issues, not just business or economic ones: 'managers have not yet faced up to the fact that they represent power – and power has to be accountable, has to be legitimate' (Drucker, 1989, p. 219). This is a new kind of power in the world and the trouble is that it is not actually accountable to anyone, save formally to shareholders whose primary (generally sole) concern is profit. True, public opinion can sometimes exert some influence – on environmental issues, for example, or sanctions against some hated regime – but it is sporadic and uncertain. Corporations are subject to various laws and regulations, but the pressure of the global economy has been towards minimising these at the very time that they are becoming more necessary, and there is anyhow no effective international agency to make and enforce rules apart from the economic agencies which grease the wheels of the global economy.

Corporations have to be responsive (rather than responsible) to their consumers – for there is no real mutual dialogue – in the sense that no one can be forced to buy their products; but the corporation's great resources for advertising and public relations, its capacity to monopolise products and brand names, and its ability to squeeze out smaller competitors all assist its sales. Its relationship with its staff and workers would seem to call for the kind of leadership which shares benefits and burdens as a matter of moral responsibility and enlightened self-interest, since a well-treated workforce should be a more co-operative one. Such attitudes can be found in business, cemented in some countries by well-established practices and traditions, but the historical record does suggest that it has taken a long period of political and union pressures to bring about a more co-operative and enlightened capitalism. Unfortunately the pressure of the global market for maximising short-run profit, the weakening of political and trade union restraints, and the growth of unemployment, have opened the door for a return to the more ruthless kind of exploitative capitalism. Lester Thurow puts the point bluntly: 'American capitalists declared class war on their workers – and they have won it' (Thurow, 1996, p. 180).

The national states retain the right and the responsibility to regulate markets but their ability to do so has been much limited by these global economic forces. An international corporation can go elsewhere if it does not like the market rules, the labour laws or the environmental standards which a government lays down; and corporations are strategically placed to play 'divide and rule' on these issues. A government's ability to act more independently is much restricted by the possibility of an adverse reaction in the money market, and its ability to borrow will be harmed by an adverse credit rating from a private international agency such as Moody's or Standard and Poor, influential organisations concerned only with the danger of default on debt. Government budgetary decisions are also constrained by the possible reactions of money markets, credit agencies and large corporations. Nearly all governments live in an international market climate over which they can, as a rule, have rather little influence, but which has a strong influence on their decisions.

The above account may exaggerate the extent to which nation states are *necessarily* constrained by global economic forces. The political embrace of market ideology has caused some governments deliberately to accept and promote these global trends without trying any compensatory action. Moreover, nations vary enormously in size and power, and the bigger ones have naturally more ability to carve out some degree of independence of action, if they choose to do so, than the host of small nations which have become highly exposed to global economic winds; yet, as the experience of the Mitterand government in its early years in France and of the Social Democrats in Sweden showed, even governments of developed countries with a contrary agenda have been defeated by these global pressures – and the British government was unable to defend sterling against the money market led by a single rich and able speculator, George Soros. Furthermore, one of the gravest problems of governments who want to pursue some independent goals is the short-term horizons of the money market and the pressures to maximise profits. An enlightened pursuit of social and environmental goals by a national government might in the longer run, through creating a more harmonious society and a better environment to live and work in, also prove itself an attractive target for investment and job creation – yet such ambitions take time to work through and the international market is not hospitable to long visions.

The global split

A crucial issue of the global economy is the relationship between the developed 'North' of the world and the relatively undeveloped 'South'. It is simply not the case that the development of Southern economies with the aid of Northern loans, investment and technology is necessarily beneficial to the local population – quite the reverse can be the case. It all depends upon the objectives and methods of development. Foreign investment helps to create a modernised sector in the economy, usually concentrated in the capital and including a relatively affluent middle class, but the mass of the population will not gain much from this development, whether they stay in rural areas or move to shanty towns around the cities as vast numbers have done. The growing of export crops to earn foreign exchange reduces the land available to support subsistence farming, which is anyhow usually inadequate to support the rural population, thus pushing more people into shanty towns. Large development projects such as hydro-electric dams, sometimes financed by the World Bank, have had devastating effects upon the local habitat and livelihood in densely populated areas. Much of the hard-won foreign exchange is spent on cars and imported goods for the new middle class, or upon 'cargo cult' luxuries such as Coca-Cola, widely advertised and drunk in poor countries which have excellent fruit drinks of their own available.

It is true that foreign investment, coupled with strong and authoritarian government policies, has produced a substantial improvement of living standards in some Asian countries, notably Malaysia and the small Asian 'tigers' (Taiwan, South Korea, Thailand, Hong Kong and Singapore), although the gains in the last two are related to their small size and special strategic position in world trade; but the overall results are less impressive, especially now that some of the 'tigers' have suffered a financial collapse. World Bank figures show that between 1965 and 1985 the share of world production in middle-income developing countries increased from 7.0 to 11.2 per cent and their share of world exports increased still more from 5.0 to 15.3 per cent; but this was matched by an actual small decline in the shares of production and exports in low-income developing countries (Strange, 1988, p. 167). Large parts of the world, in Africa particularly, have been moving backwards not forwards in terms of the claimed benefits of world trade. Those poor countries which depend upon exports of primary products are especially vulnerable, being subject to erratic and adverse terms of trade.

Moreover in the larger Asian countries – India, China, Indonesia and the Philippines – labour is often shockingly exploited. Not only are wages very low and hours long, but many children and women are put to work under conditions little different from outright slavery. It can be argued that the explosion of population in these countries, without the possible relief of mass emigration which helped European countries in the nineteenth century, is bound to create conditions of life similar to or worse than those in the Western industrial revolution; but the productivity of modern industry is such that it is quite possible to offer more reasonable wages and working conditions without a big addition to prices (the wages of some Asian workers constitute a mere 5 per cent or less of the price charged in a Western shop). A ruthless treatment of labour, whether in the West or the East, adds to the growing inequality of incomes in the world and undermines the creation of mass markets on which general economic prosperity ultimately depends.

These tendencies towards a highly uneven and environmentally destructive pattern of development are strongly reinforced when a poor country gets into debt. The history of third-world debt is now a familiar story, with the eagerly proffered Northern bank loans often misspent on imports for the local elite and repayments inflated by rising interest rates. The annual debt payments of poor countries now exceed the sums available in aid programmes, much of which is tied to commercial loans made to promote the exports of developed countries. But if the debt burden becomes too great, leading to a danger of default, the IMF and the World Bank enter the scene to assist a 'rescheduling' of debt over a longer period and to deliver a stern lecture about the requirements of the new financial orthodoxy as a condition of any help. The poor country is told to cut its budget drastically, which inevitably hurts the mass of the population with cuts in health, education and rural development. Privatisation, deregulation and drastic reductions in the public service are recommended, often regardless of local conditions and traditions. The usual orthodoxies about free trade and expanded exports are also decreed. Its citizens are thus denied an effective say over the development of their country's resources, and forced to swallow the current economic dogmas of Northern nations with different cultural traditions and at a very different stage of development.

Most Southern states are very weak players in the exercise of both economic and political power. They have tiny domestic markets compared with the European Union or NAFTA, and they are weakly placed in trade negotiations and relations with international corporations. The weapon of debt obligations has been wielded skilfully to keep them tied to the global economic system. The local elites have become tied to the North in terms of their lifestyles and their economic and political dependency. Any attempt to mobilise the masses in order to pursue more radical policies will be countered by the USA with economic and political pressure, extended if necessary to surreptitious or even overt military intervention. The unseating of even moderately radical governments, from Lumumba to Allende, and the endorsement of military or authoritarian governments provided they respect American economic interests, is evidence enough of the close relationship between global political and economic power.

The dominant principle of national policies is becoming one of equipping the nation to compete effectively in the global market. Up to now governments have backed the interests of their largest firms and economic sectors. However as corporations extend their world operations, their allegiance to any particular nation grows weaker and so may the benefits which their national base receives from their operations. They are likely to invest less, employ fewer people and pay less taxes in their home base. They are still likely to be a source of well-paid jobs in management, consultancy and research at their home base, although – given increasing global competition for ancillary activities such as accountancy and advertising – some of these activities may be shifted elsewhere. They will of course remit profits to their shareholders, but some of the shares will be owned abroad and some of their domestic shareholders may choose to live and spend their money abroad, as is indeed increasingly the case with rich and retired individuals. A very large and powerful state like the USA can still achieve a concentrated zone of prosperity from its close involvement with international trade and finance, but the contribution of an international corporation to the prosperity of its home base is becoming more selective and uncertain.

The other fashionable recipe for national competitiveness is to improve the skills and adaptability of the workforce so that the owners of capital (whether domestic or foreign) are more willing to invest and provide employment. The idea is that workers in developed economies will need to specialise in more technically advanced industries and services, while less elaborate activities are progressively hived off to more backward countries. There are obvious advantages to any one nation in improving its skill base faster than its competitors, but this doctrine (while it changes the pecking order among nations) will not itself produce a situation of sufficient effective demand in the world to mop up widespread unemployment. Indeed the staggering advances in automation mean that more investment in sophisticated industries will reduce, not increase, the supply of jobs even if they are more skilled and better paid. Behind these dreams of global market growth lies always the spectre of a large and growing *lumpenproletariat*, working in low-paid jobs or not at all.

The logical outcome of the present global economy is the social polarisation of the world along class lines. Indeed this phenomenon is already apparent. An increasing inequality of incomes, and a much sharper division between rich and poor, is apparent in both North and South, in both developed and developing countries. Just as in the USA, between 1977 and 1989, the average real income of the top 1 per cent of families rose by 78 per cent and that of the bottom 20 per cent decreased by 10.4 per cent (Korten, 1995, p. 109), so countries like Mexico and Pakistan have increasing numbers of millionaires in a sea of grim poverty and deprivation.

This social polarisation and immiseration is likely to have devastating consequences for the stability and harmony of individual nations. The aristocracy and the bourgeoisie have always been more international than the workers in terms both of culture and economic interest, but this difference becomes more corrosive when the rich no longer have any necessary and strong interest in the prosperity of their own country. To the extent that they think and act globally, and live a global lifestyle, they become detached or indifferent to the problems or sufferings of their fellow nationals. When they lock themselves away in expensive, closely guarded enclaves or live abroad, they further distance themselves from the national life. The masses have always paradoxically been more patriotic or nationalistic than the rich because they have nowhere else to go. The world wars demonstrated that workers' patriotism was much stronger than their attachment to international class co-operation, and such co-operation becomes still more difficult under conditions of surplus labour and international competition for jobs. The frustration of ordinary people with growing inequality and instability can be deliberately turned, as is increasingly the case, against immigrant groups who have an easy visibility and compete directly for jobs, rather than against the rich beneficiaries of the global economy who seem remote and invisible. The potential for fascism, communism or severe class conflict is simmering in many countries as a product of this growing social polarisation along world lines.

The politics of globalisation

As already noted, nation states have strong reasons for maintaining some degree of independence from the impact of global economic forces. This is a question partly of national security, partly of the interest of their workers in job security, partly of preserving political choice or autonomy, and partly too of balancing the different interests of domestic and international capital – the former firms being tied to the home market and often wanting some degree of protection, the latter wanting freedom to operate in international markets. It would be wrong to suppose that these national concerns and interests have disappeared, but their political impact has certainly waned in recent decades.

One reason for this change is the lower weight attached to national military security, except in the USA, the USSR (until recently) and China, because of the dependence of states upon global alliances in the event of a major war – although this consideration does not apply to regions where a local war can still occur such as the Middle East. However, these states are heavily dependent upon armaments supplied by the big powers, so that their military needs stimulate world trade. Another reason is that the cult of consumerism has been nourished by a widening global choice of products, giving the injunction to buy domestic products a rather old-fashioned ring unless supported by strong cultural tastes or a still fiery nationalism. Hence promoters of the global order can make strong play with the interests of the consumer, which many people assume to be the only important economic consideration.

Then again, the internal balance between international and domestic capital has shifted strongly in the former direction, because of the growth of international firms and the dependence of many local firms upon contracts with them. A further important factor is the interest of the principal financial centres in maintaining open access to the much expanded world of international finance. Thus the importance of both international corporations and international financial centres is greatest in the USA, Japan and Britain. In Britain the interests of the City of London seem to count for more than those of the traditional manufacturing industries of the Midlands and North, a bias strongly apparent in the policies of the Thatcher government. By contrast the labour interests hurt by globalisation have lost influence both nationally and internationally; for example, the World Trade Organisation failed to write into its rules a requirement for nations to observe at least the minimum principles of the International Labour Office. English-speaking countries are also permeated by belief in the value of a completely open consumers' market, unlike France and Japan where there is cultural resistance to the impact of globalisation on consumption choices and way of life.

An important factor is the ability of the strongest states, pre-eminently the USA, to influence the structure of the global economy so as to favour its dominant economic interests. Such policies amount to a reinforcement of the economic power of big corporations or financial institutions with the political power of the state – a formidable combination. The effect of state support is to increase the monopolistic leverage of the favoured economic interests within the rules and functioning of the international market-place (Wallerstein, 1984). National policies need not be consistent. They can combine a strong advocacy of free trade in most spheres with protective devices in others. The USA is a strong advocate of global intellectual property rights, because its major corporations have a big interest in securing and monopolising valuable technical inventions. It is equally keen on freedom of trade in films and television because of its dominance of mass culture. It also uses its political clout to back trade deals with weaker nations and to protect the foreign loans of its banks and financial institutions. On the other hand it continues with price and export subsidies for its farm products because of the strength of the farm lobby, even though agriculture is the best example of the free trade ideal since it involves competition in simple products between numerous countries and producers.

All these examples show the weight of business lobbies, especially the big corporations, in the calculations of President and Congress. Trade unions by contrast have had rather little influence, despite the periodic support of presidential aspirants such as Pat Buchanan. President Clinton was expected, from his rhetoric and credentials, to take a more populist stand on trade issues, but instead he piloted through the NAFTA free trade agreement against strong popular opposition. Many workers and ordinary people realised that competition from very cheap Mexican labour was not an attractive prospect, but many firms liked the idea of competing in the rich American market from locations across the border. Clinton fell back on the familiar rhetoric about the prospects for economic growth which would follow from an enlarged market. However when economic union was followed by the collapse of the Mexican peso, with tragic consequences for the lives of millions of Mexicans, the President was prepared to use taxpayers' money to support the banks who had made risky loans to Mexico.

The principal international economic organisations – the International Monetary Fund (IMF), World Bank and World Trade Organisation (WTO) – are all strong supporters of the development and further expansion of the global economic system. They are naturally influenced by the strongest member states, especially the USA, and their financial contributions. They also are open to direct lobbying from major business and financial interests. This is particularly true of the World Trade Organisation, whose network of advisory committees is dominated by the representatives of big corporations (Korten, 1995, pp. 174–81), and which is highly pro-active in spreading the gospel of freedom of trade and investment. These organisations take the lead in lecturing the world, especially the governments of the weaker states, on the requirements of the global order.

As said earlier, the present global system cannot be plausibly defended by traditional economic theories, and the more perceptive neo-classical theorists do not claim as much. Instead, its defence is often based upon a *political* argument – namely, the need to combat the selfish interests of any domestic industries and trade unions who seek protection against the healthy blasts of foreign competition. That such interests exist is undeniable, although it does not follow that their cause has no justification. But the boot is now very much on the other foot – that while protectionist interests were often powerful in the past, they have become heavily outweighed by those with strong vested interests in the global system.

Globalisation is vigorously pushed throughout the world by what can fairly be described as a transnational capitalist class. This class comprises leaders of business corporations with strong international interests or aspirations, major international banks and lending institutions, together with supportive politicians and bureaucrats. One important element is a supportive media, often now owned by rich proprietors with international interests, together with think-tanks and economic advisers or commentators, who supply the daily grind of publicity that is so crucial for sustaining political support or acquiescence (the key players operate much more behind the scenes, sometimes well behind them). Also necessary are the salesmen who promote a 'culture-ideology of consumerism' to encourage demand for modern market products, and for the bank loans and foreign investment which will stimulate economic growth (Sklair, 1994).

This description does not imply the existence of some massive organised global conspiracy. It is rather that there are strong interests in global growth, and as the structure of the world economy slips beyond effective political control, the peculiar logic of the system asserts itself. As the bandwagon effect grows, so more people climb aboard from expediency. This point applies especially to politicians and bureaucrats. Some of these in the Thatcher and Reagan years were highly supportive of all efforts to 'set markets free', and indeed did much – if not always intentionally – to launch the global process on its present path. Other politicians and bureaucrats were resistant to the whole project, but as global trends have accelerated, they have experienced increasing difficulty in standing out against the tide.

The continuous stress on the need for market-led growth adds to environmental problems and obstructs any basic attempt to remedy them. The advocates of the global market deny this and claim that growth can provide extra financial resources to help remedy the bad environmental effects; and they have purloined the concept of 'sustainability' so as to try to include this economic priority. However, without being an extremist, any intelligent observer can see the fallacies in this claim. They can see the extent to which soils are becoming exhausted, forests are being cut down, deserts and floods are spreading, and the atmosphere is being polluted by carbon dioxide and acid rain, as a consequence of the pressures to achieve continuous market growth.

The drive to increase sales and lower costs often adds to these effects. The competitive pressures to increase agricultural productivity, primarily to supply the richer markets whose demands for meat absorb a large part of the earth's surface, or to provide newspapers with enormous reams of paper, much of it used for advertising, exhausts soils and destroys forests which are vital for preventing erosion and protecting the world's atmosphere. The consumer market is flooded with disposable or short-life products which can achieve a rapid turnover, rather than aiming at fewer, more durable products. Energy utilities, especially where they are privatised and price-controlled, have an obvious incentive to expand their sales, rather than to promote energy conservation. The idea that increased profits from market expansion will be used to tackle environmental failures runs up against the problem of raising taxes for this purpose since governments have increasing difficulty over taxing the main sources of market profit.

It is sometimes urged that the system will correct itself as consumers and producers become more environmentally aware and selective, and as a profitable industry develops in pollution control and other remedial measures. To some extent this hope may be realised, but it is expecting a lot from voluntary environmentalism to offset the powerful trends in an opposite direction, and paradoxical to rely on a profitable pollution control industry to remedy what the profit motive has first destroyed.

The United Nations Environment Programme (UNEP) has achieved some useful international agreements but it lacks the capacity of the World Trade Organisation to make binding rules; for example, while endangered species such as dolphins do receive the protection of an international treaty, the WTO has ruled that any national ban on particular methods of fishing which indirectly threaten an endangered species like dolphins, must be disqualified internationally as unfair competition (Leveson Gower, 1977). The bogey of protectionism is cited in all sorts of contexts to support the freedom of market forces, and the upholders of the global economy turn 'sustainability' into a limited form of environmental 'management' for making minor repairs to the damage which continues to be done (Redclift, 1994).

Moreover the global expansion of trade itself intensifies environmental impacts. It requires goods to be transported over ever-increasing distances, adding to energy consumption, and it stimulates a very large volume of business travel to increase the atmospheric pollution caused by long-distance jet flights. The big hydro-electric projects and other developments financed by the World Bank have had some severe environmental effects, although under new leadership the Bank has improved its sensitivity to local conditions in recent years. An environmental cynicism underlies the argument that it is 'rational' for poor countries to make money by importing the nuclear waste and industrial spoil of rich ones, a policy that also adds to the dangers of disastrous spills of lethal chemicals in transit.

A critic may respond that surely economic growth, even if it does have some unfortunate aspects and misleading connotations, still carries enough real benefits to millions of struggling people in the world to deserve a high priority – so that while growth aims may need to be modified environmentally they should not be abandoned. The difficulty here is one of distinguishing and exploring the differences between 'growth' and genuinely sustainable development, a subject which gets more attention in the next chapter.

Global crisis

The most dramatic aspects of the failure of the global economy are the severe currency crises which have erupted recently in a series of countries, notably in Mexico soon after the creation of the NAFTA free trade treaty, followed by the successive crises which have hit Asian countries including Malaysia, Thailand, North Korea and Indonesia and severely tarnished the reputation of the famed Asian 'tigers'. Before the Asian crises had been overcome, in 1998 a severe crisis hit the Russian rouble and a fiscal crisis loomed in Brazil. Fuelling the crises are the booms and slumps in the global economy, inflated speculation in shares and property, and topping all this the large speculative movements in the exchange rate of currencies which acquire a bandwagon effect, especially when some currency is perceived to be weak and vulnerable.

Market defenders argue that a main cause of these problems in developing countries, including the leading Asian 'tigers', is considerable corruption and 'croneyism' between politicians, bureaucrats and big business, and a lack of 'transparency' in financial dealings, the implication being that there is too much government intervention in the market of the wrong kind and that more independent and neutral forms of regulation are necessary. On the other hand, it seems that governments which have controlled market forces somewhat so as to protect and develop their own economy have done better, such as Taiwan which has controlled the export of capital and fostered small domestic industries, or Singapore which has monopolised and earmarked its large superannuation funds for domestic development, as well as those countries which have tried to cool excessive property speculation. Moreover another basic cause of these crises is the flow of sometimes rash bank loans from rich to poor countries. Poor countries get the benefit of access to global sources of credit, but the benefit brings considerable costs and risks.

The responses of the world financial institutions to these successive crises are always much the same. The first imperative is to prop up the ailing financial system, lest the loss of confidence spread round the world to infect other and even the strongest centres. This is done by raising an urgent packet of financial credit for the affected country to avoid the danger of debt repudiation or other radical measures, coupled with stringent conditions about the need for market discipline and cuts in public expenditure in an effort to restore (gradually) confidence in the currency. These IMF rescue packages have become a regular feature on the world scene, modified somewhat according to the perceived danger of political turmoil in the affected country, and usually receive endorsement from political leaders in the developed world, even from Labour ones who are apt to argue that 'there is no alternative to the IMF but anarchy'. Sometimes the rescue operation comes with the pious expectation that, as 'market disciplines' are put in place successively around the world, the crisis will not be repeated – but this hope has lost plausibility.

Strongly unequal relationships are embedded in this whole sequence of events. In the first place, national economies are very unequal in their exposure to currency crises, not just because of their relative competitive 'efficiency' but because of the size of their market and financial reserves. Speculative fever in the money market can quickly overwhelm the currency reserves of a small economy, whereas the USA was able to run a huge trade deficit without incurring the wrath of the money market because of its big internal market and the accumulated value of the dollar as the world's key reserve currency.

Then again, a currency crisis does not as a rule threaten big corporations or the largest banks because they systematically hedge their bets against currency fluctuation; but it does badly hit those farmers and small businesses whose export earnings suddenly plummet. In particular, it hits whole populations dependent on the import of essential food, raw materials or energy. In Russia the grim effects of the failed transition from socialism to capitalism were compounded by soaring prices for food and other essentials. One can easily imagine the extent of the pain felt in Indonesia when its currency fell to one-fifth of its previous value within six months. An IMF 'rescue' further means that a poor country must tolerate the effects of a sharp deflation on unemployment and prices, and the deprivations – and setback to development – caused by cuts in basic public services. Countries suffer pain from a drastic currency collapse which is unfair and disproportionate to any internal failings.

The final irony is that the financial market, which claims to be self-adjusting (in time), actually has to be baled out internationally at the cost of taxpayers. Some strong believers in the market reject this solution, believing quite logically that all market players should accept the results of the game. Of course, given its entanglement with the world economy, a country in financial crisis could well plunge into political turmoil if nothing is done internationally – although the effects of an IMF package can create turmoil too. It could be that leaving a country to its fate might prod it politically, even at the cost of some heavy sacrifices, into reducing its dependence on the world system and fashioning gradually a financial system more suitable for its indigenous development. But, whether or not the IMF is better than a hypothesised 'anarchy', it is clear enough that an international rescue operation, as at present conceived, also inflicts heavy sacrifices on the afflicted country.

One may conclude that developing countries, although they gain some advantages, pay a high price when they get closely entangled in the global economy. Referring to the NAFTA free trade treaty, Martin and Schumann (1996, p. 142) conclude that the Mexican economic collapse was bound to happen when 'a hopeful developing country, itself weak in capital, joins without protection a free trade zone of developed industrial nations'; and without belonging to a free trade zone, a closely dependent relationship can still develop which ties a developing country to financial relationships and indebtedness which it can do little to control – unless it dares to cut the painter.

It is just this possibility which is most feared in the global financial centres, because it undermines their vision of freedom of capital and monetary movements, as well as trade, across the world. This chapter has tried also to show how this belief in 'globalism' is a necessary part of the parallel belief in continuous market expansion, and how the pursuit of this goal produces a high degree of turbulence and inequality in the world, in which those with the weakest financial resources go to the wall. To the financial centres, however, it is imperative to rescue an ailing currency in order to keep the recipient country, willingly or not, within the ambit and requirements of the global economy. The growing incidence of financial crises is finally (at end 1998) compelling world leaders to perceive a need to put some limits to monetary speculation, but there is not yet recognition of the more fundamental inequalities which exist in the global economy.

At the time of writing the American economy still appears to be strong and buoyant and is sometimes quoted as a capitalist success story for achieving a relatively low level of unemployment. But is this reputation justified? Some of it is due to the reserve status of the American dollar in a turbulent exchange market and to the extra affluence made possible by a large trade deficit – which will eventually of course have an adverse impact; and some of it is due to the relatively high level of employment that is only possible through the explosion of low-paid, often part-time service jobs, and the re-emergence of sweated labour in the textile, electronics and other industries. Prosperity for most Americans is real enough, but it is buttressed by America's strong power and present fortunate position in the global arena and vitiated by the large numbers living in poverty and grim environments.

Enthusiasts for the global system still put their faith in the weary dogma that prosperity will 'trickle down', or alternately argue that individuals must adjust to what is seen as an inexorable process. Economic pundits, such as *The Economist*, are fond of telling European nations that they must follow the American example and cut wages, standards and welfare provision in order to create new jobs (*The Economist*, 9 Oct. 1995). It seems a strange doctrine that, after years of economic growth and occupying a continent that is almost self-sufficient in resources, and with no change apparent in the availability of skills and savings to support a decent standard of living, there should be no cure for unemployment save through a rapid, backward march; yet the advice is offered without any apparent awareness of its paradoxical nature.

To conclude, then, the claimed theoretical beneficence of the global economy cannot stand up to an examination of how the system actually works. There is everything to be said for the gradual expansion of free trade, provided it is mutually advantageous to the countries concerned, takes place on reasonably equal terms, does not result in a destructive export abroad of capital and unemployment or a game of 'beggar-my-neighbour', does not cut hard-won social and environmental standards, and does not lead to excessive consumption of scarce or precious natural resources. The actual trading patterns in the world do not comply with these requirements, and the ill-effects are greatly accentuated by the instability of the global money market which dwarfs the requirements of trade. The most fundamental problem posed by the global economy is the lack of political accountability for its operations. There are as yet no international agencies strong or impartial enough to correct the gross instabilities and inequalities of the global economy. Unless or until they appear, it becomes essential to strengthen the political capacities of states to control their own destinies.

6
The Conflict of Beliefs

Previous chapters have examined the baleful influence of contemporary market dogmas from a variety of perspectives – those of economic theory, political thought, concepts of welfare, the role of government and the global economy. It is now desirable to confront more directly the beliefs which sustain the dominant role of capitalist markets and to consider how this situation might be changed.

The dominant ideology of modern societies is often described as 'neo-liberalism'. As Chapter 2 illustrated, this belief system draws on the liberalism of the early nineteenth century, although it exaggerates the arguments of early liberals such as Adam Smith and applies them to a very different world. Neo-liberalism assigns a central role to the market system along three interconnected dimensions – economic, social and political. Economically capitalist markets are seen as a rational system of resource allocation and as the dynamic engine of prosperity in an increasingly globalised world. Socially the market system is claimed to underpin a robust individualism which defines individual rights, responsibilities and opportunities. Politically the theory requires the state to provide an efficient legal framework for market operations, but otherwise to confine itself to those limited functions which must be provided collectively rather than as the outcome of individual market choices.

It is likely that few people swallow the full draught of this neo-liberal philosophy. It is too contrary to many familiar beliefs and values, and too unrealistic in its concepts of what is 'individual' or 'collective', since the market as well as the state is dominated by large organisations. Neo-liberalism can be seen as one extreme and currently fashionable pole in a prolonged cyclical debate between the claims of market freedom and collective responsibility, or between private self-interest and social idealism

(Hirschman, 1982). Yet the actual situation of the world does not permit this fairly comfortable conclusion. The global reach of capitalist markets is now such that corrective political action has become much harder. The expansion of the market system into spheres which were once the realm of other practices and values is matched by a decline in the feasibility and ethos of purposeful collective action. Thus, while the philosophy of neo-liberalism may indeed seem extreme, it represents the intellectual vanguard and rationalisation of these developments. Its fallacies therefore need to be clearly exposed, and an intellectual framework for alternative beliefs developed. The next three sections deal in turn with the economic, social and political claims of neo-liberalism.

But if neo-liberalism is to be rejected, what alternatives exist? Some consideration needs to be given to the concept of a 'third way' which tries to unite endorsement of capitalist markets with a new ethos of social responsibility – a theme which has been specifically advanced by New Labour in Britain and has resonance elsewhere. Finally, this chapter will consider the more radical visions of society offered by environmentalism and other social movements for the light they may shed on possible paths to reform of the existing system.

The perverse economy

Neo-liberals claim that capitalism has now proved its superiority to any possible alternative system as a way of organising production efficiently in response to the preferences of consumers. Their evidence is the ever increasing flow of marketed goods and services, and the growth of an affluent population in many countries. It is also claimed that arguments for the 'efficiency' and 'rationality' of capitalist markets have a firm theoretical foundation. Some defects in the system may be admitted, but the argument goes that they are minor compared with the system's great virtues, and that in any case they are often best treated and hopefully cured through increasing rather than reducing the application of market principles. It is also said that there is anyhow no feasible alternative to capitalism, an argument which fails to consider how far capitalism might be reformed or modified.

These claims fail to recognise the extent of the system's failings, or the fact that these seem to be increasing and not (as market theory would have it) diminishing as a result of liberating market forces. The instability and extreme inequalities which appear endemic to capitalism are growing. One is back with the paradoxes of poverty amid plenty and a serious mismatch between the massive potential of production and the inadequate and unequal distribution of consumption. The system is marred by perennial unemployment and by directions of growth which intensify grave environmental problems. A closer look at these perverse effects, as they occur primarily in developed countries, will question the neo-liberal claims and suggest explanations which are different from the orthodox theoretical defences usually put forward.

Economists lay much stress on the concept of 'micro-efficiency', or the need to minimise costs and maximise productivity. This doctrine is being given vigorous application through the rapid adoption of new technologies, the elimination of redundant labour, the ferocious cutting of costs, and the increasing specialisation of markets made possible by globalisation. The down-side of the process is the drastic impact on the labour market. The new system requires highly skilled technicians and new 'multi-skilled' workers, but the new technology destroys a great many more jobs than it creates. The relative abundance of labour leads to downward pressure on wages, job insecurity, part-time working, and substantial unemployment.

These developments seem paradoxical. One would expect the much greater productivity per worker to lead to general wage increases and cuts in working hours; but while some highly skilled workers have gained, much of the labour force has lost from this process. One might also expect much of the surplus labour to be usefully absorbed into social functions such as health, education and personal social services; the renewal and expansion of infrastructure; and environmental clean-ups and improvements. Most of these functions are relatively labour-intensive and face rising demands; yet this desirable shift of labour is simply not occurring. Governments who are largely responsible for these services are unable to expand or even to maintain them and are pursuing the same micro objective of cutting their labour force.

How is this perverse situation to be explained? An orthodox economist might still argue that the cure for unemployment is to let wages fall until some employer finds it financially worthwhile to offer workers a job. Under modern conditions that could mean wages well below the poverty line for many unskilled workers, while welfare also would have to be drastically cut to maintain any incentive to work. A more sophisticated position is that there is a 'natural level of unemployment' determined by the state of the economy; but this state is usually conceived only in market terms so that the possibility of a switch of labour into collective services gets largely ignored. In practice the more hard-headed gurus of the market have given up the quest to cure unemployment and now simply assume that there has to be a large and growing core of unemployed whose services will simply not be wanted. The capitalist economy can manage without them and the only (but very big) problem is how to stop these idle people from making trouble.

Some economists do recognise the familiar Keynesian problem of 'underconsumption' and recommend a periodic boost to the economy through monetary expansion or public expenditure to keep the system moving. But the problem is that pressure on exchange rates from the money markets now inhibits what most governments will risk doing, while there are no real means available for maintaining effective demand on a global basis. Equally the expansion of the collective sector is inhibited by the difficulties of raising taxation as well as fear of adverse market reactions. The political constraint occurs through the swallowing of market dogmas and the unprofitable party competition over tax reduction. The economic constraint is produced by an economy which will dance only to the tune of profit and its continuous expansion; any jobs which accord with this criterion, however wasteful or silly they may seem, are grist to the system; but collective services only keep the market moving where they can be privatised.

At the same time the pattern of consumption is being changed and skewed by the increased share of profit (including interest and rent) and the reduced share of wages in the national income of almost all countries. Some of this income from capital is more widely diffused than used to be the case, but it still primarily boosts the spending power of a rich minority (and especially of a very tiny but very rich minority). This development leads to a growth of jobs, many part-time, in services such as restaurants and tourism, and of personal services (domestic help, security guards, etc.) for the rich; but it weakens the volume of mass consumption and leaves many people in poverty. Curiously, the orthodox theory has nothing to say on this subject. As Chapter 3 pointed out, it seriously proposes that a theory of economic 'welfare' can be put forward without any regard to its distribution between individuals. It is accepted of course that an 'efficient' allocation of resources is always dependent upon the actual distribution of assets between individuals; but it is less often added that the theory of 'efficient allocation' is quite consistent with a society containing only millionaires and beggars. Most people would hardly consider such a society at all consistent with a tenable theory of economic welfare or progress. Yet it is clear that the actual distribution of wealth depends upon the very unequal rewards coming through the market and upon the cumulative workings or chances of the laws of inheritance; and that the global market, through increasing the share of profit in total income and reducing the possibility of corrective government measures, is adding steadily to the existing imbalance.

The instability of the whole system is quite easily explained. Even under the assumptions of the theory, investment decisions made exclusively by the owners of capital will always tend to be erratic, because they are influenced by the variable possibilities of new technologies and by calculations about future profitability which are bound to be speculative, and which in practice are strongly influenced by market psychology. This situation has always been a main cause of the cycle of booms and slumps, but it is now augmented by the size and volatility of the international money markets and speculation over exchange rates. The shifting interdependencies of the global economy compel continuous and difficult local adjustments as the flows of money and investment change directions, which also bring with them many problems of both 'frictional' and 'structural' unemployment. Orthodox economic theory offers no cure for this situation, although revisionist theories influenced by Keynes would at least want to use public measures to modify the trade cycle.

Orthodox economic theory offers a very inadequate account of how modern capitalist markets actually work. Orthodox theory does not assume that the preferences of workers, for example, over the balance between work and leisure, should be subordinated to production requirements – yet such is the current dogma. The need for continuous economic growth, so basic to today's economic 'globalisation', has no basis in the orthodox theory, which is only concerned with equilibrium between demand and supply. In fact J. S. Mill, a pioneer of this theory, was emphatic that it was fully consistent with a stable society – which he devoutly wished to see realised on population and environmental grounds that are very relevant today. The current market doctrine stresses the need to boost consumption by intense marketing, etc., whereas the orthodox theory assumes that consumption represents the unsolicited preferences of individuals, subject only to a need for information.

If the present market system accords badly with its theoretical model, how should it be described? A better description might be to see the system as a form of dynamic capitalism geared to continuous 'creative destruction' in the pursuit of profit and an expanded market. Such a theory does explain the system's dedication to market growth, efficiency of production and the boosting of consumption. This alternative theory admits that profit and capital accumulation are the driving forces behind the system, and not – as in the orthodox allocation model – just one 'factor of production' in a system of a supposed mechanical equilibrium under the pressures of 'perfect competition' and 'full information'. It also makes it easier to explain the uneven distribution of economic power, the causes of inequality and instability, the curious disjunction between the economic treatment of work and consumption, and the hostility to collective services, unless they can produce private profit.

This theory can be expressed in either a Schumpeterian or a Marxist version. In the former, the vital role is that of the capitalist entrepreneur (now often of course the managers of a big company or financial institution) over organising the use of resources effectively so as to anticipate consumer demands. The entrepreneur takes big risks and can get big rewards. His contribution (well earned) to human welfare is to speed and improve the flow of new products to an expanding market, and the result is claimed to be big increases in economic productivity. The familiar Marxist version stresses the exploitation of labour by capital and the inevitable 'contradictions' of the system which block the growth of human welfare and lead to continuous malfunctioning and crises which can only be saved by support from the state. It would be adding too far to the scope of this book to arbitrate between these two very contrasting accounts of the development of capitalism. Both seem to contain some elements of truth. One can accept the high productivity and rapid innovations associated with modern capitalism, while recognising also its strong tendencies to inequality and instability and the 'contradictions' between work and consumption, etc. which have already been sufficiently discussed.

There is, however, an important difference between the two versions. The Marxist version is consistent with all the perverse effects of the system, although it does not follow that one need accept all its explanations – such as the beliefs in economic determinism and in the system's inevitable downfall by revolution. Marx was a shrewd critic of the capitalism of his time, but it is a pity that these insights were linked with a loose revolutionary doctrine and used later to justify a tyrannical 'communist' system. On the other hand, the Schumpeterian version depends critically upon the vital and valuable role played by capitalist entrepreneurs in economic progress. Was this role really ever quite so central and necessary as the theory asserts, and, more important, does it still remain so? This theory also fails to recognise the important role which the state has taken on (and is now struggling with) for meeting a rising demand for services which cannot be equitably provided within the capitalist framework of profit. Schumpeter himself believed that, while the capitalist system was enormously productive, it would be destroyed by social resentment against the sources of its success; but might it not more likely get undermined by its failures when it seeks to absorb the whole economy?

The conclusion must be that the capitalist market system is justified by its neo-liberal enthusiasts on the basis of false beliefs about how it works. Once a clearer vision is adopted, one can better understand how the perverse aspects of the modern economy arise. They are not just the regrettable side-effects of a fundamentally sound and beneficial system, but are the inevitable results of allowing the profit motive to dominate the workings of the whole economy.

A flawed philosophy

Perhaps the most distinctive element in neo-liberalism is its social philosophy. Its justification of capitalist markets is based upon a long-lived economic theory which, as the last section argued, does not really describe the modern capitalist system. But where economic theory falters, social theory takes over and in neo-liberalism enthrones the market system as the central element in the definition of an individual's rights, responsibilities and opportunities. The philosophy is remorselessly individualistic. The market is favoured as an arena where bargains can be struck between individuals who need only consider their own interest. Individual rights refer to the freedom to acquire and use property and assets subject to not interfering with the like rights of other individuals. Individual responsibilities refer to the obligation to provide for oneself, and perhaps one's family, within the context of one's resources and opportunities. Individual liberty is defined negatively by the absences or rather the minimisation of direct coercion, which cannot in practice be measured, and positively by the freedom to use one's resources for one's own purposes and projects. More than this the contractual model influences a wide range of relationships including social and emotional ones. This point is sometimes expressed by saying that the neo-liberal model makes society more like a hotel in which independent lives coincide than the shared lives of a community.

A thoroughgoing neo-liberalism is also sympathetic to what is seen as the neutral values of a post-modern society. It takes the view that all values are subjective, a matter of personal belief and interpretation, and that public authorities should (perhaps with some extreme exceptions) take a neutral stance on social and moral issues. The market is regarded favourably as a neutral mechanism and facilitator through which individuals can pursue their chosen goals independently. These ideas are not acceptable to conservative opinion which mixes support for the market with the preservation of social and moral traditions.

The basic difficulty with this philosophy is that the market is an improbable moral terrain for the enunciation of universal rights and responsibilities because its assets and rewards are so very unevenly distributed. Ownership of capital is sometimes acquired through hard work or valued skills, but a great deal of capital is inherited or grows through market speculation and inflation of assets; for example, the inheritance or fortunate acquisition of a house is often more profitable than many years of hard work. Differences in earned income, which exceed a maximum ratio of over 100 to 1, imply very large claims about the social utility of the service earned and suggest the relevance of 'political' differences of effective bargaining power, as well as class beliefs about the appropriate payment for particular occupations. In turn these sharp differences in wealth and income greatly affect the educational, cultural and occupational opportunities of individuals and their families.

It may be reasonable to defend a right to inheritance for its contribution to social stability and the strengthening of family ties, but this principle hardly justifies an unlimited right to personal acquisition, nor would it be consistent with a society where the ownership of most capital was the outcome of passive processes of inheritance. Like inheritance, other market relationships depend crucially upon the laws of property, contract and taxation. Hence an unqualified right to property makes little sense morally and socially – or economically either, since how property is acquired and distributed plainly affects incentives to work.

Similar considerations enter into the definition of individual responsibilities. Here the assertion that the right to welfare implies a correlation to work is in principle reasonable, the practical problem being the shortage of available or suitable jobs. It is curious, however, to stress the responsibilities of the poor and unfortunate without saying anything about those of the rich and fortunate. The latter are claimed to get their wealth through the supposedly benign processes of the market, while the former depend for their pittance on the state; but this distinction makes little sense unless one has first assumed that all market outcomes are reasonably equitable.

Early capitalism was associated with religious and moral beliefs in the importance of thrift, hard work and probity. The emphasis upon personal effort and initiative, rewarded by God no doubt but depending strictly upon the individual ('God helps those who help themselves'), marked a sharp break with the more fatalistic and static beliefs of earlier times, and stimulated the efforts of early entrepreneurs to change the world as described in the writings of Weber and Tawney. Japan's strong work ethic is also supported by a pragmatic mixture of the religions of Shintoism and Confucianism, but in an age of much more efficient forms of production, a strong work ethic no longer seems so essential. As belief in the social necessity of hard work and thrift has diminished, a kind of hedonism has replaced it, and the appeal of capitalism has shifted from being a supplier of essential wants to one of offering (for those who can get them) the pleasures of abundant and never-ending consumption, in which (so the economic doctrine goes) human 'wants' are literally unlimited and endless.

The re-emergence of the old economic belief that the motive of personal material gain is the ruling principle of human behaviour and should be left to the play of 'liberated' market forces, will inevitably have an impact on individual motivations and behaviour. An economic rationalist should surely see how an unemployed youth with poor job prospects and few resources, living in a society which continually exalts the values of consumption and wealth, might quite 'rationally' turn to the pursuit of self-interest through crime (see Schotter, 1990, pp. 65–80). The crime might start with cheating the welfare office, but could go on to burglary and other more serious offences. A cost–benefit analysis might suggest that, if personal net profit is the standard, the possible rewards for burglary might exceed those from any legitimate activity by a wide enough margin to justify its considerable risks. Of course the moralist will huff and puff at this conclusion, but a sophisticated youth might respond that his reasoning is not unlike that of a rich executive going in for tax evasion or even illegality with far less need to do so in terms of his already well-nourished pursuit of 'rational self-interest'.

Then there is the great stress laid upon money itself, and its accumulation, in modern societies. Weber pointed out that the use of money for rational calculation was an essential part of 'modernity' (which he did not much like), and, since Weber wrote, the role of money has grown enormously with the expansion of trade and speculation. One effect seems to be that money, which is really a means to other ends, gets often turned into an end in itself. The more the market takes over all forms of production and exchange and supersedes other arrangements, the more important money becomes.

Public choice writers apply their assumption of 'rational self-interest' to suggest perverse political or bureaucratic behaviour;

but the same analysis can be just as well applied to the market system. There are many market situations where asymmetry of information (between 'insiders' and 'outsiders'), or a degree of monopoly, or the skilful drafting of a contract, gives plenty of scope for the opportunistic pursuit of personal gain. As the market expands to cover an increasing volume of transactions between strangers, and as trust in the probity of personal understandings declines, so more and more contingencies have to be put into formal contracts. The result can be seen in the rapid growth of litigation, especially in the USA, which represents what economists describe as a very substantial 'transaction cost'.

Some economists are now much worried by the effects of this decline of trust and probity upon the efficiency of the market itself, often described as a loss of 'social capital'. Given the great reluctance of market believers to consider political solutions, their preferred remedy is to seek some antidote to the erosion of trust within the framework of 'civil society'. For example, Fukuyama (1995) stresses the economic advantages of informal voluntary networks of individuals bound together by mutual trust and co-operation, and gives interesting examples of how such activities have raised the prosperity of immigrant groups in many countries and within some whole societies such as Japan. There is no reason to doubt his examples, but some people might wonder how far this networking among particular (usually ethnically cohesive) groups can raise the prosperity of the whole society. In Japan, for example, it might be queried whether these informal deals among business leaders and politicians have benefited the mass of the people.

Another problem for Fukuyama is the extent to which this networking can work effectively under the new conditions of the global economy. He even has some doubts about whether 'economic efficiency' should be treated as a supreme value in situations where it undermines well-established relationships of trust, as is now happening in Japan. But his faith in global capitalism is such that he ends by hoping that these informal networks can somehow adjust to the new exigencies of the global economy.

A more promising concept is that of a 'stakeholders society', which again uses economic jargon to express the desirability of giving other important affected interests (such as workers and consumers) some say in the decisions made by the owners of capital over the policies of large corporations. The examples of such joint decision-making are taken from 'Rhenish capitalism' (primarily Germany) and 'East Asian capitalism' (primarily Japan). The argument goes that both these types of capitalism, though in different ways, produce conditions of continuity, security and trust in the conduct of economic life, which are not usually present in the more free-wheeling and opportunistic conditions of 'Anglo-American capitalism', where the capitalists effectively make all the key market decisions without the participation or input of other affected groups. However, this participation of other interests in the functioning of capitalism (further discussed in the next chapter) runs quite contrary to neo-liberal thought.

These examples offer valuable suggestions about the reforms of capitalism (see next chapter). However their application, certainly in Germany, has been crucially dependent upon the state for creating the necessary co-operative framework. The development of a 'stakeholder society' requires political action to change the market's functioning.

Neo-liberalism is a coherent and logical but basically irrational social philosophy, because of its failure to realise that markets will only work well as one element within a broader social and political framework. Its cold contractual view of human relations is ethically unappealing. Its espousement of a neutral view of social values has a fashionable post-modernist ring, but is vitiated by treating the market as a neutral mechanism for expressing diverse values.

Assault on democracy?

Liberalism has a long-standing association with democracy. It is true, as Chapter 2 showed, that market capitalism and liberal democracy grew up together, and in many ways are products of the same rationalist, individualist movement. It is true also that, although conflicts between these two wings of the same movement (if it is looked at that way) have always existed, in some ways each movement can help the other.

Thus the dispersal of economic power among various individual actors – as long as it is truly dispersed – can help to prevent the over-concentration of authority in a too powerful state which the demand of a dissatisfied democratic majority might otherwise bring about. On the other side, the doctrine of economic individuation – if its claims of a career open to talents are to be taken seriously – seems to require the complementary doctrine of formal political equality. A formal equality in the political sphere provides a vital legitimising function for the laws which have to be passed, and the coercion which has sometimes to be exercised, if the capitalist market is to work. It also offers an outlet for channelling complaints against the harsher side-effects of capitalism, so long as the complaints do not basically threaten the capitalist system. The ability to point to a formal political equality is also a useful offset to the inevitable inegalitarianism of market outcomes.

However this helpful alliance can last only so long as the market does not grow too dominant or democracy become too awkward or rebellious. In the post-Second World War period some thinkers such as Hayek saw the necessary springs of market capitalism being undermined by the overgrowth of state powers under the mistaken influence of a too egalitarian democracy. If this possibility ever existed, which must be doubted, it has been clearly overwhelmed by the opposite tendency of a too powerful market system dominating through its requirements and implications, the workings of democracy. The much vaunted victory of 'liberal' capitalism and democracy over communism, and indeed (allegedly) over all 'ideologies', can now be quickly seen as a victory very much for the senior partner, with the status of democracy all around the world looking much less robust and secure, so that not just radicals, but a very successful market speculator such as George Soros, now see the ascendancy of the market to be as destructive of democracy as was communism.

Neo-liberalism also endorses the value of democracy but couples this endorsement in theory with a minimal view of desirable government functions. In practice very substantial market regulation is necessary, both to maintain the efficiency of the market itself and to achieve tolerable standards of consumer protection, environmental impact, occupational health and safety, probity in commercial dealings, monopoly pricing, the uses of confidential information, and much else. Neo-liberals want to keep all this regulation to a minimum, which runs contrary to the demands for intervention coming from workers, consumers, environmentalists and many other groups.

At the same time, however, neo-liberals need the state to be active in promoting the goals of economic growth and productive efficiency through its budgetary and financial decisions and through a variety of 'micro-economic' measures, such as competition policy, trade union legislation, education reform, tax assistance, etc. It is expected to guarantee the integrity of the currency and the banking system, provide export credit and guarantee foreign loans, and bale out the financial system as and when a crisis occurs. In other words, government is vital for the effective functioning of capitalism and plays a large and crucial part over facilitating its dominant drives; and if or when that system causes too much poverty and insecurity, or produces an economic crisis, government has to cope with the consequent distress, and if necessary prevent civil disturbance, riot or rebellion.

It is therefore necessary for capitalism to have government as a willing and co-operative partner, not the bland minimal regulator sometimes pictured. Too active a democracy appears as a threat to this relationship, because of the range of protests which it may encourage and the growth of government functions or intervention which may result. Hence neo-liberalism inclines to a narrow conception of democracy such that democracy has done its job with a periodic election between at least two (and often no more than two) political teams, and that its main if not sole function is an ability to change the winning team, or in stronger terms to 'throw the rascals out' when the public is sufficiently displaced. This very restricted conception of democracy is largely indifferent (if not secretly hostile) to political participation, it views 'public consultation' as a tool of legitimation rather than decision-making, and it seems unconcerned about low turnouts at general elections, the one great formal democratic act. Thinkers in this vein dislike the Australian rule of compulsory voting, because it is said to violate individual freedom and responsibility, although this practice does at least require all citizens to treat democracy seriously and to participate at least in this basic act. At the same time, beguiling market images permeate elections and present political choice as being between two carefully packaged and sanitised products.

These conceptions of limited democracy contradict the value of a more active democratic process. Such a process throws up a variety of claims and arguments about the good of society. Some of these claims are narrowly selfish or extreme but a balanced democratic process will try to moderate this extremism. Examples of legitimate democratic inputs are the various causes which relate to the needs of the poor, environmental problems, gender and ethnic discrimination, oppressive labour conditions and many others, which involve the efforts of many public-spirited and idealistic individuals. It is good for society that they do so.

Yet these claims are treated as illegitimate by the 'public choice' economists who support neo-liberalism and are simply written off as forms of 'rent-seeking' by sectional interests at the public expense. It is even doubted by some economists such as James Buchanan whether any such thing as the good of society or 'public interest' exists at all, although Buchanan himself soon contradicts this by arguing that there is a general interest in keeping government limited. This hostility to democratic pluralism is plainly based on the fact that many of these claims, if implemented, will affect the operations of the market system. But why should this discovery be so alarming? It merely shows how comprehensively the modern market system dominates over other social interests and values, and how the democratic process offers a reasonable opportunity for the articulating of values and interests which the market system itself neglects or overrides.

Compared with democratic politics, the market system is based upon a very limited and narrow range of social values. The dominating principles are economic efficiency and consumer choice. They are also interpreted by their advocates in a very narrow way, which does not consider their social side-effects or how both 'efficiency' and 'choice' are much influenced by institutional and sociological factors.

The resulting 'market failures', as they are called by economic theorists, were clearly recognised by some earlier economists, but today's practitioners tend to minimise or forget them. The result is a neglect of social considerations which get squeezed out by the ruthless application of this narrow economic doctrine; yet democracy, if it is to be at all active or meaningful, is necessarily concerned with a pluralism of social values, not just with the maintenance of a single-value system – one that has something to contribute to society no doubt, provided its particular logic does not overrule all other values and interests which block its path.

This does not imply that a benign and comfortable view can be taken of the workings of the democratic process. Undoubtedly the process contains much scope for opportunistic and self-regarding behaviour, and some amount of such behaviour can be expected under almost any political system. The pity is that in recent decades incorrupt and reasonably public-spirited governments, not just bad ones, have been attacked and undermined for their alleged inferiority to the rule of the market. But what is the answer to the danger of democratic degeneration? Certainly not to enthrone the market still further, and to manipulate or restrict the democratic process so as to prevent it from obstructing the market's triumphant path. That course can only lead to an authoritarian system and the danger of the extreme abuses and savage applications of political power, such as occurred in Germany and Italy when Fascism ousted democracy. Just as the failures of the market system were a main reason then for the rise of Fascism, so the same causal chain can be seen at work in many countries today. The only way to avert this result is to strengthen not weaken democracy, and to rely upon a more active and balanced democratic process to prevent the slide into social conflict and intolerance which the failings of an uncontested capitalist system so easily produces.

A mean society

Neo-liberalism makes for a politically mean society. This statement does not apply to the many voluntary organisations, their workers and supporters, who struggle unselfishly to combat poverty all round the world (including the increasing number of poor in rich countries) and to deal with the numerous crises of hunger and misery due to war, droughts, floods and other disasters. It does apply very much to official attitudes. Despite increasing deprivation in some poor countries, and the 'natural' (often man-made) disasters that afflict them, overseas aid has been cut in many Western countries to further below the modest target set earlier of 1 per cent of national income. Third world debt is endlessly 'rescheduled', but with no willingness to write the sheet clean for the hardest-hit nations. Right-wing politicians rub salt into the wound by praising the renaissance of private charity in place of government aid, while turning a deaf ear to the desperate pleas of the charities themselves for more government support for their efforts.

After the Second World War, the Marshall Plan provided massive and generous aid for the reconstruction of Europe. After the dramatic collapse of Russia and the Eastern bloc, and the ensuing turmoil and poverty, little aid was forthcoming from the West except in the form of commercial loans. Instead Western leaders (especially Mrs Thatcher and her advisers) seemed concerned only with preaching unvarnished market theory to countries in no way equipped to practise it efficiently or honestly, and to seize on the commercial opportunity for penetrating a large new market. While it may be true that the generosity of the Marshall Plan owed a lot to America's fear of communism, is there not today equal reason to fear fresh military conflicts and turbulence if ex-communist countries (some of whom possess nuclear weapons) are allowed to drift into chaos and misery?

Again the end of the Cold War offered scope for a large 'peace dividend' from lower government expenditure on armaments, and a golden opportunity to tackle afresh the running sore of the American urban ghettos and racial poverty. It seems the idea was never seriously entertained, and instead welfare support and Federal aid to impoverished cities was actually cut further.

Capitalism itself offers no compelling and certainly no morally attractive vision of the future. While there may be endless talk about the benefits of conventional economic growth, the goal held forth to American society has shifted from Roosevelt's view that economic progress should be judged by the advance of the poor to Reagan's hope that some Americans at least will always be able to become millionaires (nothing about the rest!). These opinions are poles apart in their vision for society and (despite what 'welfare economists' say) in the very definition of economic welfare and show the growth of a narrow ideology of individual self-interest.

A new third way?

Is it possible to overturn the social philosophy of neo-liberalism while keeping its commitment to global capitalism? Can social democracy be modernised so as to combine economic orthodoxy and fiscal rectitude with new social ideals which respond to the changed conditions of the economy and politics? These are the issues raised in the 1990s by the emergence of a new form of centre-left politics marked first by the election of President Clinton in 1992 and especially by the victory of New Labour in Britain in 1997. In the same period new Social Democratic governments emerged in most of the principal European countries, culminating in the 1998 victory of Gerhard Schroder and the SPD in Germany.

New Labour in Britain rejects the ideologies of both neo-liberalism and socialism. In a series of Fabian pamphlets (Blair, 1994; Brown, 1994) and elsewhere, its leaders criticised the selfish individualism and moral bankruptcy of the former doctrine which they associated with the previous Conservative regime. Their rejection of traditional Labour beliefs was more guarded because of the need to claim a continuity of ideals within the party; but it was actually more definite since the traditional Labour goals of economic planning, market intervention and public ownership were specifically discarded. Tony Blair, the British Prime Minister, vowed to avoid the political interventions in the economy which had marked previous Labour (and some Conservative) regimes; and for the first time the Bank of England was given independent authority to set interest rates.

The 'third way' does not represent a middle way between contending ideologies. Its strong commitment to capitalist markets and its belief in the importance of entrepreneurship, productivity and growth clearly rule out this position. Instead it claims a new social philosophy. 'Unlike the neo-liberal and the (older) social democrat, third way politics invokes quite a strong sense of community, of common life, of common obligation' (Plant, 1998, p. 34). Giddens (1998, p. 65) suggests that 'having abandoned collectivism, third way politics looks for a new relationship between the individual and the community', one which entails a redefinition and strengthening of mutual rights and responsibilities. The initial popularity of 'third way' politics seems to be based upon its appeal to rebuilding the life of the community as a counter to the self-interest of the market and to the considerable evidence of social disruption and conflict. But how are these concepts to be applied other than as forms of moral exhortation?

The new social democracy claims to retain the central value of equality, but to interpret it in a more relevant way, less as a question of economic redistribution and static welfare rights, more as one of enhanced individual opportunities and associated obligations. These new opportunities have to be found primarily within a dynamic market context and require a sustained pursuit of fuller employment – a goal which has always figured strongly in the social democratic litany and remains its greatest political asset. 'Third way' advocates agree with the neo-liberals about the moral hazards of welfare dependency, but they differ in insisting that economic opportunities cannot be left to the market but must be actively promoted by government. The right to welfare should be linked realistically to a duty to find enough suitable jobs.

The most distinctive policy stance of both the Clinton administration and New Labour has concerned the linkages between employment, education and welfare. One guru of a new approach was Robert Reich, Clinton's first Secretary of Labor, who argued that since global competition was moving towards a principle of equal wages for equal skills, raising the skills of the population through better education and training was the passport to higher employment and wages (Reich, 1991). This emphasis on the need to expand and improve the educational system is supported by many economists and is enthusiastically advocated by New Labour. It could strengthen the competitive position of an individual nation over attracting investment and jobs, the problem being that it can also function as a zero-sum game, which would not make much difference to the sources of global instability and inequality or prevent the export of unemployment between nations.

The second policy aim is to find new means of moving or pushing welfare recipients into jobs. President Clinton's original proposal to 'end welfare as we know it' was based on this premise. His plan was that after two years on welfare all unemployed under the age of 25 must either find themselves a job or be found one in subsidised community services. The good intentions in this proposal were cruelly destroyed by the Republican majority in Congress, who eagerly seized upon the idea of ending welfare but refused to devote adequate funds even for this limited scheme. In the end Clinton found himself acquiescing in the termination of the Federal commitment to welfare, which was passed back to the states, coupled with a very reduced provision of subsidised jobs for the young unemployed (and none for older redundant workers), and with the cost being met partly by withdrawing welfare rights from new immigrants (Crine, 1994). This was another victory for neo-liberalism and a destructive setback for new politics.

New Labour followed the precedent set by the Keating Labor government in Australia of subsidising employers or voluntary organisations to provide jobs for the young unemployed, and financed the scheme by a tax on the windfall profits made by privatised utilities. The problem is that, as happened in Australia, new jobs in the market easily disappear if and when the subsidies are withdrawn, and given New Labour's promise not to increase income tax, there is no assured source of continuing finance for the scheme. As the earlier economic analysis suggested, most of the jobs which need doing are concentrated in the hard-pressed collective sector and require new sources of finance which conflict with New Labour's market orthodoxy.

An important theme of the 'third way' is social inclusion, the idea that all individuals should contribute to the life of the community and share in its benefits. 'The new politics define equality as inclusion and inequality as exclusion' (Giddens, 1998, p. 102). The existence of an impoverished and alienated underclass represents a grim reproach to this ideal. To promote and nourish an ethic of work and participation among this class, it is essential to overcome the 'poverty trap' which often makes work little more remunerative than living on welfare. More fundamentally, if deprived individuals are to share in the common life and the enjoyment of liberty, they need at least enough resources to meet their basic or 'generic' needs (Plant, 1998, p. 30).

New Labour recognises this requirement in principle. It has endorsed the European Social Charter and established a minimum wage. It has strengthened the rights of trade unions and the legal protection against unfair dismissal. It has initiated a modest but comprehensive attempt to improve conditions in the most degraded housing estates. It would like as soon as possible to eliminate income tax on low incomes. Unlike neo-liberalism, New Labour has a positive commitment to maintaining and improving the public services and it has promised moderate increases in health and education expenditure. The problem with all these plans and intentions is that they are hard to square with the party's promises not to raise income tax, to keep a close control upon public expenditure and to leave interest rates to an independent central bank.

The other side of this new politics is its strong communitarianism. The doctrine of 'no rights without responsibilities' is applied much more widely than just to welfare recipients. There are measures to prevent truancy and increase discipline in schools; there is an American-style stress on being 'tough on crime' including minor offenders; and a desire to enlist community support over policing and shaming bad behaviour. There is also a policy of penalising bad teachers and doctors, and rewarding good ones. But this communitarian critique has so far stopped short of criticising the rich for withdrawing from society into privileged enclaves and privatised services. Nor, unlike the earlier doctrine of political liberalism, have the rich yet been told that they owe a civic duty to the disadvantaged.

The new social doctrine remains tied to market ideology. Its stress on social co-operation might suggest the importance of other motivations besides individual self-interest, such as professional standards, public service and team work; but in fact reliance continues to be placed upon financial incentives and disciplines. Again the concept of community values suggests the desirability of insulating some spheres of action, such as mutual organisations, the administration of justice and the treatment of hazardous wastes, from invasion by the profit motive, but there seems little resistance as yet to the march of privatisation. There is also a need to introduce community values into spheres dominated by market profit, such as urban development.

A broader theme is the importance of developing an effective dialogue over issues of value. Cultivating the willingness to make pragmatic adjustments over a wide range of issues is perceived as the only way to avoid destructive social conflicts or a relapse into forms of fundamentalism. The interaction of cultures produced by the global spread of information, tastes and customs, together with the erosion of older social traditions, makes an open public dialogue both possible and necessary. The idea is that individuals who disagree on specific issues may prove to share common ground on fundamental human values, and be able to reach new compromises or to remake their traditions in a novel form.

The case for 'dialogic democracy' as a means of reducing pervasive social and economic conflicts has been persuasively argued in America. The idea is not a unique property of the 'third way' – it rests on the old-fashioned belief in rational argument – but does match its experimental, modernist temper. However, the belief that such dialogue can resolve basic political conflicts between nations, classes or the sexes (Giddens, 1994) is rather naive. A dominant ideology such as exists is likely to be overcome only by the emergence of an alternative, equally potent set of beliefs, not just by open debate, although that could help. New-style political parties seem in practice quite as keen to restrict debate in the interest of the leadership as their more traditional rivals. The stress which New Labour puts upon participatory democracy is accompanied by strong attempts to keep off the agenda issues which conflict with market orthodoxy or its leaders' interpretations of community.

The new centre-left politics can be perceived as a product of the problem of political opposition, especially as this arises within a basically two-party system such as Britain's or America's. Just as after 1945 the British Conservatives accepted the dominant welfare and employment goals pursued by Labour, so New Labour has finally 'reformed' itself by adopting the dominant market ideology of the Thatcherite Conservatives, and repackaging it with a more human face as its own product. A genuinely dominant ideology will always present itself as inevitable and be absorbed in a rather different form into an opposition programme. Of course New Labour does not recognise itself as ideological, but its claimed pragmatism seems to lie much more in its social experiments than in its economic beliefs.

It would be too cynical to treat 'third way' politics as simply a piece of political opportunism or realism. Its leaders certainly feel a moral mission to forward the goals of social inclusion and solidarity and to advance the opportunities of the deprived and disadvantaged. Their general approach, as Tony Blair (1988) has said, seems very like that of the old 'positive' liberals discussed in Chapter 2, whose alliance with social democracy led on to the welfare state. The picture is still more complete when one reflects that the old liberal passion for free trade is repeated in the new liberal passion for the global economy, which is shared between both main parties in Britain and America. But a major difference is that the 'positive' liberals occupied an upswing in the move towards collectivism and state welfare, whereas New Labour seems to be located in a downswing. Increasing conflict between the economic orthodoxy and the social goals of left-centre politics seems inevitable, and it will be difficult to prevent the hard element in its ideology – the strong commitment to global capitalism – from dominating over the soft element – the search for new means of social integration.

One should also remember that this fashionable 'third way' politics is but a pale shadow of the compromise between capitalism and socialism, which was hammered out in Europe this century and which produced the actual product of the mixed economy and the welfare state. Although it has some resonance on the continent, the New Labour notion of a 'third way' is generally weaker than the belief of its continental counterparts, who are less disposed to reject the previous, more potent middle doctrine. A French leader such as Lionel Jospin has a much greater willingness to protect cultural and social values against their absorption by market capitalism. The German concept of the 'social market' may seem close to New Labour's approach, but it includes a stronger welfare system and workers' rights to participation which are non-existent in Britain. In Germany too the 1998 formation of a coalition government between the Social Democrats and the Green Party represents a political victory for environmental thinking which, while formally an element in the British 'third way', has yet to make much headway. Possible answers to the challenge of neo-liberalism are more evident on the continent of Europe than in English-speaking countries.

Alternative social visions

Who today offers positive visions for the future of the world? The capitalist market vision is one of ever bigger and brighter shopping malls, still more varied consumer goods, computer techniques to simplify domestic life and to give easy access to an enormous range of immediate information, more exotic forms of tourism (if there are any exotic places left to visit), and so on. It is all very beguiling, but is it a satisfactory or inspiring vision? It would be different if the emphasis of this market vision was upon feeding the hungry, providing decent housing and other basic equipment for the many people who are without these things, raising standards of health and education everywhere, and creating a cleaner and safer environment. No doubt the market system could contribute to these goals, if it were steered or enlisted to do so, but they are hardly central to the modern market vision – indeed in many ways they are an embarrassment since they suggest that its priorities are badly wrong. Where then are the compelling visions of the future? They lie as always with those who have strong and positive hopes for a better future, for which they will work hard and make sacrifices. Who wants to make sacrifices for the market vision? The very idea is an anachronism even for those who must supposedly wait indefinitely for prosperity to 'trickle down' to them – for market satisfactions cannot be indefinitely postponed. The whole philosophy is relentlessly selfish. By contrast, there are many people who will make great sacrifices for ethnic, nationalist or religious claims or for well-known causes of the modern world, such as environmentalism and feminism.

It is the bearers of these various causes who can transcend the moral void of the market vision. Environmentalism, it is true, can seem largely negative – a warning about the terrible things that may happen from a failure to act; or it can be rather narrow and extremist, when expressed as a concern only for 'ecology' regardless of human interests, or when canalised into single panaceas such as saving only 'noble animals' or curbing population drastically. Yet environmentalists are for the most part idealistic and sincere, not tarred with the brush of material self-interest, concerned with very real and pressing dangers and problems, and offering a vision of a society that would be less greedy or grasping and more in harmony with the natural world than the present one. Defenders of the existing order portray environmentalists as a 'special interest', for that is their way of dealing with any cause that has moral appeal.

Some version of socialism or social democracy still has moral appeal despite the fact that environmentalism has displaced socialism as the 'religion of youth'. This is because the older socialism has to be rewritten so as to achieve gender equality, to unite older humanitarian with newer environmental values, and to discard dogmatic panaceas – all of which is difficult and takes time. A reborn social democracy might be able to combine the appeal of social justice with contemporary causes and environmentalism so as to stir again the hearts of women and men.

The strongest of these contemporary causes, environmentalism, necessarily has a global reach. Inevitably the amount of interest and support for global reforms is limited because the problems are too complex and remote for most people, and popular interest is concentrated upon the social and environmental issues that are seen as pressing within a national and local context. Still there is growing involvement by many voluntary bodies in global issues, which was strikingly demonstrated at the 1992 Rio Earth conference where a wide range of non-governmental organisations (NGOs) stepped beyond the immediate issue of greenhouse gases to produce a comprehensive manifesto on the urgent need for global reforms. There is now also massive information and publicity on the severity of global environmental problems, whose impacts are dramatically demonstrated by the activities of Greenpeace.

Effective global environmental action requires proper application of the concept of sustainability. Despite attempts to change its meaning so as to incorporate the existing concept of economic growth, environmental sustainability requires at least two conditions: (a) that the rates of use of renewable resources do not exceed their rates of regeneration, and (b) that the uses of non-renewable resources do not exceed their replacement by acceptable substitutes (Daly, 1991). As the last chapter indicated, these conditions are being breached so seriously that reliance on new technology to fill the gap is clearly unworkable and in some cases – such as the extinction of wildlife and forests – irrelevant. Writing twenty years after their first comprehensive review of environmental dangers, the same authors pointed out that all the indices of pressures on resources had continued their steep upward curve, and that 'the human race is (still) not using the earth's sources and sinks sustainably . . . many sources are eroding and many sinks filling . . . soils, forests, surface waters, groundwaters, wetlands and the diversity of nature are being downgraded' (Meadows, Meadows and Randers, 1972, and 1992, p. 99).

The causes of this situation are not mysterious. They comprise the joint effects of high levels of consumption, rapid population growth and misuse of technology (ibid, 1992, p. 100). The necessary remedies involve changing the consumption habits of affluent Western populations, checking the population explosion in poor countries by raising basic standards of living, and using technology so as to conserve resources and assist grass-root forms of development.

The present capitalist system is strongly inimical to these environmental goals in two vital respects. First, while market prices may be an efficient way of allocating scarce resources in relation to economic demand, they work within a time frame which heavily discounts future scarcities or overuse of resources. It is true that a particular shortage, say of oil, may correct itself through the joint effects of more rapid exploitation and higher prices; but this hopeful scenario cannot cope with a massive destruction of environmental resources in a longer perspective (and now not so long). Moreover, in relation to many natural resources the price system fails completely; for example, competition to maximise profit can lead to the rapid extinction of a prized species, as happened with whaling in Japan.

Second, the drive for continuous economic growth works to a large extent through increasing the consumption of the already affluent. Thus every effort of salesmanship and persuasion is thrown in a contrary environmental direction, and is supported by the gains to be made out of a 'throw-away' society in which there is a rapid and abundant turnover of changing products.

World population has almost quadrupled this century, and although forecasting is hazardous, the population of today's advanced Western economies is likely to stabilise and perhaps eventually decline, but rapid growth in many poor countries is set to increase total world population by a further 50 per cent in the next thirty years (UN estimate). Developing countries will urgently need access to more resources, but the overwhelming dominance of the richer countries – about 20 per cent of global population (and it will soon be less) uses up 80 per cent of resources – adds vastly to this emerging crisis. The likelihood of mass starvation is particularly serious since in 46 developing countries food output per head is declining and many will soon be unable to feed themselves; yet the meat diets favoured by Westerners require ten times the input of energy to get the same calories, and vast areas of the world are occupied by cattle and sheep for that purpose.

It is of course unrealistic for environmentalists to hope for sudden, drastic changes of behaviour in the face of these alarming facts and prospects; but they do at the least suggest the blindness of the present quest for endless economic growth, and the need to substitute an alternative vision of balanced global development.

Such a strategy would respond to both environmental and social priorities which to a considerable extent point in the same directions. Thus the only way to check population growth in poor countries is to raise the living standards of the impoverished masses, still largely located in rural areas despite the growth of vast cities. This goal cannot be realised through the creation of a small modernised sector of the economy where Western lifestyles and consumption habits are emulated, but require a massive application of appropriate technology to grass-roots development through agricultural improvements, water supplies, small-scale industries, etc., backed by generous overseas aid for health and education. Equally there are social as much as environmental reasons for the affluent in developed countries to cut down their demands on resources, so as to eradicate poverty in their own countries, as well as giving more generous overseas aid. It is a combustible situation that inequality within the world, as well as within nations, should be growing, and that the world's richest 20 per cent get an estimated 82.7 per cent of global income as against the mere 1.4 per cent going to the world's poorest 20 per cent (UN Human Development Report, 1998). One hardly needs to be a revolutionary to see the superiority of this alternative vision over current economic doctrine.

There is currently less popular concern with economic and social inequality than with these environmental dangers. The moral drive against gross inequalities has weakened somewhat under the erroneous belief that these are unavoidable accompaniments to an efficient market economy. There is great concern among welfare groups, churches and, fitfully, the general public about the multiple deprivations of a large 'underclass', whose reappearance in developed countries has brought back conditions of poverty and disease and a need for soup kitchens and other charitable efforts to feed the hungry, which many thought had gone permanently. So long as these groups can be treated as a special problem of a generally prosperous society, their situation nags at the social conscience but need not threaten the contentment of the affluent majority, supported by a dogma of economic righteousness. However, the insecurity of life caused by the global economy may combine with growing pockets of deprivation to challenge this culture as popularised by J. K. Galbraith (1992). Meanwhile the spread of marginal groups whom society does not apparently need or want, represented in Britain by the squatters and beggars in cities and the 'travellers' in the countryside, shows how real is the social polarisation in what are formally rich societies.

In developed countries the concern with social justice has not so much evaporated as been channelled into conflicts over the rights of individuals (abortion, euthanasia, etc.) and groups (ethnic and sexual). These issues arouse strong passions and inevitably they distract attention away from the pursuit of broader social goals. Most social movements also display inner tensions which may permit identification with traditional 'left' or 'right' politics. Feminists, for example, may give priority to improving the career opportunities of professional women or may fight the re-emergence of female sweated labour. More extreme feminists can mount such a comprehensive critique of the male sex that there is no room for ordinary politics at all. Similarly ethnic politics can dominate over any broader conception of the good of society. All these developments, however understandable, make it very hard to explicate the concept of 'social justice' or to fashion a programme around it.

The political creation of a 'rainbow coalition' that can argue effectively for radically different social and environmental goals is plainly a tough proposition. The numerous groups who might participate in such a coalition get absorbed into the political world of their own special concerns, while defenders of the present orthodoxy can pursue a tactic of divide and rule. Some environmental groups recognise the close and necessary linkages between environmental and social goals, and attempt to incorporate both into their programmes. This is true of the Green Parties which have appeared in many European countries, and the formation in 1998 of a coalition government between the Social Democrats and Greens in Germany is a major step forward. Much work still needs to be done over reconciling environmental aims with the protection of the vulnerable and with social aspirations – for example the environmental case for restricting urban growth easily conflicts with that for raising housing standards.

Fundamental to a new vision is the need to shift social values and to elaborate a changed social ethic. It is not hard to sketch its character. On the environmental side there is no need to accept either the position of those concerned simply with the future of humanity or that of the 'deep ecologist', for whom humanity is but one (and possibly a dispensable) element within a total system of nature whose complete integrity must be preserved. It can be accepted that humanity has manipulated nature to an extent which cannot be reversed, but there is also a widespread if vague belief in 'respect for nature', which carries a strong bias towards the protection of wildlife and natural habitats for their own sake as well as for human use or enjoyment.

The appropriate norms would stress greater moderation and simplicity in lifestyle, and a stronger concern with the maintenance of an unpolluted, peaceful and attractive environment. These ideas are reflected in the growth of 'post-material' values among some of the affluent, but they have to be matched by a strong egalitarian concern with raising the living standards of the poor and disadvantaged in ways that are not also environmentally destructive. This is an enormously difficult challenge which calls for a redirection of the initiatives and ingenuity at present devoted to orthodox growth. A stronger sense of social priorities would naturally develop first within a primarily national context, but its global application would need to be progressively forwarded.

The aim would be to establish a much more stable society, less prone to boom and slump and more economical in its use and disposal of resources, but it would not be a static one because of the need to cope with inevitable population growth and to raise the basic standard of so many people. As J. S Mill argued long ago, a static economy need not be dull or unprogressive, but could give ample scope for the advancement of knowledge and the arts and for many forms of personal development. It probably would also be a happier society, since beyond a certain point the pursuit of material advancement seems to be injurious to happiness, and a less unequal society which cared about its weaker members would also be more harmonious and less prone to destructive conflict.

Visions of this type will of course be discounted as politically and economically unrealistic; but they do at least point up the extent to which the present economy encourages quite opposite valuations. An economy which requires individuals to change jobs frequently and young married couples to have two incomes to pay off their mortgage cannot avoid choking the environment with cars. A society whose media promotes extravagant consumption, social passivity and personal impotence (Elgin, 1981) is being driven hard away from the vision of a more stable and caring society. The idea that individuals are so wedded to the values of the present society that they can be changed only by a very prolonged period of education needs questioning. There are signs that many people would welcome a stabler and simpler society, with more attention to both environment and equity, but they do not know how to achieve this.

A revived social democracy probably has the best opportunity for incorporating these new environmental and social directions into a workable programme. That idea gets further explored in the last two chapters. Meanwhile, this brief review of some visions of a future society is not presented as a realistic basis for immediate political action, but as guidelines for challenging the pragmatism and complacency of conventional political and economic beliefs.

7
Capitalism and Human Welfare

The purpose of these last two chapters is to consider methods of reforming the capitalist market system and reinvigorating political democracy. The two aims are interlinked. It is necessary to reduce the constraints of global capitalism if political choice is to be widened so as to embrace more positive options for improving human welfare than at present seems possible; but equally it is necessary to overcome the perceived obstacles to political action if capitalism is to be reformed. While the issues overlap at many points, this chapter is primarily concerned with capitalist reform and the last chapter with political revival.

The aim of this chapter is not to set out a dogmatic blueprint for reforming the present economic system, but to probe ways of reducing the adverse impacts of global capitalism as it now operates – its tendencies to extreme instability, inequality and short-termism – while preserving the virtues of a competitive market within a modified framework. The aim should be to replace the monolithic grip upon society of modern capitalism – its single-value character which treats the profit criterion as being an adequate and acceptable guide to prosperity and welfare – with a pluralistic set of institutions and values which recognise other ways of developing human capacities and skills. Many will say that this design is impossible – that one cannot tinker with capitalism without destroying its rationale, or that at the most it can be modified only slightly. But if this is really the choice, one must doubt, as this chapter concludes, whether the present onrush of global capitalism will survive for long.

The corollary to the attempted reform of capitalism is the creation of a more effective state and a more active and egalitarian democracy. These are the themes to be developed in the final chapter. Meanwhile it will be useful first to consider the reasons for the entrenched power of the capitalist system and the lessons

189

to be derived from past political attempts to create a more balanced economy and society.

The power of capitalism

If the capitalist system has so many serious economic, moral and political defects, the nagging question returns as to how it can be so strongly entrenched and widely accepted or tolerated. Several explanations can be given.

A first one is the amazing capacity of capitalist markets to absorb and to equalise all additions to private capital. A simple example is that increases in urban land values, which even mainstream economists recognise as the by-product of urban growth not the efforts of individual landowners, once privately appropriated acquire the same validity as any other private asset. If now an attempt is made to tax land values, the answer comes that this will reduce the profits of land and development companies whose beneficiaries include many widows and orphans, etc.; and since insurance funds are the principal holders of such assets, the statement is quite true. The strong economic and ethical case for taxing or publicly appropriating increases in land values has succeeded in a few countries up to a point (Sweden, Holland), but has usually been defeated by entrenched property interests.

The same kind of argument helps capitalism to entrench other illogical private gains; for example, when householders living on expensive sites get faced with an increase in rates, the argument goes that this will hurt widows who have rich assets but low incomes, and if the local council offers to defer rate collections until the widow's death when the property can be sold, the reply comes that this is unfair to her children. In the same way, if a government is deliberately vested with the freehold ownership of its land as happened with Canberra, its control over leases gets continually attacked and whittled away on the grounds of interference with the tenants, in a way that would never happen to the large private landowners who own large chunks of London. It is assumed in all this (but why?) that private ownership of land should be the norm and that all assets should be equalised on that basis, with public ownership treated as the regrettable exception.

These examples are illustrations of the familiar point that the ownership of capital is widely spread and includes many individual owner-occupiers of houses, small proprietors and small investors in shares and bonds. Privatisation can be used to spread this net a bit wider, so that the new small investors become partners in the capitalist system, and the repeal of the measure becomes politically awkward and expensive. Yet this argument is in a sense built on sand. The great bulk of all capital is owned by a small minority of very rich people, as many studies have revealed; and a very large section of the population, even in the richest countries, own only a minute amount of personal capital or none at all. Consequently most small investors have a much greater financial interest in their wages and working conditions than in profits from their investments, but that truth is disguised by the separation of their interests and the apparent legitimation of the whole profit system as it currently operates. The big capitalist interests have always banked on the support of the small owners, a tacit coalition that is vital to the system's maintenance. This equalising and legitimising power of private capital appears to be so strong that Labour governments are often reluctant to allow an independent inquiry – only an inquiry – into the distribution of wealth, for they know very well what it would show. They fear evidence which might upset their credentials as endorsers of capitalist markets, a situation of almost pathetic dependency.

A second explanation is that capitalists cannot legitimately use direct threats or coercion of any kind, since all market transactions are supposed to be voluntary, but rely upon governments to initiate and enforce the laws and rules which capitalism requires. Of course, not all these laws are to capitalism's taste, there is some degree of counter-influence, but governments now play a widely supportive role. Moreover, when the requirements of capitalism change (as they have with the coming of the global system), governments are expected to act in all sorts of helpful ways – promoting competition policy, pushing micro-economic reform, passing more flexible and tougher trade union laws, even reducing the number of annual paid holidays, and much more besides.

These facts mean that governments, not capitalists, get the blame attached to making and enforcing laws which meet these capitalists' requirements. Governments are also constrained by market pressures from doing the good things or providing the improved services which would earn popularity. Moreover it is government, not capitalism, which in the eyes of the population carries responsibility for 'economic management', and when the market goes wrong, it is again government (or the current ruling political party) that collects the blame and is also expected to alleviate the consequent distress.

Like it or not, then, governments and their political leaders are the whipping-boys for the market's failure and unwanted impacts, the barking dogs of capitalism. If they do everything they can to comply fully with capitalist hopes or expectations, they may get some political credit as sound 'economic managers', but likewise the more they pander to these expectations, the greater the popular odium they are likely to incur over any ill-effects or unexpected disasters. Many explanations have been given for the increasing unpopularity of governments and the alienation of voters, but the most obvious explanation is the one just suggested.

One can also slot this explanation into Lindblom's (1977) analysis of the role of democratic governments as mediators between the pluralist pressures of workers, consumers, environmentalists, etc., and the interests of the business sector on whose prosperity government is largely dependent for getting the resources to meet these demands. When the terms of capitalist co-operation are sharply stiffened (as they can be indirectly, without any threat being spoken), the consequence will be to present these democratic claims with a dusty answer and an empty kitty. Here too a poor showing by government again protects the legitimacy of capitalism.

Yet a third explanation lies in the two faces of capitalism. The open face, the one turned to the sun, so to speak, is the spreading abundance of the market-place, full of goodies that anyone can buy – regardless of birth, education or other status – provided she or he has the money. The targeting of social groups – teenagers, ethnics, gays, etc. – shows a market sensitive to different tastes, styles or fads, while the happy pictures of clean, well-clad blacks, browns and whites enjoying some product together sends a reassuring message of harmony through abundance. The opposite image, the closed face, is one of tough bargaining against weak interests, labour exploitation, job instability, etc. – but that side of capitalism is less visible and some of the dirty work for enforcing it is left to government.

Finally there is an air of inevitability about the capitalist market system. It is so omnipresent that its successive expansions and inroads – its capture of more and more of what was once the work and enjoyment of households, its penetration of what were community services, its takeover of the urban landscape – go almost unnoticed. It all seems as natural as the air we breathe. People like to feel at home in their societies, to make the best of what is, not to incur the label of a persistent critic or outsider.

Aims of reform

In considering how to change this powerful embedded system, it is best to revert briefly to the mixed economy or 'Keynesian welfare state' which lasted almost thirty years from 1945 to the 1970s. Unlike the virtual reality of New Labour's present 'third way', this system represented a genuine third way between capitalism and a modified socialism; and despite the efforts of right-wing politicians to puncture its reputation, it delivered an unparalleled growth of prosperity and welfare to the populations of Western societies, together with a reduction of the economic inequality and an elimination of the severe unemployment which had existed under pre-war capitalism.

The conditions of this achievement are now well known. Economically they rested on a global boom linked with a relatively stable monetary system based on the convertibility into gold of the American dollar, supported by Keynesian demand management so as to maintain full employment. Socially they rested on the development of the welfare state, paid for out of economic growth, as well as on improvements in wages and working conditions, such as more holidays with pay, which were helped along by the strengthened power of trade unions under conditions of full employment.

It is important to distinguish the criticisms which have been directed against this mixed economy system from the reasons for its decline from the 1970s onwards. These criticisms have been wrongly used to discredit the foundations of this post-war settlement which collapsed mainly because of the resurgence of capitalism and its political supporters under much more unstable global economic conditions, but it is true enough that there were also fault lines in the post-war system.

(*a*) Macro-economic planning to sustain full employment produced inflationary conditions and expectations which could not be indefinitely tolerated. However, this problem was not insoluble. In Britain in the 1970s the leaders of both main parties wanted to introduce a statutory incomes policy to restrict wages while preserving full employment, but they were frustrated by opponents within their parties. Instead the Labour government in Britain fell back upon a policy of voluntary wage restraint in return for improvements in social services, as did the Australian Labor government in the 1980s, although both experiments eventually collapsed. But success is possible. For example, the Dutch achievement over combating the global slide into unemployment and inequality can be ascribed to the 1982 'Wassenaar agreement' between the peak trade union and employers' organisations which moderated wage increases for the next 15 years. It can still be claimed that 'with co-operative trade unions and employers it is *in principle* always possible to pursue a mix of policies which stimulates demand and so employment, but creates neither a wage–price spiral, nor a public debt spiral' – although such action would admittedly be easier at a European level than at a national level (Vandenbroucke, 1998, p. 41).

The pursuit of full employment still requires demand management to combat the deflationary tendencies of global capitalism, and ought to utilise (as in the post-war period) fiscal changes in taxation and public expenditure as well as the monetary changes in interest rates on which excessive reliance has come to be placed.

Another lesson from the history of employment policy deserves attention. The post-war settlement certainly favoured the interests of workers over those of consumers, and in Britain a legacy of strikes in public utilities, culminating in the 1978 'winter of discontent', made trade unionism unpopular and contributed to New Labour's excessive disavowal of its previous policies. Conversely the triumph of capital and the penalisation of unions has produced an extreme swing in the opposite direction which is injurious to workers' interests in reasonable security and personal development. A balance between these poles needs to be sought.

(*b*) The biggest failure alleged against the mixed economy was the extensive nationalisation of industry. Consequent political interventions subordinated commercial considerations to the expediencies of conceding wage increases or controlling prices, and these difficulties have led to the 'corporatisation' of public enter-

prises so as to shield them from unreasonable political demands.
As the use of corporatisation suggests, public enterprises can be
established on a sounder basis which combines general directions
laid down by government (for example, about environmental
goals) with a reasonable degree of commercial freedom. This
argument applies particularly to public utilities, where there is
often a strong need to conserve resources and energy, and where
responsible long-term management continues to be more important than the profit incentive to cut costs and expand sales.
The contribution of the profit motive to efficiency is anyhow
much exaggerated. As Stiglitz (1994, pp. 236–7) points out, it does
not prevent a firm's managers from having goals of their own and
'all [firms] have exactly the same problem of inducing their employers to work towards the institutional goals' (Simon, 1991,
p. 28). Thus one can accept that post-war nationalisation was
overdone and used some unsuitable methods, but public enterprises still have superior advantages in some circumstances.

(*c*) The third criticism concerns the organisation of the welfare
state. The principle of collective provision of basic social services
is a great deal too popular to be attacked directly. The critics have
fastened mainly upon delivery mechanisms which are claimed to
be too centralised and bureaucratic and not responsive to the
more diverse conditions and requirements of the public – or in
economic jargon, they are stuck in the Fordist phase of mass production rather than the post-Fordist one of selective services.

These criticisms tend also to be exaggerated. Bureaucracy is
always an easy target, and the fact that it needs to have and stick
to elaborate rules, in the interests of both equity and economic
prudence, can easily bring it the accusation of being unresponsive
and unhuman. The device of describing clients as customers is a
way of mimicking economic markets, which tends to treat (sometimes deliberately) public services as inferior to the commercial
model, since the idea that 'the customer is right' can obviously
not be as easily applied in a free health service as in a beauty
salon. The device of a 'citizen's charter', which concedes rights of
redress to dissatisfied customers, encounters the problem that
redress is often difficult (what can one do about a late train?), or
runs into the scarcity of funds which has become endemic throughout the public sector. It still remains true that improvements are
necessary in the functioning of the public services, particularly

through more effective schemes of decentralisation and flexible, varied administration – an issue taken up in the last chapter.

The conclusion of this review is that some criticisms of the post-war 'third way' were valid but much exaggerated. The pendulum has now swung much too far in the opposite direction, producing an abandonment of full employment goals, an excessive use of privatisation and some destructive applications of the profit motive to social services. Basically the goals of the post-war settlement remain sound but have now to be applied in rather different ways, not just because of reasonable criticisms but because the world has changed.

The full employment goal may no longer be capable of being pushed as far as it once was, because more flexibility is unavoidable in a modern labour market and 'overfull' employment is bound to be inflationary, but it is essential to change the situation where anything from 5 to 20 per cent (or more) of the workforce is out of work, and where unemployment is especially severe among youths and redundant workers who face years of undignified idleness. However, the goal must now be pursued not only through the revival of effective demand management, but through the new goal of 'social investment' in the skills of the unemployed so as to match useful jobs. Employment policy also needs to accommodate a more diversified and less male dominated workforce than used to exist. These methods are discussed in the last chapter.

Secondly, the old method of nationalisation made no attempt to introduce shared or decentralised systems of ownership and control, or to promote economic democracy in parallel with its political version. Yet these remain important aims which are still more salient in an era of corporate power and increasing inequality and alienation. They will be discussed later in this chapter.

Thirdly comes the aim of rehabilitating the concept of a publicly provided system of social services and social security. There is no need to repeat the arguments of Chapter 3 about the value of this system in combining three desirable elements: collective insurance in an unstable world, a bias to equality in an inegalitarian world, and a substitution of the criterion of need for that of wealth. Here too the older methods of the welfare state will not suffice. It is essential to find new sources of finance, to establish a keener sense of social priorities and to develop a broader range of public participation and support over the delivery of services. These issues also are discussed in the last chapter.

Clearly, global capitalism presents a tough terrain for the pursuit of these revised goals. As Chapter 5 showed, competition for capital, erosion of the tax base and the adverse reactions of the money market to public expenditure limit the ability of governments to pursue social objectives. Yet people still want them, so that governments become 'trapped between Scylla and Charybdis, the market and the electorate' (Horsmann and Marshall, 1994, p. 98); and in this encounter the market has usually won. The explanation is not just the power of capitalist markets, great as that is, but (as this book has tried to show) the pervasive political espousal of false market dogmas which are used to justify reactionary social policies.

Politics is about power. The error of New Labour's 'third way', discussed in the last chapter, lies in supposing that substantial social reforms can be achieved without facing the hard issues about the economic system; but no amount of evangelism, benevolence or even constitutional reform will make much difference to the sources of economic power. Confronting the capitalist system cannot be easy, but it is possible to envisage a step-by-step approach which could gradually change the system for the better.

Capitalism can take a variety of forms provided the essential principle of competitive markets is kept. 'Micro-efficiency' is the justification of the capitalist system and most economists agree on its importance, indeed wish to increase the pace of market competition; but they are not agreed upon the 'macro' problems of how to promote the economic welfare of society as a whole. It is, however, evident that all the current political and economic keenness for more 'micro-efficiency' is not meeting this broader goal – indeed, despite the orthodox economic view that there should be a linear relationship between the 'micro' and 'macro' aspects of economic welfare, a reverse relationship is occurring. Failures at the macro level, such as extensive unemployment, besieged public services, increasing inequality and instability and so on, have already been sufficiently described. Twenty years of liberated or unleashed capitalism seem to have made these failures a lot worse.

Must we really accept that desirable 'macro' aims should always be sacrificed to a narrowly defined 'economic efficiency', or else await a future of universal capitalist abundance as improbable and remote as the Marxist vision? It is vital then to search for an economic system which *can* reconcile a modified 'micro-efficiency' with a realistically defined 'macro-welfare'.

A second point is that even the praised 'economic efficiency' of capitalist markets has strong limitations. As Chapter 1 argued, actual markets are poles apart from the theoretical model of perfect competition, perfect information, etc. Joseph Stiglitz (1994) demonstrates that market failures are ubiquitous because of inadequate or asymmetrical information, incomplete markets (there are few or no markets for future risks) and elements of monopoly; and financial incentives are also inadequate in the real world to ensure that market functions get performed efficiently. It does not follow, as Stiglitz points out, that competitive markets thereby lose a relative advantage, because government is likely to suffer still more from these defects but can have compensating advantages for the pursuit of broader economic goals. Therefore governments need to play a more active part over promoting the goals which contribute to 'macro-welfare', instead of siding with the forces which are destructive of it.

The end product of this reform process should be to relocate competitive markets within a framework of greater institutional stability and equality (instead of the present largely open-ended system), and to balance them with a strong and democratic collective sector. The first part of this programme is dealt with in this chapter while the future of collective services comes in the next. The following discussion of capitalist reform does not claim to be comprehensive, but concentrates first on the pragmatic problems of 'taming' global capitalism, and then on considering some longer-term structural changes which might make capitalist institutions more democratic, responsible and stable.

Taming the global economy

The economic and political pressures to remake the world in line with the current market orthodoxy are ubiquitous and relentless, whether through a new international trade treaty, cuts in welfare, moves to privatise even basic public functions such as town planning, or local subsidies to developers to provide harbours, tunnels or other public works. It is hard for the ordinary citizen to see the connecting thread behind all these proposals and projects, but in one way or another they all favour the expansion of capitalist markets (and the interests especially of large corporations and financial institutions) over the claims of collective services, social welfare, progressive taxation and environmental progress. The aim here is to give a bird's-eye view of some possible lines of action to protect alternative interests and values. As Chapter 5 explained, there is little at the global level to check the dominance of international capitalism. Alternative interests – those of trade unions, for example – are weakly represented; non-economic concerns such as environmentalism carry rather little weight; and mechanisms for the redistribution of wealth such as national governments possess (though now more limited), do not exist at all.

The obvious starting point for reform is the gross instability of exchange rates and the international money market. The series of foreign exchange crises which hit a whole series of countries during 1997 and 1998 were so severe and destructive that international leaders and opinion makers have at last begun to see the necessity for some reforms if global capitalism is to survive. The danger is that corrective action will be too limited to remedy the basic problems of the system or to rescue the worst-hit nations from grim poverty and social turmoil. One obvious step is to increase the funds of the International Monetary Fund (IMF) so that it can support threatened national currencies more effectively. Combined with injunctions to reduce the 'cronyism' between government, banks and businesses which occur in many developing countries, some of the Asian 'tigers' who are deeply committed to global capitalism such as Thailand and South Korea can be expected to recover their economic viability after periods of depression; but these tactics are unlikely to suffice for countries with a devastated economy and a large foreign debt, such as Russia and probably Indonesia. International loans which have to be paid for are no solvent for fundamental inequalities between nations and currencies.

Much more is needed simply to give some stability to the monetary system. The best-known proposal is the 'Tobin tax' on all international financial transactions which, levied at a low rate (0.5 per cent is suggested), would not seriously affect genuine investment but would deter the vast flows of 'hot money' which dominate foreign exchange. It could also be levied at variable rates which would exclude long-term investment, but put a heavy penalty on very short-term transactions. The usual objection is that unanimous agreement on the tax would be necessary, but James Tobin has pointed out that any nation prepared to monitor its foreign lending could impose the tax successfully (Tobin, 1994). Another very desirable measure would be to establish some form of regulation and taxation over the worst excesses of the money market, such as the growth of financial 'derivatives' which are merely a highly sophisticated form of gambling, usually with other people's money.

A further measure would be to impose stronger reserve requirements on bank lending to discourage rash loans, especially to developing countries, while also ensuring that adequate finance and increased overseas aid was available for long-term development. If the USA and other powerful nations really wanted to introduce such measures, they could set the example and lean on other nations to follow, just as they do now for the purposes of liberalising trade and investment.

A similar approach could be adopted towards another global inequity, namely widespread tax evasion through the use of tax havens and the sophisticated financial juggling by multinationals. An international tax treaty could lay down a strong code of practice for determining tax liabilities from international transactions and for penalising the use of tax havens.

It is also desirable for trade treaties to include some protection against gross exploitation of labour. While recognising that wages should necessarily be a lot lower in poor than in rich countries, it is surely wrong to permit the present mass use of child labour, often for long hours under cruel conditions, and other grave abuses of humanity.

Poorer nations need protection against the destructive impacts of global capitalism. The IMF now appears to accept that it should not impose budgetary constraints which force nations in trouble to reduce their social expenditures, but this concession will not remedy the grim poverty caused by a currency crisis or foreign debt. Instead of regarding it as a bad deviation from free trade, nations should be recognised to have a legitimate interest in controlling the use of scarce foreign exchange so as to promote development rather than importing Western consumer goods. The debt burden of many poor countries is being paid for through cuts in basic public services and other hardships to the local population which are contrary to any intelligent development policy. It would not be too difficult to remit these debts and start again, given that the banks have already written off much of their bad debt and that some of it has been auctioned off at a much discounted price. The large proceeds of a Tobin tax (and any other similar measures) might also be used for this purpose, although preferably they should be applied more positively to promote the improvement of mass living standards.

Conversely it is vital to resist measures towards further enhancing the dominance of global capital such as the proposed Multilateral Agreement on Investment (MAI), promoted by the OECD. The MAI would require all participating governments to treat overseas investment on precisely the same terms as domestic investment. It would not (anyhow in theory) prevent a country from setting its own social and environmental standards, provided these applied to all investments. What it would do is to prevent a country from giving any priority or protection to the internal development of its own resources, or to favour or protect financially its own cultural tradition or way of life, or to impose any particular requirement upon foreign corporations about training, the use of local resources or care of the environment. It would impose strong disciplines upon elected governments in the interest of multinational corporations to add to their existing strategic advantages and ability to avoid local taxation and other obligations. This plan has at last raised massive opposition.

There are a whole raft of measures at both international and national levels, which would check the destruction and overuse of environmental resources:

- Stronger treaties on the preservation of wildlife linked with the promotion of public or philanthropic ownership of nature reserves, tropical forests, wilderness areas, etc. These policies would link with the moral imperative of protecting the remaining primitive peoples who inhabit remote areas.
- Environmental guidelines for foreign investment set by the UN Environment Programme, backed up and enforced by national governments. The World Bank would apply stronger environmental tests to its loans and specifically promote environmental projects such as the regeneration of forests.

- Dangerous nuclear or chemical wastes would be required by treaty to be disposed of in the country which produced them. This would stop the hazardous transportation of toxic chemicals over long distance, and deter their production, but should be followed by measures to ban all dangerous impacts upon the world's atmosphere or oceans. There should also be an international fund for helping the safe disposal of nuclear waste, such as exists in large quantities in Russia.

- One of the most useful measures would be the taxation of excessive or destructive resource uses, such as a carbon tax to reduce fuel emissions, a nitrogen tax to check the overuse of chemical fertilisers, and an advertising tax to check the logging of old forests for woodchips to supply the vast requirements of newspapers. These taxes must normally be applied at national level but international co-operation could encourage their use. They could do a great deal to moderate energy consumption and destructive forms of agri-business. The tax on advertising would preferably apply to television as well as newspapers, and would also serve to check the inflated advocacy of modern consumerism.

- Finally the Kyoto agreement on the control of greenhouse gases does at least show the possibility of more positive international action, although its targets are full of holes and it embraces market ideology through allowing emission permits to be sold – which gives a financial reward to countries like Australia who manage to raise their permitted targets.

Progress towards these goals depends upon changing the balance and structure of international institutions. Any immediate efforts have to be spent on challenging the assertive claims of the World Trade Organisation and the dogmatic prescriptions of the International Monetary Fund, while boosting the far too weak status of the United Nations Environment Programme, the International Labour Organisation and other specialised agencies of the UN. These criticisms were very effectively put together in the declaration of principles made by all the 'non-government' (voluntary) organisations at the 1992 Rio global environmental summit. Yet the weak attitude of the governments themselves to environmental goals was in striking contrast to their acquiescence over trade and investment.

The institutions created in 1946 at Bretton Woods have completely outlived their original purpose and role. The makers of this settlement, such as John Maynard Keynes, would be appalled at how the IMF, which was intended to assist a steady expansion of trade with help for the weaker nations, has been translated into the promotion of global financial freedom with no adequate regard for stability and none for equity. The IMF should be made responsible to the Economic and Social Council of the UN, its terms of reference broadened to stress social and environmental goals, and its financial powers linked with a clear responsibility to stop unstable forms of monetary speculation. The newer World Trade Organisation should be similarly realigned and required to pursue balanced objectives. The World Bank has started to develop a stronger sense of environmental and social responsibility. Its finances should be increased to enable it to make loans at low or no interest rates, directed towards the improvement of mass living standards in poor countries.

This may be a very optimistic wish list of international actions, but it must be hoped that as the belief in the innate beneficence of global capitalism gets questioned, more of these reforms will become possible. It will also be objected that those reforms would reduce the capacity of capitalism to produce goods at the lowest possible cost. That view overlooks the extent to which capitalist entrepreneurship has got diverted into short-term financial speculations which harm rather than help the growth of productive capacity; but more basically the value of cheaper production ought always to be balanced against the costs of its social and environmental impacts.

National and regional initiatives

Despite the pressures put on national governments by global capitalism, there is still a good deal of scope for independent national action *if* the political will is there. Indeed the political argument for such action is increased by the admitted difficulties of international action, and a long agenda of possible measures can be set out (see, for example, Horsmann and Marshall, 1994, pp. 234–48).

To start with, there is nothing in the global arena which compels national governments to divest themselves of their existing functions and enterprises such as transportation, public utilities and regional development. Much of the pressure to do so is a mix of ideological dogma and political opportunism. It is true that the multinational corporations who now operate and bid in these fields can sometimes claim to have reduced costs and are supposed to be the 'wave of the future'; but any government which holds out against this fashion will reduce its dependence upon international capital, retain a source of income (if the function is profitable), and often achieve advantages of network co-ordination and equitable distribution which otherwise will be lost.

Next there still remain very wide differences between nations over levels and forms of taxation, and over scale and quality of social services. While market pressures and dogmas exert a depressive effect upon public budgets and tax systems, there is clearly still much scope for choice. Hence the need to exert pressure to keep taxation progressive, close tax loopholes, and remedy emerging gaps in welfare provision. The scope for developing an adequate and progressive tax system is further discussed in the next chapter.

Much more difficult for nation states are the economic issues relating to wages, working conditions, hours of work and the taxation of enterprises. It is still possible, unless the MAI is accepted, to lay down the standards and obligations which a foreign corporation must satisfy (and very desirable to do so), but the market risks of pitching the requirements too high are considerable. Pushing hard for better social and environmental standards still has the long-term economic advantage of promoting the kind of society in which it is good to live and work.

In this situation the case for some positive national development policies, rather than simple-minded reliance on laissez-faire, is strong. Adaptive industrial policies can help domestic firms to supply the home market and compete abroad more effectively, thus also reducing dependence on foreign investment. An example is the way Singapore controls and allocates its large superannuation funds (or a high proportion of them) for internal domestic development. Once again this entails resisting the global pressures which would remove a nation's ability to plan the use of its own resources.

While many things can be fought for at the national level, even the strongest states have found it difficult to swim far against the global stream, and for many weak and dependent states this seems close to impossible. The obvious solution is for like-minded states to club together so as to shield themselves from global instability and increase their freedom of action. The most obvious arena for such joint action is the European Union. The EU comprises nations with 'developed' economies, a shared history and culture, and a commitment to democracy and human rights, although these advantages are getting somewhat diluted with the expansion of the Union (Turkey is currently the sticking point of a country excluded for incompatible values). Europe is also relatively rich, has no longer an expanding population, and could (with some exceptions) be largely self-sufficient in resources and productive capacity. Moreover, the EU already leads the world in introducing social and environmental standards which all member states are expected to follow. A stronger European Union, such as is being attempted, would enable the EU to strengthen these standards and to require all enterprises to comply with them, without encountering a fatal retaliation from global markets. The EU could also impose some public accountability upon business corporations more easily than nation states.

The economic objection to these policies is that they might cause a flight of capital from Europe to countries where labour costs are lower and environmental standards less stringent. Indeed the same problem arises inside Europe in the form of an obvious conflict between its richer and poorer countries over the levels and stringency of these standards (Scharpf, 1991). If other developed countries, pre-eminently the USA, preferred lower or no standards, it might be reasonable for Europe to adopt some modest degree of protection to maintain its own standards. This course would be helped by the fact that the European economy is already highly integrated.

A more serious issue would concern Europe's trading relations with poorer countries. Attempts to prevent gross exploitation of labour in poor countries will not alter the fact that they have a legitimate advantage in foreign trade from their low wage levels. The EU should therefore be reluctant to impose any trade restraints upon poorer countries, and it should in any case be the aim of a united, prosperous Europe to increase its foreign aid considerably.

However, critical unresolved issues still surround the future of the European Union. The introduction of a common currency (the euro), if successful, will not only strengthen political and economic integration, but will give European countries a much sounder defence against the global instability of exchange rates. The drawback is that the euro is being introduced under very restrictive conditions. Monetary policy is to be determined by an independent central bank pledged to a single-minded policy of avoiding inflation and democratically unaccountable, while participating countries are required to keep their annual budgetary deficits within 3 per cent of their GDP and their government debt within a 60 per cent limit. These conditions could make it difficult for some countries to pursue effective employment and welfare policies. A related problem is that the small size of the European budget makes it almost impossible to provide adequate relief for the regional disparities which will certainly occur in an integrated Europe with a common currency. In America, if rising oil prices bring prosperity to Texas and a setback to California, Federal taxation and expenditure will have some compensatory effect, but as yet Europe possesses only a modest fund for regional structural adjustment which will come under increasing pressure as new but poorer countries get admitted to the Union.

Europe is the habitat of resurgent Social Democratic parties seeking new ways of controlling market forces for social ends. European leaders such as Jacques Delors argue that a united and integrated Europe could pursue Keynesian economic policies and achieve social and environmental goals which have become beyond the reach of individual states. However, the leaders of European states still often view the European project in nationally competitive terms, while others like the OECD see the basic purpose of the EU as being simply to increase the scope for lower-cost global competition. There is also conflict between an expansionary approach to employment and the more restrictive approach of the Bundesbank and the new European bank. Thus a structured European Union could be a powerful vehicle for fruitful co-operative action, but its realisation will depend upon the outcomes of a continuing struggle between contending political and economic beliefs.

The only free trade area comparable to the EU is NAFTA (North American Free Trade Area), which provides American big business with easy access to Canadian raw material and the cheap labour available in Mexico. It is producing greater economic integration but contains staggering economic inequalities between the US and Mexico.

Other regional trade blocs are growing and the proportion of global trade conducted within regions has been steadily increasing (from 41 per cent in 1958 to 50 per cent in 1993). Some analysts see the direction of economic development as being regional more than global (Vandenbroucke, 1998). Trade, investment and finance seem likely to become increasingly concentrated within a few powerful blocs – North America, Europe and one or more Asian ones. It seems unlikely that APEC (Asia Pacific Economic Co-operation group) will ever achieve its goal of a free trade zone because of its wide, scattered membership and the overlapping interests of the US; but Japan is and China will become a powerful economy and they each will probably become centres of one or more blocs.

These large blocs already exhibit some degree of economic protection, and this protectionism is likely to grow if the instability of global markets produces economic depression or the domino effects of debt defaults and bank failures. Trade wars, already latent between America and Europe, are a possibility. These developments could largely insulate the few powerful blocs from global pressures but would be a disaster for poor countries, already in a dependent position because of their tiny internal markets and fragile currencies. They also could form trading blocs on the models of ASEAN (the Association of South-East Asian Nations, with six members); but even ASEAN is a weak economic unit compared with Europe or America, and many nations – those in sub-Saharan Africa, for example – face formidable obstacles to joint action or, like Australia, have no natural trading partners.

It seems likely that the weaker nations will seek to attach themselves to the strong blocs and probably to align their economies with one of the few dominant currencies. This arrangement might give them more protection but would also confirm their very dependent economic status. Thus it seems vital to develop effective measures of international or regional assistance which will enable poor countries to raise their mass living standards and check rapid population growth.

Reforming capitalist institutions

Besides the urgent need to cool global capitalism, a longer perspective suggests the need to make some fundamental changes in the institutional structure of modern capitalism. The choice here has usually been seen in terms of a conflict between capitalism and socialism. Capitalism is defined by orthodox market theory, socialism by comprehensive public ownership and control of the economy. The usual verdict is that socialism has now failed and capitalism has won. In terms of the historical conflict this is true. But this verdict falsely identifies all socialist ideals with the discredited systems of the communist bloc which were actually a tyrannical form of state capitalism. Another common opinion is that no realistic 'middle way' between capitalism and socialism is possible – one cannot have 'half a pregnancy'. But the statement is an over-simplification of possibilities. Capitalism can take a variety of forms provided the essential principle of competitive markets is kept. Socialism need not be identified with a centralised monster but can serve democratic goals. A mixed system which incorporates some traditional socialist aspirations in a new way would be very preferable to the undiluted triumph of capitalism in its present form.

Guild socialism dissented basically from the top-down version of public ownership in favour of a democratic ideal of workers' control. The co-operative movement offered one way of pursuing this goal which flourished for a time and still does so in some places. From within the capitalist camp, 'Rhenish capitalism' and the concept of a 'stakeholders' society' offer a more modest approach to making capitalism more democratic. A wide spectrum of opinions join in the belief that business corporations should be more accountable, and that the cycle of booms and slumps should be calmed and stabilised. These beliefs acquire increased relevance as the unaccountable and irresponsible tendencies of capitalism become plainer. Although they are often grounded in earlier socialist ideals, they can provide a topical agenda for modern social democracy and accord with some of the aspirations of positive liberalism. To bring the subject down to earth, four important issues will be considered here – those of ownership, participation, investment and accountability.

(a) Ownership

The case for widening the ownership of wealth has always been very strong and has become more so. It is grossly inequitable that within a system which is based upon the pursuit of profit, the bulk of profitable assets should be owned by a small minority. This extreme economic inequality also consorts badly with the principle of political equality and acts as a baleful influence upon democracy because of the enormous advantages which wealth can confer in practical politics. So much is familiar territory, and the only strange fact – which can only be attributed to the political dominance of capitalism – is that genuine democrats do not protest more vigorously at the situation.

One way of remedying this situation is through progressive taxation, which will be considered later. Another more direct way is through broadening the ownership of capital. This goal is favoured in principle by conservatives as well as radicals, and is the reason for offering subsidised shares to workers and small investors in privatised industries. This device is inequitable and largely ineffective. It deprives the ultimate owners of the public asset, including the poor who cannot buy shares, of some of its value, and it achieves only a relatively small and often temporary transfer of assets. It is virtually a bribe to co-opt small capitalists into support for the system. A desirable policy will not only widen the ownership of wealth but give workers a more direct stake in economic management. The obvious, again frequently advocated, solution is the promotion of producers' and consumers' co-operatives. The advantages are many. Ownership becomes more widely shared; workers acquire a direct stake in the profits and conduct of their firm; co-operative action is encouraged as a balance to competition; and co-operatives accord with the very desirable goal of greater decentralisation of the economy since many of them will be on a small scale and lend themselves to local initiatives.

It is often claimed that workers lack the interest and motivation to make co-operatives work successfully. In capitalist systems co-operatives seem to have difficulty in competing with large business corporations, and in socialist experiments (such as that of Yugoslavia) they are said to have failed through a lack of market incentives. The latter opinion seems to be largely true, but the

Yugoslav experiment did not enable co-operatives to compete effectively in the market. There was no individual ownership of shares and the co-operative was the common property of the workers so long as they worked in it; hence their main incentive was to maximise their annual wages, not to risk investing profits in the quest for growth which could only benefit future workers (Brus and Laski, 1989, pp. 81–102). For co-operatives which (as is assumed here) have to compete with private firms, the lessons are clear. Workers should own individual shares which must be sold back to the co-operative on an agreed formula when the worker leaves or dies. This arrangement gives workers some personal interest in increasing profits, and repayment of the workers' shares on retirement would give a bonus for any increased market value.

It would be necessary to pass enabling legislation to facilitate the growth of co-operatives. A vital factor would be their financing. One suitable agency for this purpose would be community banks, which are already quite numerous in the USA, and which could mobilise local savings and provide credit for those co-operatives which primarily served the local economy. To give the growth of co-operatives a reasonable chance as a policy goal, it would be necessary to pass new legislation to facilitate their formation and also to establish a financial institution specifically geared to meeting their requirements. One problem would be in enabling individual workers to buy shares. Some enlightened firms are prepared to offer their workers shares, and with encouragement the movement would grow, but development would be slow and ownership would remain very unequal. One indirect solution would be a drastic measure which, however, even orthodox economists sometimes support, in the form of a once-for-all 'Pigovian' lump-sum redistribution of wealth through a tax on capital assets which workers could use to buy shares in co-operatives (or in capitalist enterprises if they preferred). If this is too drastic (as it probably is), there is also the unfinished Swedish experiment of earmarking superannuation funds for eventual share acquisitions for workers. A more modest but direct way of favouring co-operatives would be tax rebates exclusively for this purpose.

The Mondragon co-operatives in the Basque area of Spain are by now a familiar success story. There are 2,000 trading co-operatives with an average workforce of 100. They are financed by a local community bank, and a central collective organisation provides health services, technical education and social security. Mondragon is an example of a democratically owned and controlled local economy which faces outwards for trade and works effectively (Porritt, 1984, pp. 140–2).

Co-operatives do find it difficult to compete against the market power and ruthless cost-cutting of capitalist enterprises, and would be helped by measures to increase the accountability and soften the methods of capitalism. To improve their competitive efficiency, there is nothing to prevent the workers collectively appointing a manager on any terms they like, since they would keep ultimate control and profits. Co-operatives could play a very useful part in a more decentralised economy, but are not a panacea for the widening of ownership and management.

(b) Participation

The concept of a 'stakeholders' society' was briefly mentioned in the last chapter as one way of protecting the 'social capital' on which the legitimacy of capitalism ultimately depends through engaging the participation of workers and consumers in the economic decisions which affect them. Some examples of how this form of participation works can be drawn from German and Japanese examples.

In Germany, a system of basic laws (the 'social market contract') guarantees workers certain basic rights and underpins these with a strong welfare system for the retired and unemployed. In Japan, the goal was achieved mainly through the practice of large firms offering security of employment for life to most of their workers, and in cultivating traditions of company loyalty and paternalism. The result in both cases has been greater security of employment for workers and a closer, more continuous relationship between banks and firms, and in Germany a system of 'co-determination' of conditions between employers and workers which enables agreed adjustments to be made to changing circumstances. By contrast the conditions of 'Anglo-American capitalism' give workers little protection against redundancy or changes in work conditions when these suit shifting opportunities for maximising profit, and they expose top executives to frequent 'head-hunting' and pressure for quick results, which adds to the lack of stability and continuity in organisational behaviour. While some companies do recognise wider responsibilities than maximising profit, this form of capitalism is destructive of mutual trust and co-operation.

In the period of general economic growth, these partnership arrangements served Germany and Japan well, with indices of growth much exceeding those of the Anglo-Saxon countries, and real wages, especially in Germany, increasing very rapidly; but a situation of lower growth, coupled with the large redundancies made possible by new technology, has produced strains in both systems. In Germany, the protected position of workers has limited the scope for the ruthless 'efficiencies' pushed through in Anglo-Saxon capitalism, and has been one cause of increased unemployment, although a larger cause has been the problem of absorbing the labour-intensive industries of East Germany into the capitalist system. In Japan, financial crisis has exposed a degree of inefficient 'cronyism' among key actors, and the security of workers has been much modified by recourse to part-time or casual forms of employment.

Nonetheless, it is certainly still the case that these systems, especially the German one, are well worth keeping and protecting against the pressures for short-term profit-making which have dominated the Anglo-American capitalist version. After all, workers have a more vital stake in their livelihood and working conditions than do shareholders in immediate profits, and the former interest should not be simply sacrificed to the latter. Workers need to be involved in taking a long-term view of the company's future, and when sacrifices are essential they should be shared fairly between all levels of the organisation. A situation where the executives give themselves large bonuses for firing workers cannot be a tolerable system.

In Germany the role of the state in creating and maintaining this type of society is vital. Without the 'social market laws' and the co-operative arrangements which they enjoined and encouraged, there would have been no widely shared 'economic miracle'. Reform requires a strong exercise of political choice, notably in the Anglo-American societies where the laws of private property are still close to sacrosanct. 'Ethical capitalism' (or 'ethical socialism', depending upon which way one looks at it) is an important tradition in British political thought, but it has never succeeded in persuading British capitalism to reform itself from within, although some companies have tried to do so. The older apostles of 'positive liberalism', as Chapter 2 showed, grasped the nettle of calling on the state to redress the balance, and modern reformers will have to do the same if their efforts are not to remain as empty talk (see 'Does stakeholding make sense?', special issue of the *Political Quarterly*, vol. 67, no. 3, July 1996). Consumers are also entitled to protection against harmful business decisions. Laws exist to require proper labelling of products, disclosure of possible harmful effects, protection against fraud and other safeguards, but they require vigilant updating under conditions of rapidly changing products, and adequate laws of this kind do not exist (or are not enforced) in many developing countries which leads to serious abuses over the sale of harmful products.

Beyond this point consumers are usually considered to be adequately protected by the option of 'exit' – if they do not like a product, they need not buy it. However, this protection can be weak if firms recognise no social responsibility to their customers. For example, Australian banks have shut their branches in country towns because they are insufficiently profitable, causing considerable inconvenience to long-standing customers who can find no alternative bank without a long journey. Similar problems arise when banks raise charges against poorer customers with small accounts and give favourable terms only to big depositors. The sheer logic of profit cumulatively adds to inequality and poverty, and needs to be combated by some sense of loyalty to customers and sensitivity to the needs of the poor and disadvantaged. Something could be achieved through a voluntary charter of social obligations which shamed businesses into better behaviour. Another remedy would be competition from a public enterprise such as a bank which would be required to recognise social obligations subject to reasonable commercial limits.

This discussion leads back to a broader conclusion. Capitalism only becomes morally acceptable when it is embodied within some type of social compact which restricts its excesses and gives a proper weight to other interests and values besides that of profit maximisation. A commonsense view of capitalist morality accepts the existence of profit but believes that the profit should be 'fair' (not excessive) and conditional upon good service and socially responsible behaviour. Gradually a compact of this kind has been worked out through a long period of political striving, first being consciously achieved by the Swedish Democrats in pre-war Sweden and subsequently developing more loosely in many Western societies. This latent compact needs to be protected against the turbulent impact of aggressive global capitalism.

(c) Investment

The case for some degree of public control over capital investment raises difficult and important questions. The main rationale for the role of the entrepreneur is his or her willingness to take the large risks of investing capital in the production of some good or service which will sell profitably on the market. Often the decision is taken by some corporate board, but it always requires skilful and shrewd calculations and risk-taking. However, this claim does not apply so plausibly to the financial entrepreneurship seeking profit out of the assembly or disposal of existing company assets, or from speculation in financial markets. Capitalist entrepreneurship has become a complex world in which productive investment is overlaid and entangled with financial speculation, much of which has a very doubtful claim to providing an economically useful function.

At the same time there is a strong 'public interest' in the timing and directions of capitalist investment. This investment is highly speculative in itself and subject to fluctuating market expectations or fashions, causing the familiar but socially destructive trade cycles. Private investment also tends to favour relatively short-term projects, since future profits get heavily discounted in financial markets. Moreover much investment is the product of co-operative research by scientists and others, assisted strongly by publicly financed education and public research funds. It seems wrong that all those who have contributed to economic development should be unrepresented in the critical investment decisions which utilise their knowledge.

Keynes saw the answer to booms and slumps as requiring a 'somewhat comprehensive socialisation of investment'. This might seem a possible solution, although in the Keynesian period it was not really tried, reliance being placed instead upon short-term demand management to maintain employment. The difficulty is that a competitive market system entails risk-taking over new investment, which could not be comprehensively controlled without vitiating the system. However, there are other ways of bringing some degree of 'public interest' to bear upon private investment decisions.

In the post-war period, planning agencies, such as the French Economic Planning Commission and, later and more modestly, the British National Economic Development Council (NEDC), were set up to assist the co-ordination of investment. They did not use direction but methods of mutual consultation, information and advice known as 'indicative planning'. Industries were encouraged to take a long-term view of their developments through consultative mechanisms such as the 'little Neddies' in Britain. In the rush towards market liberalisation all this machinery was jettisoned, but it remains a possible model for a new effort to co-ordinate investment sufficiently to reduce violent economic swings.

A more novel approach would be the creation of a National Investment Board to take a more balanced view of the desirability and timing of new investments. Its members, who would report to a legislative committee, would include besides responsible financial experts, individuals who could offer scientific, environmental and socially relevant advice about the effects of different investments. Such a body could offer valuable advice to consumers about (for example) the environmental effects of new products and to government and universities about the use of research funds. It could also provide useful information for checking the credentials of foreign firms wishing to invest in the country and of any firm seeking government support or tax concessions for a proposed investment.

It would be inadequate to rely simply on an advisory body to influence investment. A National Investment Board could not only play a part in the investment decisions of public enterprises, but should be given a substantial slice of funds to invest on broader criteria than those of the private capital market. The obvious source for this purpose are the large superannuation funds which exist in most developed countries and are a major source of private investment. A stipulated proportion of these funds would be made available for longer-term investments which would yield environmental benefits (such as more durable products or energy savings), or which would make a socially informed use of the many new and disturbing inventions (such as genetic engineering) which otherwise will be left to commercial exploitation. These funds could also apply the new techniques of the 'information revolution' to social purposes, such as public education. The fund would be restricted to stipulated aims and could have important demonstration effects.

The familiar objection is that savers are entitled to get the best returns possible from the market, as judged by their fund managers. However, these savers have usually the benefit of tax concessions, in return for which some conditions about the use of the funds seem reasonable; and it might also be provided that, if profits from the funds fell significantly below the market average over a period of years, some further tax concession would be added by way of compensation. It would be vital, however, to allow this form of 'social investment' to prove itself over a sufficiently long period and to accept that some lower return can be worth accepting where it brings other advantages.

(d) Accountability

The hardest reform of all is to influence the behaviour and establish the accountability of business corporations. Part of the problem is the enormous political influence which these bodies can and do wield through political donations, lobbying, the use of non-profit subsidiaries, advertising, etc. Even charitable giving can be and is quite often used to advance business interests until almost every event, including even work in the classroom, has to be 'proudly sponsored' – and influenced – by some business corporation. The story of the American boy who was dismissed from school for wearing the shirt of a soft-drink company which was a rival to the school's sponsors illustrates the absurd limits of this influence. This octopus-like influence helps corporations to achieve tax advantages, resist wage claims and environmental requirements, and escape anti-monopoly laws. Can there be a more striking example of political influence than the ability of a few rich proprietors to dominate all forms of media at the same time as governments are enforcing more competition in many spheres (public and private)? And is not competition in news and opinion the most vital of all in a democracy?

There seems to be no logical reason why a corporation set up to run some business should not be banned by its charter from political activities, and be liable to lose its charter if it failed to satisfy certain standards (Korten, 1995, pp. 308–20). Such a degree of reform may seem utopian, but it certainly is possible for a national government to remove any tax exemption for a corporation's advertising, political or 'educational' activities and (perhaps with some exceptions) charities, and further to limit political expenditure generally. It could also reform the media through strict limits on market share, favourable treatment for educational or philanthropic trusts, more assistance to public and educational outlets, and stronger requirements upon private television companies to cover the full range of public and political opinion (including a ban on short television election advertisements). A vigorous public opinion ought to demand all these measures, which are not only necessary for democracy (the first consideration) but would also achieve a better balance of economic influence in societies.

The goal has to be one of imposing some form of public accountability upon private corporations for their standards and behaviour. A start might be made with the appointment of some independent body to monitor the behaviour of corporations, publicise the results, and advise government on the fitness of the corporation to operate in the country or to receive government assistance. From this basis one might move to the establishment of appropriate international standards. Another important improvement would be changes in the laws governing commercial contracts to give more protection to the weaker parties. It is practicable to make big business more accountable; the problem is its power to block reform (Crouch, 1998, pp. 240–3).

The suggestions made here fall a long way short of what might be called 'socialist'. They amount rather to significant modifications of the capitalist economy in the direction of broadening ownership and participation, influencing investment and making business more accountable. As such they run the risks not only of being called impracticable, because they are bound to meet considerable opposition, but of not going far enough to achieve effective changes. Alec Nove sets out the 'economics of feasible socialism' in a much bolder spirit (Nove, 1983). He recognises, indeed stresses, the need for socialised firms to accept that rewards must be based upon market performance, and not simply upon socialist conceptions of equity, although equity would have a place in limiting the permissible differences between incomes. Socialism (unlike in Marx's view) should be concerned with 'efficient allocation, calculation and valuation'. It was, Nove argues, failures on these points which doomed the socialist experiments in Eastern Europe (see also Brus and Laski, 1989). However, Nove hopes (with some doubts) that it would be possible to achieve market efficiency in a system where private enterprise was confined to small businesses with a limit on size, and the rest of the economy consisted of public corporations, socialised enterprises (in which workers had a limited say) and producer co-operatives. He concedes, however, that the range of political decisions which would have to be taken about the organisation of such an economy would be a formidable challenge to the capacities and integrity of a political democracy.

Whether Nove's version of an efficient socialism is feasible or not, it may be wiser to proceed more cautiously if the benefits of competitive markets are to be kept. Whilst a political democracy ought to have some supervisory powers and authority over its economic system, there is an obvious danger of severe 'political failures' if this supervision attempts to be too extensive. The first need is to establish a more balanced system, which introduces some measure of stability and equity into the capitalist system. The problem is that, as pointed out earlier, capitalism is entrenched within a seemingly logical structure (although the logic is not consistently applied to the big actors) which resists piecemeal amendment. Any alternative structure will look less logical and tidy simply because it recognises the pluralism of values. It will not be the worse for that fact, but there are difficult issues of 'social engineering' in moving to a different system. But what will happen if efforts at reform fail?

Collapse or reform?

Social scientists have a poor record over forecasting the future. This is because of their endemic tendency towards 'trend planning' – for simply extrapolating present trends into the future.

But the future is often unexpected and surprising. Who after the Second World War foresaw the end of full employment policies, the assault on the welfare state, the collapse of trade unionism, the orgy of privatisation, the sudden end of communism and the Cold War? Effective prophesies of the future are more likely to come from those with a scientific or literary imagination, such as H. G. Wells and Aldous Huxley and the best science fiction writers.

At present, social scientists, and economists in particular, foresee little beyond inexorable progress of the capitalist economy, mounting statistics of economic growth, and an unbelievable degree of affluence and mobility for the economically successful. The darker side of these forecasts is the fear of the growth of a large proletariat of idle, casual or part-time workers suffering impoverishment among plenty, or even of the emergence of a 20–80 society, the 20 per cent very affluent and the 80 per cent struggling or poor. These gloomy thoughts are not enough to drive out the upbeat assumption that global market growth will somehow find a way through these problems. Others are already arguing that the 'greenhouse effect' and other troublesome environmental impacts must be tolerated and coped with as the inevitable consequences of the continuation on a world scale of existing patterns of production and consumption. Those who welcome or expect to gain from the global market economy have a wonderfully stoical attitude towards the misfortunes of others which must be expected to accompany its triumphal path.

There are many possible (many would say probable) events which may upset these beliefs and cast a pall over the prospects of global capitalism. These prospects are after all strongly dependent upon certain necessary facilities, including the maintenance of quick and rapid communications around the globe, easy and safe movement of capital and money, and reasonably stable or anyhow entrenched national regimes capable of sustaining and enforcing the laws necessary for global market operations. These facilities are all very vulnerable to a range of possible crises and disasters, including local wars, civil conflicts and rebellions, the escalation of terrorist attacks, sophisticated forms of disruption or robbery, severe environmental problems caused by the loss of forests, the erosion of soils, the greenhouse problem, extensive famine caused by these disasters and by pressure of population on limited resources – to say nothing of the risk of wider wars or the use of nuclear weapons.

Another possibility (perhaps in conjunction with other troubles) is that the capitalist system might collapse from within, under its own failings. The fall of communism in Russia and Eastern Europe was a striking (and largely unexpected) demonstration of how an apparently powerful and strongly entrenched system can suddenly disintegrate because of the enormous gap between the theoretical claims and rationale of the regime and people's actual experience of how it worked. At least under suitable 'triggering' conditions, capitalism might seem open to the possibility of a similar collapse from within. After all, there are many situations where people's experience of capitalist markets is very dismal compared with theoretical claims, as when widespread impoverishment occurs with the collapse of a currency, or increased productivity leads simply to massive redundancies, or poverty amidst plenty becomes starkly apparent. Yet capitalism is also much better protected and insulated from revolt than was communism, by virtue of its global reach, its use of the state (especially where legitimated by formal democracy) to support its requirements and to absorb complaints, and its greater 'indirectness' and complexity; and the least likely scenario now is the traditional one of a capitalist collapse due to the united action of the 'workers of the world'.

However real these various threats to the capitalist system may in the event prove to be, they hardly provide any basis for optimistic scenarios. A partial collapse of global capitalism could still leave the system entrenched in particular countries and centres, and probably linked to a military capacity to defend its claims and possibly to recapture defaulting areas (especially ones of economic and strategic significance). There might simultaneously be a development of different regimes and economies in some parts of the world. However, conditions of disaster and turmoil are much more likely to produce versions of strongly authoritarian rather than democratic regimes, whatever their aims; while the prospects of a world split again into competing military camps or plagued with fierce ethnic rivalries, or of whole regions slipping backwards into very primitive conditions, seem also to be all too likely outcomes of these various disasters.

Hence it is hardly open to any rational person to hope for or rely upon drastic transformation of the capitalist system occurring through a series of disasters. On the contrary, the real possibility of such situations increases the urgency to reform the system while time is available. Indeed the failure to do so seems already to be leading to the re-emergence of fascist-type movements as a political response to experienced (but only dimly understood) market failures, and could lead on to irrational fascist or authoritarian regimes. The idea that the present system is 'inevitable' can only be believed in by an economic determinist, who supposes that society is necessarily dominated by the requirements of a particular economic system. One is looking at the inverted face of Marxism, and it is strange indeed if that is the most that can be said for the capitalist system. Thus one must hope that collective democratic action can mend a defective system if the defects are clearly exposed.

8
The Revival of Political Choice

This chapter is concerned with ways of exercising political choice in modern democratic societies. In the future more decisions are likely to be taken internationally or regionally, and, it is hoped, also locally, so as to reduce the historic sovereignty of the nation state. Both movements of functions – upwards and downwards – correspond with economic and social changes in the world, and are clearly evident in Europe, where the transfer of powers to the European Union has gone hand in hand with other transfers to the elected regional bodies which exist in Germany, France, Spain and elsewhere. However, for the foreseeable future the nation state will remain the key player in political life, because international political power is still too weak and fragmented, and localised sources of political power – however valuable – cannot possibly cope with global impacts. The nation state still has a vital and in some respects expanding role to play in devising a more balanced and equitable framework for the market system and in organising a comprehensive but partly devolved system of public services.

Accordingly, the chapter will start by drawing together the book's conclusions into a discussion of the future character and role of democratic states, followed by a consideration of how the state might relate more effectively to community opinion and initiatives. The third section seeks a solution to perhaps the state's greatest failure, the missing links between work and welfare. Finally comes consideration of how economic thought needs to be drastically altered to take account of its neglected or overridden social impacts, and how a democratically elected counter-revolution of ideas might be established.

The regenerated state?

The nation state has become a beleaguered institution. Some see it as failing to meet its responsibilities. Others see it as too remote and authoritarian for the requirements of an increasingly individualist society. A favourite remedy is to fall back upon the more voluntaristic basis of civil society. This viewpoint has important merits and lessons for both the state and the economy, but also strong limitations. A more vibrant civil society can in practice only flourish within the framework of a supportive and purposeful state, which shares and expresses similar democratic values.

As Chapter 4 demonstrated, the notion of a minimum state with few functions is a chimerical one. The factors which influenced the growth of the state – the impacts of industrialisation, urbanisation, technology and rapid economic and social change – are proceeding faster than ever. The withering of the state would not anyhow be possible without a parallel withering of the global economy, and the latter process is harder since economic power is entrenched at the global not the national level.

Neo-liberals and libertarians seem to want to combine an extreme freedom of the individual from any form of state intervention with a simple endorsement of the global capitalist economy. This is an impossible combination, which is met with some fanciful beliefs. Thus writers such as Nozick (1974) make play with a utopia in which any group of people can choose to live in the kind of economic and social system which they prefer. This idea would only work at all if a strong state protected these groups from external pressures, especially the strong ones for global market penetration.

As this book has amply demonstrated, capitalism could not work effectively without the support of a wide array of public functions. Capitalist markets depend comprehensively upon a framework of laws and regulations established by the state, and the triumph of capitalism has been dependent upon supportive political measures which could be reversed or modified. Market liberalisation and privatisation can work tolerably and effectively only with the aid of an increased range of public regulations – over abuses of monopoly, dangerous drugs, consumer protection, environmental impacts and much else. The state is expected to sacrifice cherished social objectives in order to assist market 'efficiency', yet capitalism depends completely upon the social infrastructure provided by the state for producing educated, capable and fit workers, services which could never be provided for the mass of the population on a profitable basis. The state must also cope with all the casualties of the market system as well as the discontents and frustrations which its erratic course produces.

Many politicians now see the first aim of the state as being to promote the international competitiveness of the national economy. Other goals must be subordinated to this supreme aim. The argument goes that if a nation fails to attract sufficient investment and jobs in the highly competitive international arena, it will sink into economic decline and its social aims will be frustrated. This seems to be the ruling belief even of a centre-left party such as New Labour in Britain, while in one powerful version European unity is desirable, not for the better protection of social and environmental standards, but for forging a powerful competitive bloc in the global arena.

Against this position it can be claimed that the state is essential for protecting social and community values which are being persistently undermined by global capitalism. Also the capitalist 'virtues' of competition and consumers' choice are often applied inappropriately or operate perversely on closer examination. Because of the dependence of capitalism upon the state, the state has both a right and a duty to make capitalism more equitable and socially responsive.

Given the remoteness of exercises of economic power, the state should do all it can to assist the decentralisation of the economy. Some measures to this effect, such as support for community banks and producer co-operatives, were suggested in the last chapter. Reversion to a more localised economy would probably do more than anything else to restore social trust in the market. The state could make capitalism more equitable and acceptable through giving more protection to the weaker parties in the law of contract, and putting limits to the acquisition and inheritance of capital. It could demonstrate the virtues of co-operative working in its own services instead of slavishly and often inappropriately copying market disciplines and incentives. A more balanced relationship between the state and capitalism would itself check the destructively imperialist tendencies of the latter.

A second vital mission for the state is to rehabilitate its role and credentials as a service provider, which has been damaged by exaggerated and indiscriminate attacks upon bureaucracy. The public choice theory that bureaucrats have an inevitable tendency to pervert public policy to their own personal advantage, amounts to guilt by association and has no empirical roots in a sociological analysis of actual bureaucracies whose behaviour varies widely. Yet this impressionistic reasoning buttresses the familiar belief that governments are big, bloated and 'inefficient' compared with business enterprises. These assertions miss the point that the functional requirements of the state have been expanding for sound reasons. The greater labour intensity of many public services increases their proportionate demand on the economy; demands for education and health are naturally increasing, and developments in medical technology bring a sharp and continuous escalation in costs; the rising number of old people and of children needing care and protection places heavier demands on the personal social services; public environmental responsibilities and many forms of regulation are growing rapidly. It is often pointed out that the stringent controls since the 1970s checked the growth but failed in most Western countries to reduce the size of public expenditure as a proportion of national income. Politicians, armed with market dogmas, continue to argue that cuts can always be covered by increased efficiency, and to blame bureaucrats for any consequent service failures. But given the demonstrable reason for growth in so many spheres of the public domain, this result looks not a failure but a remarkable degree of containment.

It has become politically unfashionable to say so, but there are good reasons for understanding and accepting, not just opposing, the growth of the public sector. Actually, as Chapter 3 showed, the resources devoted to public service consumption are relatively modest – under one-fifth of gross domestic product in OECD countries, the balance of public expenditure consisting of transfer payments which have also needed to increase because of more unemployment and poverty. Chapter 3 also gave reasons for keeping the expanding requirements of social services within a democratic political framework of comprehensive coverage, rather than accepting their gradual erosion by privatisation until only a still substantial but inferior public system remains. There is no need to repeat those arguments. They are central to any reasonable view of equality of opportunity, and they represent a form of collective social insurance which is relatively cheap and a main source of social cohesion. It does not follow that these collective services need to be centrally provided and tightly controlled. The future role of the state is better seen as orchestrating the operations of a variety of service providers. However, the framework still needs to combine the case for diversity with a reasonable degree of equality in access to services. It is not an easy balance to achieve.

The present image of the state is a strongly negative one. Political leaders give the impression of disbelief in the worth of the state's functions and rarely are political voices raised in praise of what the state does or could accomplish. All eyes are fixed upon the supposed wonders and benefits of economic competition and growth. It is no wonder then that there is much ignorance about the actual range, benefits and problems of public functions. The 'public' has become an almost dirty word under the weight of the ruling market dogmas.

A revived democratic state could be expected to pursue more positive purposes. It would seek new means of stimulating and channelling the energies and resources of society so as to meet neglected social goals and aspirations. Its role would be less to order or coerce and more to energise and orchestrate within a new framework of enabling legislation and resource allocation. Resources will always remain too limited in terms of the state's tasks, but the need for a substantial public sector would be accepted and not denigrated. Present political beliefs minimise the value of research and planning for distinctive public purposes and rely upon crude political management. A more purposive stance would enlist intelligent and dedicated public servants to assist in the pursuit of complex goals.

The state's support for capitalist markets carries with it an endorsement of the values of that system as it currently operates. Economic goals are continually allowed to override their own adverse impacts, as when governments respond to mounting evidence of the grim effects of addictive gambling, not by ending their support for casinos but by requiring them to make a small contribution towards alleviating the disease they have first produced. At present, legislators seem quite unable to relate the severe social problems which they encounter in their constituencies to the economic 'imperatives' which they continue to pursue. A more purposive state, however, would be prepared to question the values of the market and, with enough community support, actively promote alternative values and goals.

Many may consider that this sketch of a more active state, less beholden to the market and more socially responsive, is an unrealistic reversion to the past. Certainly there would need to be a drastic transformation in the state's present orientations, without which few would be keen to strengthen its capacities. The state is in danger of losing democratic trust. It still remains the creature of a political process and could be regenerated by the emergence of a more active and responsible democracy, and by a reversion to the quest for a common good, which can be described as 'a set of shared purposes and standards which are fundamental to the way of life prized together by the participants' (Connolly, 1981, p. 91). Sceptics sneer at the notion of a common good, which Brennan and Buchanan (1985, pp. 37–9) see as a vain quest or 'organismic monstrosity'. But, if there is no such thing as common good, why should we embrace such purposes as 'free market' or economic growth? The common good is a contestable term and the quest will always be open-ended. There is no warranty that a more active democracy would pursue any particular goals and it could have different priorities from those espoused here, but there are also reasons to suppose that a greater stress on social considerations and objectives is congruent with basic democratic values.

These values turn on interpretations of equality and liberty. A genuine democracy is egalitarian in the sense that it accords equal moral worth to each individual. There can never be equal political influence and there will always be wide variations in political participation. Many individuals can quite reasonably opt to leave policy issues to their chosen representatives, but what they need anyhow to judge is the social values of their chosen representative rather than his technical political skills. At the same time more direct political participation is itself a good to be encouraged and fostered. In particular, if participation is to be more of a reality, it is vital to reduce the baleful political influence of wealth and economic power which contribute a lot to the alienation of ordinary citizens.

Liberty when intelligently understood implies always a balance between the pulls of private freedom to lead one's own life, and a social responsibility to contribute to the common good. Liberty then implies a responsible exercise of democratic rights. In human terms the individual's engagement with her immediate social environment may always be greater than with the more formal and often remote political environment; yet the political is a necessary framework for the social. It is because of this situation that efforts to promote a responsible, and discourage a frivolous, treatment of citizenship are so important. A genuinely democratic society would promote all forms of free discussion and debate, and repudiate commercial attempts to subordinate democratic concerns to market criteria.

Engaging with community

Both the state and the market are increasingly seen as the sources of remote decisions which bear harshly on the lives of ordinary people. The communitarian movement is a natural response to these feelings of powerlessness and alienation, as well as embodying a broader concern with the general condition of Western society. It sees society as comprising a whole series of communities (local, voluntary, professional, etc. extending upwards to national and international levels), in which the spirit of mutual concern and co-operation needs to be rekindled. The location of community is left fluid, although there is a bias to the local level as the simplest and most understandable, and the message comes across in several forms.

Philosophically, communitarianism rejects the identification of liberalism with the rights and interests of isolated individuals, claiming that personal freedom can emerge only within a context of social roots and responsibilities (Mulhall and Swift, 1992) – a position that is highly critical of market ideology. Morally it stresses that individual conscience, while ultimately sovereign, cannot function effectively without the support of shared moral norms of approval or disapproval. Politically it seeks the empowerment of the many intermediate or local associations and bodies which constitute civil society – a position which goes back to the warnings of Alexis de Tocqueville that only in such a society will genuine democracy and liberty prevail (Etzioni, 1995; Selznick, 1992).

Claus Offe (1998) argues that 'community' is the third element, besides state and market, that is necessary for the design of successful institutions. In his view the state should embody collective reason (in the Weberian sense of rational laws); the market responds to individual economic interest; and community represents the passion of affective attachment to a place or group. Institutional pathologies arise when one element is too dominant or too absent. Adapting Offe's analysis, it seems that the market and its ideology are too powerful, community is too weak and the state is caught in an unhappy position in which it is failing both to balance the market and to relate effectively to community; but how could more space be made for community initiatives, especially at a local level?

One obvious answer is that the state should delegate more of its functions to partly autonomous local agencies. Examples are the transfer of responsibility for the management of public housing to tenant co-operatives and of schools to elected or representative school boards. A wider range of social services could be delivered by voluntary bodies who represent a vital source of community interest and energy. Again more functions should be handed down to elected local governments. For a long time in Britain powers have been going upwards to national departments or appointed boards on grounds of technical efficiency and uniform service; but the democratic aim of involving the local community should count for more, and the technical arguments for less, in decisions about the location and conduct of public services.

Democratic decentralisation still has its limitations and problems. One obvious example is finance. Local governments vary greatly in their resources and these differences are becoming larger with the social polarisation of the modern economy; hence it is imperative on equity grounds (whatever form of local financing is being used) for the central government to distribute equalisation grants to the poorer localities. Voluntary bodies need financial support to deliver public services. Inevitably government will lay down some conditions which will interfere with the freedom of voluntary bodies to pursue their own aims and choose their own clients. Government faces the problem that otherwise the service may not be impartially and economically delivered; the voluntary body that it will be co-opted into ends not its own. An intelligent democracy and government can come to terms with these problems. It can sacrifice some degree of national equality and accountability in the interest of facilitating the diverse energies and aims of local or voluntary bodies; but the tradeoff is not easy or costless.

Democratic decentralisation is also one way of responding to the large and growing volume of protest against the changes being wrought, through both market and state, in the quality of ordinary life. Territorial defence is the local response to proposals for motorways, airports, nuclear power stations, redevelopment projects, etc. and for the defence of commons, woodlands, nature reserves and other environmental resources. Quite a lot of this is 'nimbyism', the defence of one's own backyard regardless of alternatives; but a lot of it can be seen as a defence by communities of threatened common facilities – such as public transport, open space, safe streets and an unpolluted environment – or as resistance to the priority given to the stronger groups – to developers over residents, motorists over pedestrians, tourists over locals – which make community life noisier, uglier and less safe.

One answer to this problem lies in giving local communities greater power to plan their areas, protect their amenities and control unwanted developments. It would not be enough to strengthen their regulatory powers, they need to be able also to promote desirable developments in the most suitable locations. The difficulty here is that many local councils are swayed by real-estate lobbies and their own financial interest into approving any development that can claim to confer an economic benefit. Some European cities have successfully protected their city centres from traffic blight, facilitated cycling and walking and linked major developments to easy access by public transport. Other examples exist of the 'greening' of cities with small parks and tree plantings as well as large green belts or other reservations, and the effective rehabilitation of degraded areas. To achieve positive planning, however, municipal councils much need the backing of land legislation, such as exists in Holland and Sweden, which enables them to acquire land at prices that exclude potential development value and allocate it to preferred public or private purposes (Thornley and Neuman, 1996).

Many communitarians, especially in America, are now clear that the moral debasement and criminal activities that stem from the abuse of drugs, alcohol, prostitution, pornography, etc., and which ruin the lives of whole communities, have to be met by a return to stronger moral codes than liberal agnosticism offers. However, the necessary legal and political support for co-operative action to attack these evils faces strong opposition from very extreme claims about individual rights. The state and the judiciary are caught in a crossfire between opposing positions which extends to other social issues such as abortion and euthanasia. While some of these conflicts involve almost irreconcilable principles, and there is no quick way of curing criminal or pathological behaviour, at least the victims and by-standers could be helped if the state threw its weight behind local community action.

Local opinion may help to shame delinquents into better behaviour but 'shaming' will not on its own change the degraded environments and lack of constructive opportunities which contribute to such behaviour. Part of the answer lies in strengthening the capacity of local communities to improve degraded housing estates and provide adequate remedial and social services. National governments have passed new responsibilities to local government without providing additional resources; for example, the closure of many mental institutions transferred the care of their patients to local community care without proper funding. The cure for social problems cannot come simply from moral exhortation or penal measures, but requires positive measures and additional resources to protect community life.

Instead of tension or hostility between state and community, there are many opportunities for fruitful co-operation. There is or should be a common interest in the promotion of democracy, the improvement of public services, the stabilisation of community life, the alleviation of unemployment and the protection of the victims of crime and vice. Voluntary bodies are often seen as alternatives to state action, but the evidence is that their members actually take a more positive interest in public policies than do more passive citizens (Wuthnow, 1995). Their involvement contributes to democratic education. Indeed, as John Stuart Mill saw clearly, widespread involvement of individuals in local government and voluntary organisations provides the essential basis for a democratic society. One learns by participating.

The state needs to develop new and more flexible methods of working which win the co-operation of other organisations. There needs to be more harmony between the roles of state, community and market. One version is that of 'strategic management', whereby government devolves responsibility for functions to other organisations (private as well as public), while concentrating on creating a system of guidelines and monitoring sufficient to achieve broad public purposes (Kooiman, 1993). This approach, pioneered in the Netherlands, reflects the orderly and systematic processes of European states. It requires a high degree of intelligent planning at the centre which mirrors on a wider canvas the kind of comprehensive planning undertaken by a multinational corporation. Here is another anomaly: why should planning be a good thing for a big business organisation yet treated as undesirable or impracticable for the more socially basic tasks of government?

An alternative American version is that of 'reinventing government' (Osborne and Gaebler, 1992) which turns on the concept of public officials acting entrepreneurially instead of bureaucratically to solve community problems through harnessing local resources in novel ways. It is an approach better suited (in the USA) to action by states and localities, and it leads to a great deal of experiment and variety which, while good in itself, does preclude more comprehensive or egalitarian solutions – unless the best results are taken up and generalised at Federal level. It also tends to be based upon a strong faith in market solutions and local economic development, which can be a limiting or zero-sum activity. Nonetheless the entrepreneurial approach has also got value as an alternative to traditional bureaucracy. It is matched by the development of a new breed of private social entrepreneurs who have the skills to assemble manpower, buildings and money from multiple sources, and whose greatest asset is the accumulation of trust and co-operation (Leadbeater, 1997).

One can expect also a considerable growth of the local 'informal' economy, especially if capitalist markets are unreformed. The increases in redundancies, youth unemployment and part-time working will stimulate household production and 'do it yourself' by many people who have plenty of time and not much money. There will be an increase in informal economic co-operation, which can already be seen in such devices as local currencies available only for services rendered. More people will retreat to low-paid local work as preferable to the instability of the wider employment market. If one must accept these developments, local governments and voluntary bodies could – if allowed – do quite a lot to facilitate them beneficially: for example, by providing small allotments for vegetable production, protecting the open spaces and common facilities which more people will now use, assisting local co-operative action, promoting adult education and using town planning to enhance the narrow opportunities available to the poor and unemployed. It is possible to envisage a more positive outcome for local initiatives. Robert Putnam (1993) demonstrates the value of both democratic decentralisation and an active civic spirit for achieving regional economic and social development. Among the Italian elected governments he studied, those which performed well (such as Emilia-Romagna, Umbria and Toscana) had a strong civic tradition and were marked by active organisations of local businesses and workers with flexible interrelations and links with government. Their regions scored well on civic attitudes and interest in public issues. Putnam argues that Olson was wrong to see interest groups as a barrier to economic development, and that the success of these regions showed the value of creating trust through frequent encounters between the participants in local economic and political life. By contrast, Italian regions which lacked these conditions and featured strong vertical lines of power, such as those in Southern Italy, scored badly on indices of both economic and governmental performance.

The community spirit is beneficial if it builds on common attachments and loyalties so as to encourage fruitful co-operation, but not if it has too much passion for the interests of a particular group. This issue of balance has to be faced – for example, an academic community is valuable if it reflects a shared concern for the disinterested pursuit of knowledge and the democratic management of its affairs, but not if it acts purely selfishly in relation to the concerns of the rest of society. Ethnic communities can express a vibrant cultural tradition and be a big source of mutual support, but tendencies to ethnic intolerance or complete segregation have to be resisted. Local communities can be narrowly selfish and can be deliberately crafted to be so – as with the small American local governments set up to protect the rich and to 'zone poverty out of existence' (through restrictive planning) in order to stay that way.

Communitarianism offers a strong answer to the atomistic liberalism of neo-liberal thought, but as a doctrine it tends to expect too much from autonomous movements within a society and to pay too little attention to the importance of the political framework, both for restraining excesses of communitarian zeal and for promoting its positive benefits. Democratic governments should bend over backwards to devolve functions and initiatives downwards into society, but they still need to organise some redistribution of resources to assist poorer communities, some basic standards of public services and a framework of common rights and duties for all citizens. The balance cannot be an easy one, but as Putnam's work demonstrates, effective engagement with community is necessary to the development of a democratic and prosperous society.

Work and welfare

A sort of collective moral blindness has set in on the subject of work and welfare. Everyone agrees that involuntary unemployment is a very undesirable situation; but this knowledge is rarely translated into a full appreciation of the sheer waste of human spirit and the loss of hope and pride inflicted on millions of individuals and families, especially by the growing phenomenon of long-term unemployment. Others too are badly hurt by the present distribution of work. Large numbers of children are being brought up by one or two jobless parents, or in a family dependent upon a single casual or poorly paid job. Social surveys indicate that, while poverty has declined among the aged in the last twenty years, it has increased sharply among children, so that in America nearly a quarter of all children live below the poverty line. At the opposite extreme, many small children again suffer – not from poverty (they may be lavishly indulged), but from neglect – by the fact that both parents are struggling hard with demanding careers.

Unemployment, poverty and family breakdowns are associated with a host of regressive social conditions. In Britain there have been very big increases since 1980 in the number of reported juvenile crimes, youth suicides and deaths from drug abuse, as well as declines in literacy and the reappearance of once prevalent diseases of poverty (Young and Halsey, 1995). The violence and drug abuse are to be found mainly among the young, the older unemployed being more prone to quiet despair. The main political reaction has been to press for tough sanctions against young delinquents and irresponsible parents, but this approach fails to consider how far 'the primacy given to the material economy has undermined the moral economy' (ibid, p. 13). While the impacts of social and economic change are difficult to disentangle, the fact that all the statistics of social deprivation and breakdown have soared since the advent of market liberalisation speaks for itself.

The argument that yet more attention to the pursuit of economic growth and competitiveness will alleviate these social evils looks increasingly absurd and contradictory. As Chapter 6 pointed out, capitalism on its own without political action has never avoided substantial if fluctuating unemployment, and the massive redundancies involved in capitalist restructuring make it unlikely that the market will find enough additional jobs for the unemployed even in an economic upswing. Although their ideas are more positive, the aim of left-centre politicians to invest heavily in skilling the unemployed is unlikely to achieve its aim, if reliance is still placed upon market growth to absorb the newly skilled workers. This policy only makes sense in the context of a broader and more determinate plan for the development of new jobs.

One obvious way of tackling both unemployment and overwork is to share out available work more equitably. This entails persuading workers to accept reductions in hours rather than increases in pay in future wage settlements, perhaps with the carrot of a modest tax rebate. Another method is to persuade older people to accept phased rather than sudden retirement. A third, important method would be to offer a 'parent allowance' to either parent who will stay at home to look after an infant.

The greatest obstacle to such measures is the competitive attitudes prevalent in the modern economic system. Mothers are reluctant to stay at home with young children if the result is to lose some career advantage. Individuals feel a need to maximise their economic opportunities and employers take similar attitudes. These attitudes are anachronistic in economies with high productivity and with too many people involved in tasks of social control and manipulation instead of having time for community tasks or personal development. A more rational sharing of work should also compensate for its economic cost through reducing social evils. In Europe, governments have traditionally pioneered helpful arrangements for maternity and parental leave and over flexible working hours. One of the many social costs of privatisation is that it usually leads to more reactionary policies on these matters, and another virtue of the revival of the public realm would be that a more favourable attitude to work innovations could be restored and taken a lot further.

Developments in work-sharing are likely to be slow and a larger and more urgent aim is a genuinely effective plan to create jobs for the unemployed. Efforts to date have offered only training and a limited nucleus of temporary, subsidised jobs, without any durability or assurance that the training will not be wasted. The basic mistake lies in the political unwillingness to recognise that most potential useful jobs are in the traditional public sector. This failure is partly ideological – the silly idea that only jobs in the market are really 'productive' – but is based primarily upon the assumption that it is impossible to finance any expansion of public services when government is being continually urged to cut back.

Against this one needs to recognise the enormous advantages of such a plan. Additional labour could certainly be well employed in the social services, especially perhaps in the care of children and the elderly, and in neglected environmental and infrastructure services. Training could be geared from the start to jobs that were actually going to be available, not merely hypothetical. There is also greater scope for employing relatively unskilled labour in the collective sector, and many unemployed people will not be capable of developing specialised skills or wish to do so. Moreover, as suggested earlier, while the government would necessarily have to organise and initially finance this project, it could be largely operated on a decentralised basis by local governments, voluntary organisations, business and other agencies. There could be plenty of scope for local initiatives within the general framework.

Finally and above all, the social impacts of this plan would be enormously valuable. It would bring new hope to workless individuals and families, with further benefits for the health, succour and education of their children, and it would raise the morale of deprived communities.

Given all these gains, can it really be the case that affluent societies could not afford such a plan? Cynics will note that far more than the necessary expenditure would swiftly be found if the nation were going to war, whereas this civilian plan could actually to a large extent pay for itself. There would be substantial savings on unemployment benefit and modest additions to tax revenue from the new employed, and also savings from the consequential reduction of crime, drug abuse and vandalism. In some cases the cost of new jobs could be at least partly met by charges, and some part of these new activities could be turned into profitable enterprises, either public or private. A substantial initial investment would be needed, but the eventual charge upon the public purse could be expected to be relatively modest.

The idea of introducing a year of community service as a partial answer to youth unemployment has gained ground. It would do much to counter the widespread cynicism and alienation of young people with the experience of participating in social goals and ideals. The three possible options of work on the environment, in welfare services or in overseas aid cover the ground naturally, and represent also a corrective to the dominance of market beliefs. It would not entail much loss of time from useful work, especially as many young people now extend their education and are slow to settle down. There are understandable objections to the use of compulsion, but a year of community service would have much more positive purposes than military conscription which is still sometimes utilised and justified. It would raise the experience and understanding of young people about urgent social and environmental problems, take them away from the influence of a narrow utilitarianism, and improve them as citizens. It could also do a lot to bridge the growing social divide between rich and poor. To achieve these results and to be equitable, the scheme would have to be both compulsory and universal.

There remains the basic problem of funding, not just a new project, but the strengthened range of public or collective services that has been elucidated in this book. Economic answers are possible, as Chapter 3 pointed out. In the first place, the wide variations between countries, with the level of taxation in Sweden twice that of Switzerland, suggest that there is no insuperable economic obstacle to higher taxation in most countries. Secondly, taxation becomes more acceptable and fair when it is genuinely progressive, but this principle has been watered down under the influence of market dogmas; for example, income tax in Britain has become only mildly progressive and the total tax system is not progressive at all – a very reactionary situation when one reflects that the top quintile of households has seven times that of the bottom quintile (Le Grand *et al.*, 1992, pp. 187, 209–10). The principle of progressiveness needs to be recovered and applied also to social security contributions and indirect taxation.

Tax reform could greatly assist employment objectives, through raising the generally and often miserly low income tax threshold, thus providing a stronger incentive to work, and shifting any taxation of low-income individuals to taxes on consumption. The poor thereby get more freedom to spend their small resources as they prefer. It is still necessary to exclude some necessities such as food from indirect taxation and possible to levy higher taxes on luxury items. Chapter 3 also suggested a number of special taxes which would raise revenue for desirable social and environmental objectives.

The expansion of collective services does establish a case for raising some revenues from users and sometimes for limiting expenditure by a system of priorities, the most obvious example being health services. It may also be possible, through devolving parts of the health and other social services to voluntary bodies or friendly societies, to achieve more willing contributions from local users. Such arrangements are preferable to dismantling or undercutting the collective framework of these services, and valuable where they increase democratic participation; but they have to be applied with caution so as not to undercut the basic concepts of equity and need.

Thus it is certainly possible to devise a fair and adequate system of revenue to meet the rising requirements of the public services, through widening the sources of revenue, relating some sources to specific objectives, ensuring progressivity, and introducing an element of user pay in suitable cases. The obvious problem is to summon the necessary political will. The existence of the original welfare state was predicated upon a tacit social compact, and there are now critical doubts in European countries as to whether this compact can be renewed under modern conditions of greater individualism and global pressures (Scharpf, 1991). But the situation is not quite so hopeless as this.

Essentially we are looking at a basic political choice about the future of democratic societies. Are we to go yet further down the imperialist market track or can we recover the benefits of wise collective choices? As long as this issue is not clearly posed, the welfare state will suffer continuous erosion and privatisation under the competitive pressures for reducing or at the least stabilising taxation. It still is not realised that this process will lead to an inegalitarian and inefficient pattern of services, which will not in fact, as Chapter 4 pointed out, conform to the belief that concentrating public resources upon the relatively poor will lead to better public services. Much could be gained if political leaders explained the reasons for the increasing pressure on public services, and discussed more positively their requirements and justification.

The concept of collective choice has come under a cloud because of the belief, nourished by public choice economics, that it is only 'rational' to pursue one's own personal advantage and not to subsume that advantage within some collective goal. But collective action can be just as rational (and sometimes, too, as selfish) as the pursuit of self-interest. Given the very marginal political influence of one individual, it is surely rational for individuals to combine for ends which can only be achieved through group action. Such action can also bring much personal satisfaction from the pursuit of a common cause, as opposed to the often corroding experience of concentrating narrowly upon self-interest. The Chicago School are correct in seeing temptations for an individual to 'free ride' on the back of group effort, but this argument overlooks the significance of group norms for sustaining any co-operative effort, including those of business. If social norms are 'running down' in modern society, it seems likely that they will have to be revived in the interest of survival – if not democratically, then by authoritarian means. The question is how they get revived.

It is true that political and voting habits have become more individualistic than when a large majority of the population tended to conform to some dominant group pattern of behaviour. This result is clear from the decline of membership and participation in political parties and the increase in floating voters. Even so, new collective loyalties have sprung up, relating to environmentalism, feminism and other causes, and are to some extent filling this empty space. Also one can surely expect a strengthening of collective interest in political parties, to the extent that any party genuinely responds to rising social concerns about the impacts of the global economy.

Under such conditions one cannot prophesy how far a future popular majority might refuse to be bound by the supposed 'inevitability' of global economic pressures. Some writers already question the necessary weight of those pressures (e.g. Hirst and Thompson, 1996), and a considerable element in the power of globalisation has come from supportive and compliant political leaders. The results of changing those attitudes and leadership have still to be experienced.

The economic and the social

What is the relationship between the economic and the social? Is there an inevitable clash between economic and social values, or is this ultimately a false antithesis? These issues are latent in the previous discussion and their resolution is important for economic advice and government policies.

Orthodox economic theory is logical and coherent given its assumptions; but the assumptions are too rarely clarified and questioned. Economists stress rightly that there is no such thing as a free lunch; that most resources have alternative uses (although some resources are 'sunk costs' and cannot be shifted) and that there is an 'opportunity cost' in using resources in one way rather than another. Market theory argues that there is an optimal way of using resources in a given situation which is settled by the processes of supply and demand. Economic competition and consumers' choice are the chosen instruments for ensuring that the market works efficiently and rationally.

The theory assumes that the market values all resources correctly, including the services of human beings; but human beings need to be fed, clothed, housed and trained appropriately before they can fill their niche in the market machine. Human beings also belong to families and communities, they have personal aims and ideals, they share traditions and prized ways of life. Human beings are not like pawns on an economic chess board.

There seems an obvious clash between market efficiency and social values. The efficiency argument assumes that it is the prime interest of all individuals to purchase goods as cheaply as possible and to get the maximum wage (if any) that the market can offer; but human beings have other interests and values, and two in particular are threatened by the workings of the global economy.

First, remote economic decisions, made by either business or government on efficiency grounds, impinge strongly upon the work, life and habits of communities, whose members can suffer a loss of meaning and value. Second, the efficiency criterion assumes that individuals will respond to continuous economic changes by regrouping as quickly as possible so as to fit the changed work pattern; but there are considerable difficulties over making these adjustments and many people cannot make them at all – for example, if young people migrate to look for a new job, they may leave behind a sad community of aged and unemployed individuals. Another economic shock will quite likely occur before adjustments to the first one are complete. These 'transaction costs', as economists call them, are socially important but figure little or not at all in economic models, presently because they are tiresome and unquantifiable.

It used to be better recognised that commercial profit was a quite inadequate test of human welfare. Today the 'economic efficiency' test rules the roost. Businesses such as banks deny that they should have any consideration for poor or remote customers if that is unprofitable. They argue that if social factors are important governments should pay for them, which usually they are unwilling or unable to do. Governments have also adopted a narrow concept of economic efficiency for their own operations which tries to ignore social impacts. 'Competition policy' requires all public authorities to open up their services to competition for the lowest bidder. This poses as an anti-monopoly policy, although sometimes the eventual result is to substitute a larger private for a local public monopoly, but it also weakens local democratic control and local enterprises. Competition policy has even been applied in Canberra to such a palpable municipal function as the management of cemeteries, despite local objections.

The application of the principles of economic competition and consumers' choice has intrinsic limitations in relation to social services, and clashes with other criteria such as need, equity and professional standards and teamwork (Le Grand *et al.*, 1992). The 'quasi-market' introduced into the British health service had some merits in strengthening the capacity of general practitioners and local health authorities to buy the best services for their patients, but it required large overheads and damaged internal co-operation, and it has been largely reversed by New Labour.

However, these principles can also be questioned in arenas where it is often assumed that economic tests should be dominant. Three cases will be briefly examined to show the narrowness of orthodox economic thought in different situations.

(a) Cultural issues   Economic theory argues that there is no need to restrict free trade on cultural grounds since competition is always beneficial to consumers. This argument overlooks the unfair differences in market power, for example in the film industry where Hollywood can buy up and control film-making in smaller countries unless it is protected. May not some protection for local culture be intrinsically desirable in any case? The creation of a global mass market in culture, sport and entertainment and a global élite of highly paid top performers may help to bring the world together, but has a destructive effect on local customs, tastes and ways of life.

Moreover, the economic test is often applied on a misreading of the existence of competition. A good example is the way that a television owner such as Rupert Murdoch can transform a whole sport by creating a 'super-league' of top teams to be shown on television. This act is not only a case of oligopolistic market power, but of the unfair leverage available from a large advertising revenue which disguises the fact that consumers are paying handsomely for super-league through purchases in the shops. There is competition of a kind for viewers, but no genuine consumer choice over the organisation or allocation of resources for sport. The local communities who lose their local football team have little means of protest and may not understand what has happened.

(b) Agricultural subsidies   The issue on which economists most readily agree is the wickedness of agricultural subsidies, so to question their finding may seem perverse. Agricultural subsidies do often represent a perverse political concession, as with payments to large farmers who do not need them or with the European Union's accumulation of a useless 'butter mountain' and other surplus food stocks; but there are counter-arguments for supporting at least some forms of farming.

Most economists see the problem of low farm incomes as due to too many people on the land, and their usual solution (which paradoxically reduces competition) is rural migration and the creation of larger farms. In developed countries this process is steadily replacing small family farmers with large units or 'agri-businesses' which can produce a higher output per worker. In theory the displaced farmers should shift to better-paid jobs, but this result does not necessarily occur, and farming as a choice of occupation and way of life becomes increasingly difficult unless one has plenty of capital. Local communities suffer and become less viable. In some areas the farmers will be replaced by com-muters or retired people, but these do not necessarily contribute much to the local economy or community.

Environmental considerations are also left out of the economic calculus. Higher productivity is obtained through large inputs of chemical fertilisers and pesticides which erode the soil and have other adverse effects. More organic and balanced farming can be as or more productive but is more labour-intensive. While more farm production may not be demanded in richer countries, the soil needs to be used responsibly and help given to the many countries which have miserably inadequate agricultural resources. In Bangladesh, for example, there is just 0.4 hectares of land avail-able per worker on the land (about the same as a large suburban housing plot), and many developing countries now rely upon substantial imports of cereals (Bairoch, 1993, p. 130). The only solution for these countries must be intensive small-scale family farm-ing, helped by imports and technical aid from better-endowed countries.

It is worth reflecting that in the past political philosophers and practical men too regarded the distribution of occupations as a vital factor in the health, freedom and vigour of a nation. Indeed for both Rousseau and de Tocqueville, who otherwise disagreed about so much, a society of small proprietors – not too rich or poor – was essential for liberty and democracy. The logic of the market is so dominant today that these arguments are treated as irrelevant – but are they really so?

(c) Town planning Town planning developed as a public func-tion which attempts to improve the functioning, livability and environmental quality of cities through the regulation of urban growth. It is a complex and controversial activity, but the close inter-actions of land use in a modern city, the impact of transportation

systems and the salience of environmental impacts all mean that town planning continues to be necessary and important, even in an age of market liberalisation.

However, town planning is increasingly perverted by market pressures and dogmas. The concept of competition is invoked to suggest that town planning, a quintessential public function, should be privatised, and professional planning staff is apt to be sidelined in favour of political decisions made with the support of compliant consultants. The concept of economic growth is invoked to suggest that quick support should be given to any proposal for new development, without much consideration of its impact upon the rest of the city. Thus office skyscrapers in central areas get approved, regardless of the public cost of providing the necessary transport for their workers – though some economists do see the logical case for a 'congestion charge' on central area offices, as has been applied in Paris to support public transport.

A further aspect of this crude development philosophy is to encourage a costly competition between cities over the attraction of new investment through subsidies, planning concessions and fast-track procedures, and the provision of supporting facilities and amenities at public expense. This competition between cities is parallel to that between nations, and most cities feel obliged to join in if the others are doing it – but it is a wasteful process even if one accepts the argument that cities have to compete to find their appropriate specialisation or 'niche' within the global economy. The result is that cities have fewer resources to assist their less favoured areas and that the power of the market blocks the creative uses of planning to improve the city's functioning for the population as a whole.

All these three cases suggest lines of public policy preferable to conventional economic recipes. In the first example, there are good reasons for protecting both national and local cultures against free trade impacts, but their extent must be a matter of social opinion. In the second example, there is a case for supporting desirable forms of small-scale farming, as well as the taxation of agricultural chemicals. In the third example, there is a need to restore the 'public interest' concept to town planning and to limit wasteful competition between cities by co-operative action or regional planning.

The defects of orthodox economic theory act as a massive barrier to any reconciliation of the economic and the social. These defects include:

- Its neglect of the sociology of economic behaviour which often offers a better explanation than economic theory – for example, over the alternative rivalry and co-operation between entrepreneurs or the behaviour of mass audiences.
- Its weak treatment of institutional factors, due to the dominance of pure theory based upon a false analogy with physics. Hence a failure to understand how developments in economic behaviour and organisation are related to 'embedded' institutional arrangements (Granovetter, in Etzioni and Laurence, 1991, pp. 75–84).
- Its monopolistic treatment of resources which ignores alternative descriptions, for example in terms of the logic of the transformation of energy or of ecological balance.
- Its neglect in recent years of the many cases of market failure where economic competition works weakly or perversely.
- Its absurd and destructive attempt to develop a pure theory of economic efficiency or wealth maximisation that is completely divorced from the distribution of welfare. Admittedly not all economists fall into this trap, although they have difficulty finding answers within a conventional framework.

Some distinguished economists now recognise the need to introduce social norms into their theories (see Swedborg, 1990: contributions by Sen, Elster, Solow and Smelser). This is an important advance, but are social norms to be viewed as obstacles to 'economic rationality' which need to be circumvented? Or do they deserve respect as valued ways of life and a legitimate reason at least for modifying or even abandoning some economic criteria? The latter option is the preferable approach in terms of social harmony. However, many social norms are conservative and can block changes that may be socially desirable. Social norms are vital for the pursuit of collective aims and they need to be renewed for this purpose as well as sometimes respected for their past contributions.

Economic thought needs to be substantially revised to help bridge the gap between the economic and the social. An important way of doing this is to rediscover and rejuvenate social economics. Social economics is concerned not just with the maximisation of marketable commodities but with multiple tests of the welfare of human beings, as explained in Chapter 3. It strips away market dogmas in order to analyse and investigate market failures. It makes no assumption that a market system is intrinsically superior to some form of collective system but looks at their relative advantages and drawbacks. Above all perhaps, it recognises that the distribution and content of economic production are not irrelevant but central for any meaningful concept of human well-being. 'The interest in the world of commodities is a derivative one and the ultimate concern has to be with the lives we can or cannot lead' (Sen, in Swedborg, 1990, pp. 249–67).

It would be optimistic to suppose that some new form of socio-economic theory could incorporate all the missing sociological, institutional and environmental factors within some general framework. Economists have to become more modest and recognise that they should form part of a broader team both for investigating human behaviour and advising government. Team-work would not deal with the status of the social values which underlie any theoretical beliefs as well as any piece of political advice. It should be clear by now that orthodox economic theory is not value-free but is better seen as a rigorous logical system (the 'scientific part') placed at the service of a particular social philosophy. Significant differences in value assumptions already exist, for example between Keynesians and Friedmanites who differ not only in their views of how the economic system works, but in the value they attach to such outcomes as inflation and unemployment. A widening of the economic framework will increase the variety of underlying value judgements and assumptions.

There is no need to regret this fact. A world in which conflicts between social values are specifically recognised and debated is very preferable to one where dominant beliefs rest upon the supposed support of a neutral science. This conclusion legitimates the promotion of important social goals, such as the reconciliation of work with welfare. While economics can assist the pursuit of such goals, their practicality does not depend upon economic theory, but upon whether a democratic society will make the effort and initial sacrifices needed to overcome a patent social evil.

An important aspect of a broadened economics would be the rediscovery of 'public economics', as an important study in its own right, not a subset of market economics. Collective choice has its own rationality as a form of personal investment and commitment, and collective decisions entail difficult balances between contending factors or interests which do not arise within the simplified nexus of profit. Their exploration would complement and assist the revival of democratic political choice.

Democratic counter-revolution?

This chapter has assumed that a democratic revival is possible. But what does a more active, equal and responsible democracy entail? It is often assumed that Western societies exhibit the basic requisites of democracy and attention is fixed upon fine-tuning of their procedures and safeguards; but this approach fails to consider the wider social and political conditions within which democracies actually function. If democracy is to become a more meaningful element in the life of society, and hence in the constructive exercise of political choice, three lines of reform need to be pursued, which will be briefly summarised.

First, the workings of democracy should be spread more widely throughout society so as to permeate other institutions besides the state. The development of economic democracy through the promotion of co-operation and consultation in the workplace, as discussed in Chapter 7, would be one element in this process. The strengthening of elected local government and voluntary bodies is vital both for developing more informed political participation and for delivering public services in an acceptable way. More than this, one must regret the monopolisation of office by a narrow political class and look for ways of injecting a broader range of representation into legislatures. One such method is to have the upper house of the legislature elected by a variety of organisations, such as the professions, academia, business, trade unions, local governments and so on. While an acceptable scheme of this kind is difficult to devise, the principle behind it offers the bridge between the state and civil society which many people want to build.

Second, democracy will continue to be halt and lame so long as the possession of wealth and property exercise such disproportionate political influence, both indirectly and directly. Obvious measures here are to place strong curbs upon political donations and electoral expenses, to limit total electoral expenditure and to provide some assistance to poorer candidates from a public fund. More basically it is hard to see democracy working fairly without a reduction in the extreme economic inequalities of modern societies, especially the concentration of wealth in a tiny class of the very rich. Sooner or later some limit must be placed on the unlimited rights of personal acquisition and the inheritance of vast fortunes.

Third, the responsible exercise of democratic rights, which is surely the ultimate point of citizenship, requires clear political support. Essential measures here are to reduce the permitted limits of media ownership, require more space for informed political discussion as a condition of television licences, promote independent public broadcasting systems, prohibit quick and slick electoral advertising, tax media advertising, and assist the emergence of a wider variety of media outlets. All these measures are within the existing powers of governments and represent little more than elementary conditions of a responsible democracy.

While efforts to strengthen democracy face formidable obstacles, they will be helped by widening perceptions of the need for change. Until recently, political pressures for reform were weak and the personal need to adapt to a rapidly changing economic system seemed dominant. The future was liberally greased with promises about economic growth, and reform efforts were sublimated (as they still are) into the never-ending quests to 'increase the competitiveness' of some industry, occupation, city, region or nation. The world was (and still is) presented as a vast arena of competition which rewarded the worthy and punished the lazy. It was overlooked that this competition did not occur on a level playing field and had many of the attributes of a zero-sum game. However, perspectives are changing rapidly. In the two years since this book's inception, protest against the capitalist market system has grown from a trickle into a stream of critical books, articles and letters.

Political mobilisation is the necessary means for pursuing new goals. It is both helped and hindered by the single-issue politics which is a feature of modern society. These various causes pursue their own agenda and can sometimes be appeased by minor concessions made within the framework of the dominant orthodoxy. However, the need for integrated action is becoming more apparent. Environmentalists are hardening in their opposition to the principles of the global economy, but effective progress with their aims requires an equally sensitive understanding of social frustrations and aspirations. Feminist efforts to make competitive entry into senior positions as open to women as men needs to be combined with advocacy for the numerous women suffering from new forms of economic exploitation. Ethnic groups are particularly liable to economic disadvantage, but their response needs to be the advocacy of better economic policies not attempts at social segregation and an elusive self-sufficiency or autonomy. These various currents can come together within a framework which reasserts the interests of workers against the dominance of the profit motive, of citizens against the erosion of common resources, and of the disadvantaged against their neglect and marginalisation.

The battle of ideas is central to this reform project. It is necessary to challenge the ruling interpretation of liberal individualism. The liberal concept that an individual should be free to choose his own beliefs and lifestyle so long as he does not seriously harm others represented in its day an important advance in freedom and toleration; but its founders never imagined that it could be used to justify a 'hands off' approach to the regulation of severely depraved activities which cause grave harm to others as well as their perpetrators. It is time to recognise that there is a difference between vice and virtue which society needs to blame or condemn, even if not too dogmatically. Governments have a direct responsibility to regulate activities which do serious harm to others and to assist the efforts of schools and communities to instil those virtues which make for social harmony and co-operation as well as tolerance.

Liberal theorists have rediscovered the need for social responsibility as the condition of individual freedom. This welcome discovery has still to be made politically effective in a world where 'liberalism' is crudely identified with the assertion of individual rights. In particular, the rights to private property and unlimited acquisition have been pushed to the point of highly destructive effects upon the common life and interests of society. It is important to demonstrate these effects and to show how the possession of common assets is essential to a satisfactory life (especially for the poor) and can be sensibly managed. What sort of 'common good' can exist in a world where the affluent isolate themselves in gated communities and where predatory activities become normal?

The revolution in economic ideas ought already to have started with the many intellectual demolitions of the orthodox neo-classical model. That so many people still cling to it may be ascribed to its usefulness (actually a much qualified one) for appearing to justify capitalist markets, in much the same way as the medieval scholastics could argue about how many angels can dance on the top of a needle and still be a useful aid to the power of the medieval church. There is no need to reject the use of formal models as such because, even with unrealistic assumptions, they may offer some insight into reality. The trouble with the neo-classical model lies not only in its degree of unrealism, but with assumptions which are socially and ethically mistaken; labour and land, for example, cannot and should not be treated as simply 'commodities', nor is it right to treat individual preferences as 'exogenous' and independent of their social formation.

It may be questioned whether it is possible to produce a satisfactory model which combines economic and social elements. But whether this is so or not, economics can offer only limited guidance on such issues as desirable patterns of ownership, the distribution of wealth, and the importance of public services, and cannot say much about largely 'non-quantitative' matters such as the quality of life or the conditions of social co-operation. Economic policy works within the possible limits of the system which it is serving, so that a different system will mean a changed spectrum of economic possibilities which cannot be constructed out of theories tied to unconstrained market relationships and interpreted along capitalist lines.

The future is uncertain. It may be that the logic of capitalist markets has become too tight-knit, and the supporting interests too strong, for any piecemeal reform to prove possible. Capitalism might then be eventually superseded by a system whose character can only be guessed at. This book has been written in the hope that piecemeal reform *is* possible, and that the better aspects of competitive markets can be retained within a more balanced and stable system, which will be more socially oriented and less environmentally destructive. From a limited start further progress towards these goals should be possible; but even a limited start entails an awakening of the latent power of what David Lilienthal (1945) once termed (in the context of the Tennessee Valley Authority) 'democracy on the march'.

Bibliography

Adams, J., *Transport Planning: Vision and Practice* (Routledge & Kegan Paul, 1981)

Arrow, K. J., *Social Choice and Individual Values* (John Wiley, 1963)

Bairoch, P., *Economics and World History: Myths and Paradoxes* (University of Chicago Press, 1993)

Baldwin, P., *The Politics of Social Solidarity: Class Bases of the European Welfare State 1875–1975* (Cambridge University Press, 1990)

Barberis, P., *The Elite of the Elite: Permanent Secretaries in the British Higher Civil Service* (Dartmouth Publishing Co., 1996)

Baumol, W. J., 'Health Care, Education and the Cost Disease: A Looming Crisis for Public Choice', *Public Choice*, 77, pp. 23–5 (1993)

Beiner, R., *What's the Matter with Liberalism?* (University of California Press, 1992)

Bell, D., 'Models and Reality in Economics Discourse', in D. Bell and I. Kristol (eds), *The Crisis in Economic Theory* (Basic Books, 1981)

Bellah, R. N. *et al.*, *The Good Society* (A. A. Knopf, 1991)

Bentham, J., *Works*, ed. J. Bowring (London, 1943)

Berlin, I., 'Two Concepts of Liberty', in I. Berlin, *Four Essays on Liberty* (Oxford University Press, 2nd edn, 1969)

Blair, T., *Socialism* (Fabian Pamphlet 565, 1994)

Blair, T., *The Third Way* (Fabian Society, London, 1998)

Blaug, M., *The Methodology of Economics* (Cambridge University Press, 2nd edn, 1992)

Bleaney, M., *The Rise and Fall of Keynesian Economics* (Macmillan, 1985)

Boldeman, L., 'Supershopper and the New Religion', *Australian Rationalist*, 39, pp. 50–6 (1996)

Braybrooke, D., *Meeting Needs* (Princeton University Press, 1987)

Brennan, G. and Buchanan, J. H., *The Reason of Rules: Constitutional Political Economy* (Cambridge University Press, 1985)

Brown, G., *Fair Is Efficient* (Fabian Pamphlet 563, 1994)

Brus, W. and Laski, K., *From Marx to the Market* (Oxford University Press, 1989)

Buchanan, J. M., *Liberty, Market and State* (Wheatsheaf, 1986)

Campbell, C. and Wilson, G., *The End of Whitehall* (Blackwell, 1995)

Cockett, R., *Thinking the Unthinkable: Think Tanks and the Economic Counter-Revolution, 1931–1983* (HarperCollins, 1983)

Coles, R. (ed.), *The End of Public Housing?* (Urban Research Program, Australian National University, 1997)

Colvin, P., *The Economic Ideal in British Government* (Manchester University Press, 1985)

Connolly, W. E., *Appearance and Reality in Politics* (Cambridge University Press, 1981)

Crine, S., *Reforming Welfare: American Lessons* (Fabian Pamphlet 567, 1994)

Crouch, C., 'The Social Contract and the Problem of the Firm', in M. Rhodes and Y. Meny (eds), *The Future of European Welfare* (Macmillan, 1998)

Crouch, C. and Marquand, D. (eds), *Ethics and Markets* (Blackwell, 1993)

Dahl, R. A., *A Preface to Economic Democracy* (University of California Press, 1985)

Daly, H. E., *Steady-State Economics* (Island Press, Washington D.C., 2nd edn, 1991)

Day, P., *Land* (Australian Academic Press, Brisbane, 1995)

Deane, P., *The State and the Economic System* (Oxford University Press, 1989)

Diesendorf, M. and Hamilton, C., *Human Ecology, Human Economy* (Allen & Unwin, Australia, 1997)

Dodds, S., 'Economic Growth and Human Well-Being', in Diesendorf and Hamilton (1997)

Douglass, R. B., Mara, C. R. and Richardson, H. S. (eds), *Liberalism and the Good* (Routledge, 1990)

Drucker, P., *The New Realities: In Government and Politics, in Economics and Business, in Society and World View* (Harper & Row, 1989)

Dunleavy, P., *Democracy, Bureaucracy and Public Choice* (Harvester Wheatsheaf, 1991)

Elgin, D., *Voluntary Simplicity* (New York, 1981)

Etzioni, A. (ed.), *New Communitarian Thinking* (University Press of Virginia, 1995)

Etzioni, A. and Laurence, P. (eds), *Socio-Economics: Towards A New Synthesis* (M. E. Sharpe, London, 1991)

Etzioni-Halevy, E., *Bureaucracy and Democracy* (Routledge & Kegan Paul, 1983)

Finding a Balance: Towards Fair Trading in Australia, Report by House of Representatives Standing Committee on Industry, Science and Technology (Australian Parliament, 1997)

Foster, C. D. and Plowden, F. J., *The State under Stress* (Open University Press, 1996)

Freeden, M., *Ideologies and Political Theory* (Oxford University Press, 1996)

Fukuyama, F., *Trust: The Social Virtues and the Creation of Prosperity* (Hamish Hamilton, 1995)

Fusfeld, D. R., *The Age of the Economist* (Scott, Foresman, 5th edn, 1986)

Galbraith, J., *American Capitalism: The Concept of Countervailing Power* (Hamilton, 1957)

Galbraith, J. K., *The Culture of Contentment* (Houghton Mifflin, 1992)

Galston, W. A., *Liberal Purposes: Goods, Virtues and Diversity in the Liberal State* (Cambridge University Press N.Y., 1991).

Gerth, H. H., and Mills, C. W. (eds), *From Max Weber: Essays in Sociology* (Kegan, Paul, Trench & Trubner, 1947)

Giddens, A., *Between Left and Right* (Polity Press, 1994)

Giddens, A., *The Third Way* (Polity Press, 1998)

Grant, G., *Technology and Empire* (Anansi, Toronto, 1969)

Gray, J., *Liberalism* (Open University Press, 1986)

Gray, J., *Liberalism* (Routledge, 1989)

Hamilton, C. and Quiggin, J., *The Privatisation of CSL* (The Australia Institute, Canberra, 1995)

Hamilton, C. with Saddler, H., *The Genuine Progress Indicator for Australia* (Australia Institute, Canberra, Discussion Paper 12, 1997)

Harcourt, G. C., 'Economic Theory and Economic Policy: Two Views', (Seventh Colin Clark Lecture, mimeo, 1997)

Hardin, G., 'The Tragedy of the Commons', *Science*, 162: 3859, pp. 1243–8 (1968)

Hartz, L., *The Liberal Tradition in America* (Harcourt, Brace & World, 1955)

Hayek, F. A., *The Road to Serfdom* (Routledge & Kegan Paul, 1944)

Hayek, F. A., *Individualism and Economic Order* (Routledge & Kegan Paul, 1949)

Hayek, F. A., *The Constitution of Liberty* (Chicago University Press, 1960)

Heclo, H., *Modern Social Politics in Britain and Sweden* (Yale University Press, 1974)

Heelo, Hugh, *A Government of Strangers: Executive Polities in Washington* (The Brookings Institute, 1977)

Heilbroner, R. and Milberg, W., *The Crisis of Vision in Modern Economic Thought* (Cambridge University Press, 1995)

Hennessy, P., 'Demystifying Whitehall: The Great British Civil Service Debate, 1980 Style', in C. Campbell and B. G. Peters (eds), *Organizing Governance: Governing Organizations* (University of Pittsburgh Press, 1988)

Hills, J. R., 'The Bridge that Failed: The Changing Distribution of Income and Wealth in the UK', in H. Sasson and D. Diamond (eds), *LSE on Social Science* (London School of Economics, 1996)

Hirsch, F., *Social Limits to Growth* (Harvard University Press, 1976)

Hirschman, A., *Shifting Involvements* (Princeton University Press, 1982)

Hirst, P. and Thompson, G., *Globalisation in Question* (Polity Press, 1996)

Hobhouse, L. T., *Liberalism* (Oxford University Press, 1964)

Hood, C., 'A Public Management for All Seasons', *Public Administration*, 69: 1, pp. 21–39 (1991)

Horsmann, M. and Marshall, A., *After the Nation State* (HarperCollins, 1994)

Hutchison, T. W., *The Politics and Philosophy of Economics* (Blackwell, 1981)

Industry Commission, *Inquiry into Public Housing: Report* (Australian Government Printing Service, Canberra, 1993)

Kaldor, N., 'Welfare Propositions and Interpersonal Comparisons of Utility', *Economic Journal* (Sept. 1939), pp. 549–52

Kalecki, M., 'Political Aspects of Full Employment', in J. Osiatynski (ed.), *Collected Works of Michael Kalecki*, Vol. 1 (Oxford University Press, 1990)

Keynes, J. M., *The General Theory of Employment, Interest and Money* (Macmillan, 1936)

Kirzner, I. H., 'The Austrian Perspective', in D. Bell and I. Kristol (eds), *The Crisis in Economic Theory* (Basic Books, 1981)

Kooiman, J. (ed.), *Modern Governance: New Government–Society Interactions* (Sage, 1993)

Korten, D. C., *When Corporations Rule The World* (Earthscan, 1995)

Kristol, I., 'Rationalism in Economics', in D. Bell and I. Kristol (eds), *The Crisis in Economic Theory* (Basic Books, 1981)

Krugman, Paul, *The Age of Diminished Expectations* (MIT Press, 1990)

Lane, R., *The Market Experience* (Cambridge University Press, 1991)

Le Grand, J., Propper, C. and Robinson, R., *The Economics of Social Problems* (Macmillan, 3rd edn, 1992)

Leadbeater, C., *The Rise of the Social Entrepreneur* (Demos, London, 1997)

Leveson-Gower, H., 'Trade and the Environment', in M. Diesendorf and C. Hamilton (eds), *Human Ecology, Human Economy* (Allen & Unwin, Australia, 1997)

Lilienthal, D., *TVA: Democracy on the March* (Penguin Books, 1945)

Lindblom, C. E., *Politics and Markets* (Basic Books, 1977)

Lipsey, R. G. and Lancaster, K., 'The General Theory of the Second Best', *Review of Economic Studies*, vol. 24, pp. 11–32 (1956)

Locke, J., *Two Treatises on Government*, ed. P. Laslett (Cambridge University Press, 1970)

Lutz, H. A. and Lux, K., *Humanistic Economics: The New Challenge* (Bootstrap Press, New York, 1988)

MacIntyre, A., *Whose Justice? Which Rationality?* (University of Notre Dame Press, 1988)

Marshall, A., *Principles of Economics* (Macmillan, 1890; 8th edn, Macmillan 1947)

Marshall, T. H., 'Citizenship and Social Class', in T. H. Marshall, *Sociology at the Crossroads* (Heinemann, 1963)

Martin, H. P. and Schumann, H., *The Global Trap* (Zed Books, London, 1996)

Maslow, A. H., *Motivation and Personality* (Harper & Row, 1954)

Meadows, D. H., Meadows, D. L. and Randers, J., *Limits to Growth* (Universe Books, 1972)

Meadows, D. H., Meadows, D. L. and Randers, J., *Beyond The Limits* (Chelsea Green Publishing Co., Post Mills, Vermont, 1992)

Mill, J. S., *Autobiography* (Oxford, 1969)

Mill, J. S., *Chapters on Socialism, Collected Works* (London, 1983)

Mill, J. S. and Bentham, J., *Utilitarianism and Other Essays*, ed. A. Ryan (Penguin Books, 1987)

Mishan, E. J., *The Economic Growth Debate* (George Allen & Unwin, 1977)

Mulhall, S. and Swift, A., *Liberals and Communitarians* (Blackwell, 1996)

Musgrave, R. A., *Essays in Fiscal Federalism* (Brookings Institute, 1965)

Muth, J. F., 'Rational Expectations and the Theory of Price Movements', *Econometrics*, vol. 29, pp. 315–35 (1961)

Myrdal, C., *The Political Element in the Development of Economic Theory* (Routledge & Kegan Paul, 1953)

Neutze, M., *Private Sector Involvement in Public Infrastructure* (Australia Institute, Canberra, 1995)

Niskanen, W. A., *Bureaucracy and Representative Government* (Aldine-Atherton, 1971)

Nove, A., *The Economics of Feasible Socialism* (Allen & Unwin, 1983)

Nozick, R., *Anarchy, State and Utopia* (Blackwell, 1974)

Nussbaum, M., 'Aristotelian Social Democracy', in R. B. Douglass, C. R. Mara and H. S. Richardson (eds), *Liberalism and the Good* (Routledge, 1990)

Offe, C., *Contradictions of the Welfare State* (MIT Press, 1984)

Offe, C., 'The Present Historical Transition and Some Basic Design Options for Societal Institutions' (mimeo, 1998)

Ohmae, K., *The End of the Nation State* (Harper Collins, 1995)

Okun, A. M., *Equality and Efficiency: The Big Trade Off* (The Brookings Institute, 1975)

Olson, M., *The Rise and Decline of Nations* (Yale University Press, 1982)

Ormerod, P., *The Death of Economics* (Faber, 1995)

Osborne, D., 'Between Left and Right: A New Political Paradigm', in A. Etzioni (ed.), *New Communitarian Thinking* (University Press of Virginia, 1995)

Osborne, D. and Gaebler, T., *Reinventing Government* (Addison-Wesley, 1992)

Perrow, C., 'Economic Theories of Organization', *Theory and Society*, vol. 15, pp. 11–45 (1986)

Peters, B. Guy, *The Politics of Bureaucracy: A Comparative Perspective* (Longman, 1978)

Plant, R., *New Labour: A Third Way?* (European Policy Forum, London, 1998)

Plowden, W., *Ministers and Mandarins* (Institute for Public Policy Research, London, 1994)

Polanyi, H., *The Great Transformation* (Rinehart, 1944)

Porrit, J., *Seeing Green* (Blackwell, 1984)

Putnam, R., *Making Democracy Work* (Princeton University Press, 1993)

Quiggin, J., *Does Privatisation Pay?* (The Australia Insititute, Canberra, 1994)

Rawls, J. R., *A Theory of Justice* (Harvard University Press, 1971)

Redclift, M., 'Development and the Environment', in L. Sklair (ed.), *Capitalism and Development* (Routledge, 1994)

Reich, R. B., *The Work of Nations* (Alfred A. Knopf, 1991)

Rhoads, S. E., *The Economist's View of the World* (Cambridge University Press, 1985)

Rhodes, M. and Meny, Y., *The Future of European Welfare* (Macmillan, 1998)

Robbins, L., *An Essay on the Nature and Significance of Economic Science* (Macmillan, 1935)

Robinson, J., *Economic Philosophy* (Pelican Books, 1964)

Roll, E., *A History of Economic Thought* (Faber, 5th edn, 1992)

Ryan, A., 'Liberalism', in R. E. Goodin and P. Pettit (eds), *A Companion to Contemporary Political Philosophy* (Blackwell, 1993)

Samuelson, P., *Economics* (McGraw-Hill, 6th edn, 1964)

Saunders, P., 'Recent Trends in the Size and Growth of Government in OECD Countries', in N. Bemmel (ed.), *The Growth of the Public Sector* (Edward Elgar, 1993)

Scharpf, F. W., *Crisis and Choice in European Social Democracy* (Cornell University Press, 1991)

Schotter, A., *Free Market Economics: A Critical Appraisal* (Blackwell, 2nd edn, 1990)

Schumacher, E. F., *Small Is Beautiful: A Study of Economics As If People Mattered* (Blond & Briggs, 1973)

Schumpeter, J. A., *The Theory of Economic Development* (Harvard University Press, 1949)

Schumpeter, J. A., *Ten Great Economists* (Allen & Unwin, 1952)

Schumpeter, J. A., *Capitalism, Socialism and Democracy* (Allen & Unwin, 1976)

Self, P., *Econocrats and the Policy Process* (Macmillan, 1975)

Self, P., *Administrative Theories and Politics* (Allen & Unwin, 2nd edn, 1977)

Self, P., *Political Theories of Modern Government* (Allen & Unwin, 1985)

Self, P., *Government by the Market? The Politics of Public Choice* (Macmillan, 1993)

Self, P., 'What's Happened to Administrative Theories?', *Public Policy and Administration* (Glasgow), vol. 12, no. 2, pp. 8–20 (1997)

Selznick, P., *The Moral Commonwealth* (University of California Press, 1992)

Simon, Herbert, *Administrative Behaviour* (Macmillan, 2nd edn, 1957)

Simon, H. A., 'Organisations and Markets', *Journal of Economic Perspectives*, vol. 5, pp. 25–41 (1991)

Skidelsky, R., 'Keynes's Political Legacy', in O. F. Hamoude and J. M. Smithin (eds), *Keynes and Public Policy after Fifty Years*, Vol. 1 (New York University Press, 1988)

Sklair, L., 'Capitalism and Development in Global Perspective', in L. Sklair (ed.), *Capitalism and Development* (Routledge, 1994)

Sklair, L., 'Who Are the Globalisers?', *Journal of Australian Political Economy*, vol. 38 (Dec. 1996), pp. 1–30

Smith, A., *An Inquiry into the Nature and Causes of the Wealth of Nations* (1776) (New York Modern Library, 1937)

Spencer, H., *The Man Versus the State* (Penguin Books, 1969)

Stiglitz, J. E., *Whither Socialism?* (Massachusetts Institute of Technology, 1994)

Stiglitz, J. E. *et al.*, *The Economic Role of the State* (Blackwell, 1989)

Stilwell, F., 'Neo-Classical Economics: A Long Cul-de-Sac', in G. Argyrous and F. Stilwell (eds), *Economics As a Social Science* (Pluto Press, Australia, 1996).

Strange, S., *Casino Capitalism* (Basil Blackwell, 1986)

Strange, S., *States and Markets* (London, Pinter, 1988)

Stretton, H. and Orchard, L., *Public Goods, Public Enterprise, Public Choice* (Macmillan, 1994)

Swedborg, R., *Economics and Sociology* (Princeton University Press, 1990)

Taylor, E., 'Irreducibly Social Goods', in G. Brennan and C. Walsh (eds), *Rationality, Individualism and Public Policy* (Australian National University, Canberra, 1990)

The Economist, 'A Survey of Multi-Nationals' (special supplement, 27 March 1993), p. 6

The Economist, 'Doleful' (9 Oct. 1993), p. 17

The Economist, 'Inequality' (5 Nov. 1996), pp. 19–23

The Economist, *Book of Vital World Statistics* (Hutchinson Business Books, 1992)

The Political Quarterly, 'Does Stakeholding Make Sense?', vol. 67, no. 3 (July–Sept. 1996)

Thornley, A. and Neuman, P., *Urban Planning in Europe* (Routledge, 1996)

Thurow, L., *The Future of Capitalism* (Allen & Unwin, 1996)

Titmuss, R., *The Gift Relationship* (Allen & Unwin, 1971)

Tobin, J., 'A Tax on International Currency Transactions', in UNDP Human Development Report (Oxford University Press, 1994)

Vandenbroucke, Frank, *Globalisation, Inequality and Social Democracy* (Institute for Public Policy Research, London, 1998)

Veblen, T., *The Theory of the Leisure Class* (1924, reprinted Unwin Books 1970)

Vincent, A. and Plant, R. *Philosophy, Politics and Citizenship* (Blackwell, 1984)

Wallerstein, I., *The Politics of the World-Economy* (Cambridge University Press, 1984)

Ward, C., 'Parish Pump Politics', *Town and Country Planning* (UK), 87. 8 (Feb. 1997)

Williamson, O., *The Economic Insitutions of Capitalism: Firms, Markets, Relational Contracting* (The Free Press, 1985)

Wilson, J. Q., *Political Organizations* (Basic Books, 1993)

Wuthnow, R., 'Between the State and the Market: Voluntarism and the Difference It Makes', in A. Etzioni (ed.), *New Communitarian Thinking* (University Press of Virginia, 1995)

Young, M. and Halsey, A. H., *Family and Community Socialism* (Institute for Public Policy Research, London, 1995)

Index